P9-DNY-839

My Life in 'toons

My Life in 'toons

From Flatbush to Bedrock in Under a Century

Joseph Barbera

Turner Publishing, Inc.

ATLANTA

Published by Turner Publishing, Inc.
A Subsidiary of Turner Broadcasting System, Inc.
1050 Techwood Drive, N.W.
Atlanta, Georgia 30318

First Edition 10 9 8 7 6 5 4 3 2 1

Library of Congress Cataloging-in-Publication Data

Barbera, Joseph.
My life in 'toons: from Flatbush to Bedrock in under a century / by Joseph Barbera. -- 1st ed.
p. cm.
ISBN 1-57036-042-1 : $19.95
1. Barbera, Joseph. 2. Animators—United States—Biography.
I. Title.
NC1766.U52B3 1994
741.5'8'092—dc20
[B]

94-7721
CIP

Distributed by Andrews and McMeel
A Universal Press Syndicate Company
4900 Main Street
Kansas City, Missouri 64112

Printed in the U.S.A.

To my wife, Sheila,
without whom this
could never
have happened.

Advance Praise for *My Life in 'toons*

"On a weekly basis, Joe Barbera frequented our living room in the guise of Fred and Wilma, Barney and Betty. I will never forget him and his partner, William Hanna, for the lasting and laughing impressions in a whole series of groundbreaking animated sitcoms. When we marvel at the success of *The Simpsons*, we must also marvel at the millions of miles of pipe first laid by this animation pioneer."

– STEVEN SPIELBERG, DIRECTOR/PRODUCER

"Joe Barbera is a unique and creative man who, along with Walt Disney and very few others, pioneered animation as an art form. This wonderful and spirited individual ushered me into understanding animation and comedy and character development, and plain old fun. Joe Barbera, during my stewardship of ABC Children's programs, was not only the backbone of ABC's Saturday morning schedule, but the other two networks as well."

– MICHAEL D. EISNER,
CHAIRMAN AND CEO, WALT DISNEY COMPANY

"*My Life in 'toons* brought back memories of some great times with Joe Barbera. He was a joy to work with—for he was, and is, singularly the most creative, energetic, and caring producer in the business. Great book, Joe!"

– FRED SILVERMAN, TELEVISION PRODUCER

"Joe Barbera is the greatest storyteller I have ever met. He should be declared a National Treasure. The creator of the richest characters, the funniest dialogue, the best stories, the most heartwarming entertainment. He is a timeless genius!"

— ANDY HEYWARD, PRESIDENT, DIC ENTERTAINMENT

"Joe Barbera is one of the great talents of the animation industry. His incredible skills are widely diverse. He can draw and write and develop characters with a magic touch. He is a true gentleman from whom I have learned so much. His humor and charm, combined with his talent, make working with him a joy."

**— MARGARET LOESCH,
PRESIDENT, FOX CHILDREN'S NETWORK**

"Having worked with animated films a bit, I have come to one solid conclusion: Animators are a bit nuts. Joe Barbera is no exception. His tools—pen, ink, and paper—lead a relentless assault on one's sense of humor in his always-perfect execution of the perfect joke. His new book, *My Life in 'toons*, proves that with great humor in hand, great humanity isn't far behind. My friend Joe has touched us all."

— HENRY MANCINI, COMPOSER

"Joe and I have been friends and neighbors through fires, floods, and earthquakes, and his sense of humor has always pulled us through. Joe Barbera has found the fountain of youth and I thank him for sharing it with us all."

— RICHARD CRENNA, ACTOR

Contents

1
CHAPTER ONE:
A PRISONER OF THE SHERRY-NETHERLAND

17
CHAPTER TWO:
WHOLLY INNOCENT

43
CHAPTER THREE:
THE LEAST YOU'LL TAKE

61
CHAPTER FOUR:
INTO THE LION'S DEN

81
CHAPTER FIVE:
CAT AND MOUSE GAMES

111
CHAPTER SIX:
ROUGH BUT READY

131
CHAPTER SEVEN:
BALANCING ACT

159
CHAPTER EIGHT:
ON THE MAP

179
CHAPTER NINE:
RISKS AND REWARDS

201
CHAPTER TEN:
TAKE AND GIVE

225
CHAPTER ELEVEN:
A FULL CIRCLE

245
EPILOGUE:
PROLOGUE TO THE NEXT VOLUME

Chapter One

A PRISONER OF THE SHERRY-NETHERLAND

AS PRISONS GO, the Sherry-Netherland Hotel was not all that bad. Planted on a sedate stretch of Fifth Avenue overlooking Central Park, it was never as flashy as the Plaza just half a block away. The Sherry was dark inside, with lots of mahogany, mellow old brass, and thick woolen carpeting. The hall ceilings were coved, the doors to the rooms dark and extra heavy. Everyone was polite. It felt to me more European than American. But after eight weeks, even a nice hotel becomes a dungeon.

Eight weeks. I was vaguely aware of the changing seasons in Central Park, a sliver of which I could glimpse through the slats of the venetian blinds, rather like the Man in the Iron Mask—whose story had been a favorite of mine as a kid: His only contact with the outside world came through a slit where the wall joined the ceiling of his tomblike cell. When I arrived in New York and settled in at the Sherry, snow blanketed the ground, and the single tree I saw was bare. Then, as if I were watching some long, drawn-out nature movie, I beheld daily the passage of the seasons: the retreat of the snow, the first buds on what had been bare branches, the reappearance of the swans on the pond, the leafing of the branches, and the sprouting of the grass.

Even as early as the second week, however, I began to smell like the hotel—a blend of lemon oil, brass polish, and cigarette smoke. By the fourth week, I became morbidly interested in an electrical outlet along the baseboard of my room. Sprouting five cords, all heavily painted over, apparently year after year after year, it was fossilized, like some weird, long-encrusted octopus. I pictured that overloaded octopus heating up as I lay sleeping in the middle of the night. It would sizzle, throwing off a spark or two, the ancient layers of paint beginning to smolder. Then a tongue of flame. The carpeting, the heavy drapery, the deep-upholstered chairs, the bed, me—all up in flames.

It was not the first time I had staked my life on a cartoon, and it would not be the last time that I would risk my life for one.

This was 1960. Just three years earlier, in 1957, Bill Hanna and I were calm, comfortable, and self-satisfied at the MGM studios. For two decades, we had been making Tom and Jerry cartoons, living off the fat capital of characters we had created two decades before, in 1940. When I got into animation in the early 1930s, I started at twenty-five dollars a week. At MGM, in 1957, my salary was up to more than seven hundred dollars a week, and I was pleasantly perched at the top of the heap.

That, as they say, was then. But this was now.

By the late 1950s, television was cutting deep inroads into traditional Hollywood's bottom line. MGM was no exception, and, floundering in red ink, studio heads were desperately groping for corners to cut. One corner they found was ours. The Tom and Jerry cartoons were tremendously successful and showed no signs of flagging. But the studio's Arthur Loew, Sr., reviewed the books and concluded that re-releasing an old Tom and Jerry would bring in 90 percent of the income generated by a brand-new one—without, of course, *any* of the cost of new production. At the time, early in 1957, it was Bill and I who ran the MGM cartoon studio. But the call—and it was just a single phone call—came down from the front office, not to us, but to our business manager: "Close the studio. Lay everybody off."

With that phone call, conveyed to us secondhand, a whole career disappeared.

Or so Bill and I thought—at the first shock of it. In fact, all that had really disappeared was an illusion, an illusion that people working for many giant corporations share, an illusion of absolute and permanent security. In reality, it was the end of one career, but the beginning of another. The only difference was that theatrical movie cartoons were already very much around when Bill and I got into them. The business of television animation—well, that we would have to invent ourselves, and I'll tell that story in its place. For now, you should know that, in the space of three years, between 1957 and 1960, Hanna-Barbera produced "The Ruff and Reddy Show," "Huckleberry Hound," "Pixie and Dixie," "Augie Doggie and Doggie Daddy," "Quick Draw McGraw," "Snooper and Blabber," "Yakky Doodle," "Yogi Bear," "Hokey Wolf," and "Snagglepuss."

Now, with all those shows going, I found myself betting my future, my business, and the welfare of my wife and children on a family of Neanderthals in a neolithic suburb called Bedrock. And it got worse. Because, after eight weeks of pitching "The Flagstones," as we first called the show, to ad agency and network executives—to the J. Walter Thompson people, to William Esty, to Foote, Cone and Belding, and representatives of CBS and NBC—I was clearly losing the bet. Pitch after pitch to faces gathered around this table or that. Each pitch was a vaudeville show. I'd tack up the storyboards, papering three walls of a room with sketches, each about four by five inches—some four hundred of them—then stand the bigger pieces of artwork against another wall. I'd go from drawing to drawing, acting out each frame, with voices, gestures, sound effects. Much of this took place—over and over again—in a meeting room at Screen Gems, our distributor at 729 Broadway in Manhattan.

Nobody ever denied *liking* the show. In fact, I was told that my presentations were becoming the talk of Madison Avenue. Account executives were telling their colleagues: *You gotta see this guy down at Screen Gems. He's* really *funny*. But nobody took out a checkbook, either—face after face, conference after conference, pitch after pitch.

Well, I thought, staring at the electric octopus in my dungeon cell, how could I have ever hoped to win? Months before, back in California at the LaBrea Studios where we had our offices, the very studios in which Charlie Chaplin had, decades earlier, worked his magic, John Mitchell, our Screen Gems contact, suggested that Bill Hanna and I create a thirty-minute prime-time animated series. Back then and there, we both said sure, because we had learned that you say "sure" to everything with the remotest prospect of money attached to it, no matter how crazy. But the very idea of a prime-time television cartoon show was *extremely* crazy.

To begin with, the logistics of the thing were simply insane. At MGM, we made five or six five-minute cartoons a year. True, we were now doing a lot more work than that for TV, but Mitchell was proposing that we animate a half hour each week, clearly an impossible task, especially with the ongoing burden of production we were already carrying.

We would gladly have pushed John Mitchell's idea onto the backest back burner we could find, but he was a strong, persistent bulldog of a man, who kept after us about the show. Besides, at the end of fifties and the start of the sixties, television was very, very hungry for children's programming, and if Hanna-Barbera was not there to feed it, a lot of others would start getting the idea that *they* could. With a medium to feed and our own families to feed, the delirious notion of a half-hour prime-time cartoon began to look more and more like a realistic, reasonable opportunity to tap a new and very rich market. Yes, the idea—mad as it was—of breaking new ground in the prime-time province of live-action situation comedy began to appeal to us, and we started to kick it, ever more hopefully, around.

It was not as if Bill Hanna, Dan Gordon—an artist and storyboard man whom I had first met back in the 1930s at New York's Van Beuren Studios—and I locked ourselves in a room and emerged with "The Flintstones." Hanna was ear-deep most of the time in production of the ongoing shows. My days were mostly consumed in working on these also, as well as developing and/or pitching new ones. Then, in the evening, I'd direct the recording sessions for "Quick Draw," "Huckleberry," and the rest.

But the new show, the half-hour show, evolved nevertheless. Really, it was a sort of process of *reverse* evolution. We decided from the beginning that going for a half-hour of laughs on TV meant writing a situation comedy, an animated "Ozzie and Harriet" or "Father Knows Best," a show revolving around a family.

But what kind of family? We thought of an ordinary American family, like any other on television at the time. We thought about a family with kids, without kids, with a tall husband, a short wife, a nagging mother-in-law, a dog, a cat, no pets. Then we thought about a farmer and his family, which led to a hillbilly family. And, soon, we were slipping backward in history. We came up with a Pilgrim family, with wide collars and high hats, then a Roman family, with togas and helmets.

Nothing worked. Nothing clicked. And the weeks and months glided by. The project seemed pretty much a lost cause.

I CANNOT SAY WHO, precisely, came up the idea of a Stone Age family. As I say, it seemed simply to evolve—or, rather, *devolve*. But, suddenly, it all started coming together. It was the objects, the gadgets, the everyday modern *things* translated into terms of the Stone Age that really drove the creation of the show. First, we came up with the Stoneway piano, and that led to gag after gag. The cave was not the cold and brutal firelit hollow from which Victor Mature emerged in *One Million B.C.*, but a tastefully appointed suburban bungalow—

except that the telephone was a ram's horn, the phonograph was a stone disk with a bird who used his beak as a tonearm and needle, the vacuum cleaner was a small mastodon mounted on wheels, equipped with a forked stick for a handle and a trunk that sucked up dust as effectively as any contemporary Hoover. (That particular appliance originated in a ceramic mastodon piggy-bank I kept—and still keep—in my office.) There was the family's pet—Dino the dinosaur. There was the family's car, constructed of logs, stone rollers (for the wheel as such had yet to be invented), topped with ragged cloth or animal hide, and powered by the driver's bare feet protruding through the floorboard.

Then there were the names—all resulting from a collision between the neolithic universe and our own modern, middle-class world: the Stoneway piano, the Polarock camera, the actress Ann-Margrock (voiced by Ann-Margret), the actors Cary Granite and Stony Curtis (voiced by Tony Curtis), the conductor Leonard Bernstone, boxer Floyd Patterstone, and, of course, the monarch of Sunday evening television, Ed Sullystone. We originally called our family the Flagstones, but we received a letter from the creator of the "Hi and Lois" comic strip, who pointed out that the surname of his characters, the Flagstons, was too close for comfort, and he was prepared to so advise his attorneys. Reluctantly, we redubbed our family the Gladstones and later moved on to the Flintstones and planted them in the town of Bedrock, Cobblestone County, elevation 250 feet *below* sea level.

To sell the show, Dan Gordon and I wrote the simplest situation comedy story we could think of, and Dan did the storyboards. Fred Flintstone and his neighbor, Barney Rubble, who are supposed to go to the opera with their wives, Wilma and Betty, hatch a scheme that will allow them to do what they *really* want to do: go bowling. Now, such a plot was hardly original. Chester Riley, on "The Life of Riley," must have done something like this a dozen times, and Ralph Kramden, on "The Honeymooners," must have done it *two* dozen. It was, quite literally, prehistoric comedy—a classic plot from the Stone

Age of TV sitcoms. And from the very beginning there have been no shortage of people to tell me that "The Flintstones" borrowed (or stole) very heavily from "The Honeymooners"—an observation (or accusation) I always take as the highest compliment possible, because The Great One really was, and "The Honeymooners" was a landmark in the history of television comedy.

But I also point out that "The Honeymooners" did not have a Stoneway piano, and Ralph Kramden and Ed Norton certainly did not have access to the Stone Age technology we made available to Fred and Barney. Barney invented a helicopter, foot-pedal-powered and resembling nothing more than a very large eggbeater, to transport Fred and himself to and from the bowling alley without the wives catching wise. Nor was neolithic bowling quite the sport Ralph and Ed would have been familiar with. To begin with, Fred bowled with a rock—a round rock, but a rock nevertheless—and when he threw it down the alley, it began to chip apart until it was reduced to a tiny pebble by the time it reached the kingpin, not with a crash, but a *plink*, which sent all of the pins down, domino-fashion. That first storyboard also featured the bowler's dreaded split. But when Fred rolled a split, it really was a *split*. His rock-ball would break in half, each half knocking over a pin and thereby scoring the spare.

We were delighted with Dan's storyboards and started a second, but already we were getting anxious to begin presenting "The Flintstones" to the agencies and the networks. Hey, I was told, fly to New York, check in at the Sherry-Netherland, do the song-and-dance, come home, and the rest will be television history.

But, as I said, it was one disappointment after another. Everyone we showed it to loved "The Flintstones." But a prime-time *animated* series? No, thanks.

Screen Gems's John Mitchell took each turndown in stride and lined up more and more meetings. About nine one night, he came to me in my cell at the Sherry. He knew how much I hated to fly, but he set up a meeting with Armour, the meat packer in Chicago. "Look," he said smoothly and reassuringly, "we'll pick you up at seven in the morning, and you'll be nice and comfortable in the limo, and we'll go to LaGuardia. We just gotta go into Chicago, make one presentation, and we'll come back."

IT WAS THE DEAD OF WINTER, and in Chicago winter is very dead indeed—maybe thirteen below, maybe colder. I got off the plane, and the wind—the cold cuts off your breath. That's when I saw that *everyone* else walked around with their chins buried in multiple layers of mufflers. Just trying to stay alive. Nor were the hanging judges who made up the meat packer's executive corps much warmer than the weather. I did what I always did: papered the walls with the storyboards, then put on the show, a one-man, hyper-charged version of vaudeville. Only these guys were stiff as boards and didn't so much as crack a smile.

It was still winter when John made me fly out with him next to St. Louis, to pitch the show to Ralston Purina. We got out to St. Louis okay, but then a blizzard roars through town. I sit in that airport, watching the snow not so much fall as shoot by *horizontally*, and I think to myself: *Why do I have to do this?* I'm saying to God: *Who cares? Who cares this much about a goddamned cartoon?*

To my tremendous relief all flights are grounded. But John Mitchell is not about to allow nature or God or the FAA to ground anything. He says to me, "Wait here," and, setting his chin bulldog-fashion, stalks off and disappears.

I'm still saying to myself: *God, thank you, God. We're not leaving. Thank you.* Then I look up and here comes this bull moose through the crowd—bodies flying left and right.

"Get your bags. Follow me."

He leads me out into the storm. There's a stairway up against the plane, a 707. We climb it, get in, and, with maybe ten other doomed souls, take our seats. There's no safety spiel, or greeting, or, in fact, any announcement of any kind. The jockey on the flight deck revs up the motors, wheels the plane around in a tight circle like he's in a parking lot—no stopping, nobody telling us to fasten our seat belts—just *zoom* down the runway. *We're getting outta here*. And into, as they say, the teeth of the storm.

All to sell a cartoon show to makers of cereal and dog food.

IT WAS BACK TO NEW YORK, the Sherry, and discouragement. NBC turned us down. Jim Aubrey, the new president of CBS, turned us down after I pitched the show in a hot, crowded, stuffy little room that was so dark nobody could see the storyboards. And then there was the pitch to Bristol-Meyers—one of my best presentations. I gave everything I had to a room packed full, got a great reaction, and wasn't finished until the end of the day, four or five in the afternoon. I staggered back to the Sherry, laid myself out corpselike on the bed, then *rrring, rrring,* and I pick up the phone. It seems that the one person missing from the audience was the president of the company. Could I come back—*now*—and do the whole thing all over again?

No problem.

Exhausted, we were at last about to give up. There was only one network left to pitch—the new kid on the block, ABC, which had an uphill struggle against the more established NBC and CBS, who regarded the fledgling contender with no little contempt. But instead of developing an inferiority complex, ABC took an aggressive and innovative stance.

I got little enough time to sleep during the eight-week marathon of pitching, and when I did get the time, I didn't sleep well. The morning of the ABC presentation was no exception. I was roused from fitful slumber at eight in the morning by drums: boom, boom, boom.

The noise was coming from Fifth Avenue below my window. It was St. Patrick's Day, and this was the start of the parade. The prospect of plowing through a sea of marchers and spectators while lugging four hundred storyboards and other assorted pieces of artwork did not appeal to me. Besides, I could already hear the variations in beat among the drummers, and that meant only one thing: They had started fortifying themselves early. When I was a kid growing up in Brooklyn, my Uncle Jim, neither a Catholic nor an Irishman, loved to march in New York's St. Patrick's Day parade. He had a bass drum, and he liked to beat it, but what he liked even more was the good cheer that came when the drummers took a break from the bracing winds of March to knock back a shot or two of whiskey. By late afternoon, what you had was a parade of bombed drummers.

Somehow I cut through the onlookers and marchers, and I set up shop in the conference room at Screen Gems, which had become as sickeningly familiar to me as my hotel room. As usual we decided to furnish those at the meeting with sweet rolls and coffee hastily purchased at the corner deli. While I was rushing to make the meeting and fighting the jostling crowds, a lot of the scalding hot coffee had sloshed out of the cup, over my hand, down my wrist, and soaked my cuff and shirtsleeve. This, I could tell, was going to be a lot of fun.

After the ABC people had assembled, including top executives Leonard Goldenson, Danny Melnick, and Ollie Treyz, I launched into the show. After eight weeks, and within fifteen minutes, "The Flintstones" was sold.

End of story?

I certainly thought so, and I got on a plane for L.A., felt the sun again, saw the grass again, settled into my own office again. Then the phone rang.

"You gotta come back."

"Wh-what?" There was a tremor in my voice.

We had sold the show to the network. Now it was up to us to sell the show to some sponsors—and, it was decided, I was the only one who could make the pitch. We were, then, only halfway home. Without sponsorship, "The Flintstones" could still fail to become a reality.

SAM NORTHCROSS of the William Esty agency, one of whose biggest clients was R. J. Reynolds, took the train with me to Winston-Salem, North Carolina, to pitch the show to the tobacco giant. I hate flying and love trains, but I've never been able to sleep on them, and we arrived in the Southland bleary-eyed and in no mood to behold the company's gorgeous offices, sumptuously paneled in the richest of fine wood. All I could say was: "We can't stick tacks in this." So I got Scotch tape and neatly, tediously, with infinite care, affixed four hundred four-by-five-inch drawings to the corporate walls, using exactly one piece of tape per drawing.

"What time are we starting?"

"Right after lunch."

So Northcross and I went out to get a badly needed jolt of caffeine. When we returned and opened the door of the conference room, we saw that every single drawing had fallen to the floor. Not one remained on the walls. With meeting time closing in, we worked feverishly to tape them up again, this time using two pieces of tape per drawing, thereby doubling our work.

We had just finished, when the door opened and the executive corps entered: the president and his lieutenants, stiff in their freshly laundered white shirts and conservative ties, and the chairman of the board, an aging southern gentleman named Bowman Gray, who, painfully afflicted with gout, leaned heavily on a cane.

They were all polite in the traditional southern way, but, rigorously following the lead of their visibly suffering chief, all utterly unsmiling. I explained that it was best to stand behind me during the presentation, so that they could view the storyboards clearly.

"All right, Mr. Barbera," Bowman Gray muttered through clenched teeth. And as he took up his position, leaning heavily on his cane, his troops lined up behind him. I regarded Mr. Gray closely and with considerable concern. His face was contorted in agony, and here I was, about to launch into forty-five minutes of goofy voices, bizarre gestures, and weird sound effects.

He was, in fact, highly attentive. Indeed, as I would move from one set of drawings to another, he would move with me, stumping with his cane, his troops following him in perfectly synchronized lockstep. I'd move slowly left to right, then quickly back to the left to get to the next row of drawings. And they followed right along, like the carriage of an old-fashioned typewriter: click-click-click-click, zoom, click-

click-click-click, zoom.

Through it all, the same face, unchanging in its expression of pain, with not the slightest hint of a twitch heralding even so much as an embryonic smile. And the troops, like good soldiers, mirrored their chief exactly.

I concluded, lamely enough, "Well, sir, that's the story," accepted his thanks, was ushered out, staggered back to my hotel room, and thought: *It is hopeless.*

Then, after some time, Sam Northcross appeared at my door, his hat pushed well back on his head.

"Sold the show," he announced.

All I could manage was, "*How?*"

"Well, they said, at least there was no blood and guts running in the streets."

Even the labors of Hercules knew an end, and surely mine were now at last concluded. But, no.

R. J. Reynolds had bought only *half* the show.

I WAS A ZOMBIE when John Mitchell put me on a midnight plane bound for Chicago and Miles Laboratories, the vitamin maker. Of all the miserable airplane rides I've had, and I've had many, this was the worst—perhaps, in fact, the roughest ride in aviation history. It was as if a dog had gotten hold of the aircraft and was shaking it like an old sock. The plane was a brand-new Electra, which was destined to go down in the annals of commercial flight as one of its great disasters. The first Electra crashed spectacularly in 1959 and, thereafter, Electras seemed to crash so frequently that about a dozen large corporations barred their traveling executives from flying on them, and people made jokes like, "Have you read the new Electra book, *Look Ma, No Wings*?"

We reached Chicago in the wee hours of the morning and had to prepare for an eight A.M. meeting. I have discovered that one of the immutable laws of nature, as inevitable as gravity and as absolute as the speed of light, is that meetings with agencies and network executives always occur at eight o'clock in the morning. My thumb was bleeding from pushing pushpins through storyboards and walls. I grabbed an hour's sleep in my hotel room, then showed up, a pale, green thing, to make the pitch.

Miles Laboratories bought the other half of "The Flintstones" and has been involved with the show and the characters ever since, even marketing the highly successful Flintstones Chewable Vitamins for children.

ALL MY BATTLES WON, I journeyed back to LaBrea, to Huck, Yogi, Quick Draw, and the spirit of Charlie Chaplin. Not that this was a time to rest. We were struggling to keep in motion what we already had going even as we worked to get the production machinery rolling on "The Flintstones."

I walked into the studio one morning and saw Bill Hanna sitting at his desk, looking grim.

"What's the matter?" I asked

"Joe."

"What?"

"Joe."

"*What?*"

"We can't deliver the show."

By now, for a fact, it simply did not mean anything to me. I rarely raise my voice, and I did not raise it then. I said: "Well, we can't deliver the show? Call 'em. Go ahead. Call 'em in New York. Tell 'em."

So Bill dialed the phone. He didn't get John Mitchell, but Jerry Hyams, the president of Screen Gems, the man they called the "Diamond in the Rough," with emphasis on *rough*. He had on occasion taken his cue from Soviet Premier Nikita Khrushchev and at more than one meeting had removed his shoe and used it to pound home a particularly salient point. Now this was New York on the other end of Bill's telephone, and there were four-letter words—some of them invented that very day, I believe.

Mild-mannered Bill Hanna announced: "Jerry, you know, we can't deliver the show."

The phone disintegrated.

It wasn't a speaker phone, but you could hear most of the other end of the conversation. What came through loudest and clearest were "*suing you*" and "*cocksuckers*."

They jumped the red eye and were at the LaBrea Studios the next day—at eight o'clock in the morning, of course. Like B-movie gangsters, they demanded: "What do you got? Let's see what you got!"

And we showed them.

"Nothing wrong with that. What's the matter with that?"

In its way, it was the vote of confidence we needed. The net result was that we did deliver, thanks to Jerry Hyams.

AND WE STILL FOUND TIME for the finishing touches. After we had the first five shows in the can, I found myself strangely discontented. Something was not right. After all we had been through, something was still not right.

As important as the story, the gags, and the look of the characters are, if you don't have just the right voices, you don't have a successful cartoon. And with five shows done but yet to be telecast, I realized that we did not have the right voices.

I recast and redubbed the voices of Fred Flintstone and Barney Rubble in all five half-hours, giving Alan Reed—best known as Falstaff Openshaw on Fred Allen's classic radio show—the role of Fred and assigning the great Mel Blanc, long the versatile voice of Warner Bros. cartoons, to Barney Rubble.

If "The Flintstones" is identified with any *single* thing, it is the phrase "Yabba-dabba-doo!" Now, I've checked the Third Edition of *The American Heritage Dictionary*, the most progressive, up-to-date, and adventurous dictionary in the English language, and I was disappointed to find that *yabba-dabba-doo* is not included as an entry. Yet, beyond question, the expression has become ingrained in universal speech, and I am confident that, come the Fourth Edition, it *will* be included.

How did this momentous artifact come to be a part of "The Flintstones"? Originally, the script called for Fred to shout "Yahoo!" At a recording session, Alan Reed turned to me and asked, "Can I say 'yabba-dabba-doo' here?"

In a stroke of blinding genius born of years of experience, I replied, "Okay."

My whole life, in and out of 'toons, has turned on moments just like this, has been determined by perfectly casual, almost thoughtless decisions and actions, some of them mine, some of them others'. You'll see what I mean as you read on. But, look, I was born in 1911, so I admit, grudgingly, that I am no longer a young man. Yet, to this very day, I sometimes wake up in a cold sweat, struck by the thought that, after eight weeks alone in a hotel room, I had about given up on "The Flintstones." I might have returned to Los Angeles at any time before I pitched ABC. "The Flintstones" came within weeks, days, even hours of never having been born. Where would I be today without the citizens of Bedrock?

I could speculate on this or any number of untaken forks in the road, but, as it turned out, I did sell the show, and I made a great life for myself in 'toons. And now, if you care to read on, I'll take you back to the very beginning, on the Lower East Side, then onto Flatbush in Brooklyn, and then to a very strange place called Los Angeles.

Chapter Two

WHOLLY INNOCENT

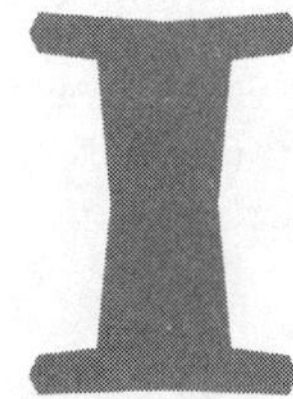

WAS EIGHTY-TWO YEARS OLD before *Who's Who* thought I was enough of a big shot to do a piece on me. Among the questions they asked me was "Whom do you most admire?" I told them it was my grandmother, Francesca Calvacca, who came to the Lower East Side of New York City from the little country town of Schiacca on the southern coast of Sicily in about 1898. She raised five sons, and she helped my mother, also named Francesca, look after me and my brothers, Larry and Ted. Except for me, no one in my family could draw, but the gift my grandmother had in abundance was a great sense of humor. Rearing and helping to rear a total of nine Sicilians requires a most acute sense of humor—mainly to prevent bloodshed.

Anyway, I like to think that I inherited at least some of her wit.

I was born on the Lower East Side, at 10 Delancey Street, in Little Italy, but moved with my family to Flatbush, Brooklyn, when I was only four months old. That was a step up for an immigrant family in those days, and, indeed, Flatbush then was a delightful place: a neighborhood of tree-lined streets and parkways with names like Buckingham Road, Rugby Road, Argyle Road, and Albemarle Road. Because I left the Lower East Side before I was a year old, I remember nothing of it, but, later, I was visiting some of my family's friends there, and, yes, the apartments were tiny—long, narrow, and dark—but they were immaculate, everything kept in perfect order with pride and care. The people who lived in them never asked for a dime but worked at any job they could get, and worked hard and with determination to succeed. My grandfather rolled cigars for a living, and two of my mother's brothers, as boys, sold newspapers in Chinatown, which was and still is adjacent to Little Italy. It didn't do them any harm—and maybe even did them a lot of good. Uncle Emil went on to study at Williams College and then Princeton, putting himself through undergraduate and graduate school by playing the violin at fancy restaurants. He became a professor of languages. Uncle Michael, whom we all called "the Little One," made it through New York University and Tufts Medical College, then returned to a tough Brooklyn neighborhood to practice medicine.

If my parents had thought to leave the Lower East Side behind them when they moved to Flatbush, well, my mother couldn't quite do it. Married at sixteen, she absorbed everything the neighborhood had to offer. Years later, when I was a boy, I was shopping with her at a little mom-and-pop Jewish deli in Flatbush, and the mom said something to the pop in Yiddish. They were standing by the butter cask. Back then, butter was delivered to the store in a wooden cask, and you bought it by weight, the storekeeper scooping out onto a scale whatever quantity you wanted. Apparently the couple was discussing something concerning the butter.

That's when my mother interrupted them.

"Never mind that," she said *in Yiddish*. "Let me have the fresh butter." On the streets of the Lower East Side my Sicilian mother had become fluent enough in Yiddish—and in how many other languages I do not know—to understand that the wife had told her husband to "sell the old butter first."

In perfect unison, the couple did a double take as funny as anything I ever put into a cartoon, though without the sound effects. Later, when I was in high school, I worked in that deli after classes.

My father was a barber, but not your ordinary, everyday barber. He cut men's hair as well as women's, specializing in what was called the Marcel wave, which consisted of fashioning deep, regular waves in the customer's hair with a curling iron. The style was much in demand, but not everyone could do it. The net result was that my father made enough money to expand. By the time he was twenty-five, he had three shops in Brooklyn—on Church Avenue, Newkirk Avenue, and Cortelyou Road—all of which made a ton of money for him.

He used some of his profits to create and maintain an image of elegance that was a thing of wonder to me. Next door to one of his shops was the shop of a little Armenian tailor named Drazian, and I remember watching Mr. Drazian fit my father for suit after suit. If you've ever watched a man getting fitted for suit today, chances are what you've seen is a stiff, uncomfortable, self-conscious, even slightly embarrassed figure. Not my father. He stood for his fittings as if he had been born to such things.

We all should have been living pretty well off the proceeds of my father's business, but as the money started coming in, we saw less and less of Vincent Barbera, and he, in turn, saw less and less of what he called "the shops." Instead of attending to business, he communed with the horses at Aqueduct and Belmont. Once, when I was about five years old, he took me with him to the track and had me mark his racing form. I picked a horse called Gray Lag, my old man placed a bet, and the horse won. My father embraced me, proclaimed me an oracle, and even laid out a career for me as a jockey.

It is true that I was puny enough at age five to suggest that I had the makings of good jockey material. The year before, I was playing in our neighborhood on a wintry afternoon when I saw a tub under a rainspout beside a neat little Brooklyn house. The tub was maybe two feet high, and the water had frozen, so I climbed up on top of the ice and started sliding around. I remember laughing and laughing, and I remember the cracking noise and a rush of cold. Then all I remember is opening my eyes and seeing my mother and a doctor hovering over me.

That, I learned, was nine days later. I had gotten double pneumonia, and it looked so bad that my mother was approached by a particularly aggressive undertaker. But she refused to give up on me and promised God that she would go to mass every morning for a year if He would only let me recover.

Well, I didn't die—though it seemed to me that, perversely enough, after saving my life, my mother tried to kill me. From the time I was back on my feet until I left my mother's house as a young man, I was made to drink a mixture of a quart of milk, a pint of cream, and three raw eggs each and every day. As if that weren't enough to stop my arteries cold, I was given a tablespoonful of something called cream of cod liver oil. It came out of a bottle that bore a label showing a little kid wearing a yellow slicker and sou'wester with a great big codfish slung over his shoulder. I hated that little kid.

As for my mother, she made good on her promise to the Lord, and left the house at 5:30 each and every morning for one year, through rain, snow, and gloom of night—or predawn morning—to attend mass. A vow, she said, was a vow.

For all her high-cholesterol ministrations, I failed to fatten. The second time my father took me to the track, he once again gave me the card to mark. This time, my horse did not even show. In fact, the triumph of Gray Lag was my first and last success as a handicapper. After a few more failures, my father stopped taking me to the track, and there was no further talk of my future as a jockey.

AS TIME WENT ON, we rarely saw him around the house. Once in a while, he'd show up and throw money on the table for my mother—

on occasion a bankroll of two or three thousand dollars. At one point, he tried to become a responsible real estate investor and bought an entire apartment building for six thousand dollars. Within a day or two of buying the building, he sold it for, I think, nine thousand dollars. It was a nice quick profit, but he could have held the building, made long-term money in rents, and ultimately could have bought the entire block for next to nothing. But that kind of business was too slow for my old man, who became increasingly restless and temperamental, often flaring into violence—though most of that consisted of yelling, gesturing, and stamping about the parlor.

My mother, exasperated, would yell at him that he wasn't holding my brothers and me in check, and in response he would threaten us.

I remember waiting for him to show up after I had committed this or that misdemeanor. When I heard him come in, then listened to the characteristic exchange between him and my mother, I would retreat to my refuge, which was under the bed in my room. It was a bed with old-fashioned box springs, and I discovered that I could hook my feet between the springs at one end of the bed and grab the springs at the other end with my hands, then pull myself up off the floor.

My father would come fuming into the room, unbuckle his belt, pull it through the loops, and begin flogging the floor and the furniture with it, all the while hurling threats. Hanging from the box springs, I'd watch his feet going back and forth and I'd listen to the crack of the belt. When I saw the feet at last retreat out the door, I'd ease myself down, self-satisfied in the knowledge that I had put one over on the old man.

As I think about it now, I hadn't won at all. My old man *preferred* yelling, demonstrating, and exercising his wrath on the floor and furnishings to actually hitting me or my brothers. In this he was remarkably similar to the manager of the little movie house on Cortelyou Road. When I was eight or nine years old, on matinee days, two friends and I used to wait for some of the people to come out of the theater, and we'd sneak in. Who had a dime for a movie back then? So we'd come in from a bright, sunny Brooklyn afternoon into the blackness of the theater, and we'd scrunch down in the seats, trying to make ourselves totally invisible.

That ended when the manager stormed down the aisle, yanked us out our seats, and took us into his office. With the three of us sitting there, terrified, he'd slip off his belt and start slamming the floor and the furniture with it, hurling threats at us the whole time. It was as if he and my old man had compared notes.

My father's performances succeeded sufficiently in terrorizing me while somewhat appeasing my mother, allowing her feel for a few moments that he was discharging his fatherly duty. Then my father could return to the track relatively undisturbed.

I can't honestly say just when it was that my father officially left us, because he didn't so much *leave* as he *phased himself out*. We just saw less and less of him, and then, one day, we realized that we weren't seeing him at all. At that point—I was about fifteen—we moved into my grandmother and grandfather's small two-family house.

IN CONTRAST TO MY FATHER, mother, brothers, and me, who moved repeatedly from place to place in Flatbush—Eighteenth Street and Church Avenue; Argyle Road and Church Avenue; Fifteenth Street and Newkirk; 343 Twenty-sixth near Clarendon Road; 262 East Twenty-sixth near Coretlyou Road; and a number of others I'm forgetting—my grandfather and grandmother had, like so many immigrant families, a dream of owning some little piece of America, buying it, and staying in it all their lives.

My grandfather made wine in his basement and had a good little business delivering such Italian staples as parmesan cheese, salami, and olive oil door to door. On Saturdays I'd have to help him on his rounds, which were made by subway and trolley car. He'd ring a doorbell, and a gracious Italian lady would answer. We would step in and enact the ritual courtesies of discussing the health and welfare of our respective families while taking a sip of coffee. You didn't drink directly from the cup, but carefully poured a small puddle of the liquid into your saucer and drank it from that.

Among the many stupid and ridiculous things I've done in my life, the stupidest was generally to scorn my Italian heritage. I deliberately refused to pick up any of the language. I looked down my nose at all the wonderful food—somehow forgetting how I used to spear with a fork as many of the exquisite little meatballs simmering on the stove before my mother could hit me with her long-handled spoon. And I remember with particular shame how I allowed myself to feel embarrassed when I took my mother to meet my future mother-in-law, and she drank her coffee from the saucer.

At the conclusion of his visits, my grandfather would fill the lady's order, cutting a slice from a great wheel of parmesan. It was perfectly smooth and yellow, yielding freely to his sharp knife. Then we would take our leave, go to the next house, and repeat the process. By the end of our Saturday rounds, I was awash in Italian coffee and thoroughly buzzed.

WELL INTO MY HIGH SCHOOL YEARS, I maintained some minimal contact with my absent father when, like my brothers, I called at one of his shops to claim a free haircut. That much he seemed to consider his sacred duty, although there was no father-and-son warmth to these visits. And there was also one occasion when I went to him, very much hat in hand, to plead for the loan of some money to rent a dinner jacket for a dance at Erasmus Hall High School. I think it was the hardest money I've ever gotten out of anyone.

There came a point when even these brief contacts ceased, and I lost track of my father entirely. Many years later, when I was living in Los Angeles, my brother Larry told me that he had seen the old man running a shabby little one-chair barber shop way out on Avenue S, which I guessed was in the vicinity of Coney Island.

Increasingly, during later childhood, my Uncle Jim stood in for my father. It was not something he had deliberately set out to do. It's just that Jim, one of my mother's brothers, had it in his nature, a nature that was kind, generous, and, in a word, wonderful. For a week each summer, he would take me to the Catskills, where for ten dollars we got room and board with John Steele and his wife, a bona-fide farm couple who took in guests during the summer. There was a boat and beautiful lake, which I would row or swim across. Sometimes we would journey up the Hudson, rent a large, two-person tent, and set up camp just below West Point. I even swam in the Hudson—until one day the bloated and discolored carcass of a pig floated by and met my horrified gaze, open eye to open eye. That was when I retired from river swims.

Then there was Jim's wife, Aunt Tess, who loved these trips almost as much as I did, but who was deathly afraid of bugs and insects of all kinds.

Folks would pitch their tents in a kind of colony or encampment near the river, and I remember more than one night when the silence was pierced by her screams. The whole tent colony would emerge from their shelters, wondering what assailant or apparition had invaded the peaceful banks of the Hudson.

"For godsakes," Uncle Jim would say to her, "it's only a little bug."

"But, James, I can't go back in there until you get rid of it."

And, with infinite patience, that is just what he would do. Years later, in California, I had the pleasure of watching Jim "adopt" my own young son, Neal, just as he had adopted me in Brooklyn.

I DON'T KNOW THAT I SPENT any more time alone than any other kid, but being by myself never bothered me. I liked to dream and daydream, and on one rainy afternoon when I was eight years old and found myself alone with nothing in particular to do, I made an important discovery.

I found out that I could draw.

I was lying on the carpet in our apartment on Newkirk Avenue and Fifteenth Street, looking at some pictures. I happened on an illustration of a puppy playing with a kitten. It was a perfectly ordinary picture, but it fascinated me. So I got some paper, and I started drawing the two animals—not tracing them, but *drawing* them, *duplicating* them.

There was no great fanfare to accompany this event. No rays of light flooded into the room. And no one in my family took particular notice of it, although my mother must have thought something of it, since she saved the picture, and I have it to this day, three-quarters of a century later. At the time, I didn't even think much about it. Drawing was just something to do on a rainy day. But it was the first inkling I had that I could do something that nobody else *I* knew could do. It seemed to me that God had looked around, saw me, and just said: *You can draw*. And that's all there was to it.

To this day, I also keep on a shelf in my office a complete set of *The Book of Knowledge*, some twenty volumes, which my mother bought, through a subscription at, I think, $1.47 per month, payable for just about the rest of your life. My mother and I regarded these books as precious. From time to time, I'd ask her for one of the volumes, to read about some hero of myth or ancient history and, perhaps, to copy a picture. My mother would get her key, walk down the hall to a high mahogany cabinet, unlock it, and ask me which volume I wanted. They were numbered, kept two on a shelf on ten shelves in the cabinet.

"Number three."

And she would take the book from the shelf, make a jacket for it out of brown paper, then hand it to me. It was a combination of ritual and game, for me almost a magical incantation. I'd pull a number out of the air, then endure the eager anticipation as I watched my mother wrap the volume, imagining what wonders would be revealed to me in volume three, or five, or twelve.

IN THE FIRST GRADE, I was enrolled at a Catholic elementary school called Holy Innocents. It did not take long for the nuns there to discover that I could draw. Far from wielding a knuckle-rapping ruler to discourage me in this, they put me to work. They planted me up at the blackboard with a big book of Bible illustrations propped up on the ledge. I remember one picture in particular, a double-page spread of Jesus entering Jerusalem. There were palms and people waving. I duplicated this and others in white chalk on the board.

Once the nuns had discovered that I could do this, drawing Bible pictures became all that I ever did. The nuns would bring visitors into the classroom to watch me work. I never had to study, and I never had homework to do. I did acquire a film of chalk dust on my head, and, later, when I read about Michelangelo lying on his back for four years to paint the ceiling of the Sistine Chapel, I confess that I identified myself—coated in chalk—with the "agony and the ecstasy" of the great artist of the Italian Renaissance, covered in plaster and paint.

By and by, my mother must have connected the chalk dust I brought home with the fact that, as the weeks and months passed, I was learning absolutely nothing. Reading I had picked up on my own, but I couldn't add, subtract, divide, or multiply—a disability that remains with me to this day, despite the fact that my first "adult" job was filling out tax forms in the trust department of a bank for six dreadful years. So, horrified and outraged, my mother yanked me out of Holy Innocents and put me into PS 139, a public school. There, for a time, I turned from drawing to sports, when I discovered that I was a very good high jumper. I would jump over the bar on my right side, until one day I tried jumping on my left side—and added four additional inches of height. I won a championship.

WHEN I GOT OLDER, I worked after school. My father had struck a bargain with Mr. Drazian, the little Armenian tailor who made his suits, to give me work as a delivery boy. The best thing about this was that my father bought me a secondhand bicycle for five dollars—no fenders, just bare tires, but it beat walking. Mr. Drazian would call me in, have me extend one arm, then fold a suitcoat in his particularly deliberate, neat, and methodical way, and drape it over my arm. Next would come a pair of pants, similarly folded, then a dress, perhaps, and another suitcoat. With one arm thus occupied, I'd mount my bike and ride up Buckingham Road, Rugby Road, Argyle Road, Albemarle Road, making the prescribed round of deliveries, leaving a bill or collecting cash, depending on the customer.

For me it was a lovely occupation, through the beautiful streets of Flatbush, which had grass and flowers running down the middle. On one trip, however, I hit a rut, flew over the handlebars, and landed headfirst in the grass. I got to my feet, felt of myself, and, concluding that I was still in one piece, set about collecting the clothes strewn over the parkway. I worked assiduously to pick off the dirt and grass and weeds, but I couldn't hope to refold the garments as Mr. Drazian had. If there was any outrage among the Armenian's customers, I never heard anything about it, and I kept my mouth shut about the accident.

I didn't even tell my best friend at Drazian's, a tall, slender black man I knew only as Clarence, who, with aspirations of becoming a professional dancer, worked for the tailor as a presser. He would spend hours telling me stories, and he made the most of his tedious day job by meticulously pressing his own super stylish bell-bottom pants until their crease was razor sharp. I was only nine or ten at the time, but with the elegant example of my father firmly planted in my imagination, I had a keen appreciation of *style*, and I thought: *If only I had a pair of pants like those*.

One day Clarence motioned to me.

"I want to give you something," he said.

And he handed me a pair of freshly pressed trousers. They were an old pair of his, greatly cut down, because he was over six feet tall. But we were both slender, and the pants fit perfectly. They weren't the longed-for bell bottoms, but, with a large portion of my father's income going to the track, there wasn't a lot of money for clothes, and I gratefully accepted the gift, wearing the pants to school the very next day.

It was after classes when I was making my bicycle rounds for Drazian that a problem developed. All of a sudden, my rear end was bathed in cool air. With one arm occupied in holding my deliveries, I couldn't reach behind me to confirm what I strongly feared was the case: The seat of the pants, worn paper thin, had utterly disintegrated.

This incident hardly foretold what would be one of the three distinctions I was later to earn in high school. Although we fought constantly, my girlfriend Dorothy Earl—beautiful and possessed of a powerful personality—and I would be proclaimed "Romeo and Juliet" in the senior yearbook. I would also be named "Handsomest Boy," and, finally, "Beau Brummel." It was true that I did dress with style and elegance in high school—but that was due to the good taste of Uncle Emil, who had gone to Princeton and traveled all over Europe, and who handed down to me his ultra-sophisticated cast-offs, which were considerably less worn than Clarence's gift.

IT WAS IN HIGH SCHOOL at Erasmus Hall that I rediscovered drawing. I was perhaps thirteen at the time, and I was sitting across the room from a girl—a pretty blonde named Stephanie Bates—in music class. I began sketching her, never saying a word to her. Then I gave her the sketches, and I took her out to a movie—once. I never even held her hand, but, fifty years later, I got a call from her. Of all things, she was working in a nunnery.

I also entered some art contests while I was at Erasmus Hall, and I won them. I became editor of the school newspaper, *The Dutchman*, to which I also contributed a number of cartoons. At this point, however, art meant less to me than literature. In English class I wrote a story about Cossacks attacking a village, the whole thing seen through the eyes of a wounded soldier. My teacher was sufficiently impressed with what I had done to have me read it aloud to the class.

I have always been attracted to adventure stories. Hanna-Barbera made its name with a cat and a mouse, a scheming bear with a porkpie hat, a horse who wore a ten-gallon hat and packed a six-shooter, a drawling blue hound dog, a family of Stone Age suburbanites, and others. But some of my favorite shows have been the action adventure series we did: "Jonny Quest," "The Herculoids," "The Fantastic Four," and so on. I was one of those kids who read voraciously anything having to do with action and adventure. I would read into the night well past my bedtime, under the covers with a flashlight, and I did this to the eternal annoyance of my father, who would burst into my room and snatch both book and flashlight from my hands. On one occasion he tore the book in half—something for which I never quite forgave him.

I would, of course, pore through *The Book of Knowledge* and rivet on the myths, legends, and tales of heroic deeds. I read about Roland, the hero of the medieval epic *Chanson de Roland*. During one of the Crusades, Roland's uncle, Charlemagne, left him to defend Roncevalles as he and his knights beat their retreat. Attacked by Saracens, Roland, steeped in his magnificent chivalric code, repeatedly refused his friend Oliver's pleas to blow the horn that would summon help. When he finally did blow the horn, it was too late, and both he and Oliver were slain. *The Book of Knowledge* had a picture of Roland defending the bridge at Roncevalles, sword in hand, with a band of warriors fighting like crazy in the background.

The story of Roland captivated me, as did the name, which sounded like another favorite of mine—Raoul—which I frequently encountered in the stories of Dumas. As I neared age thirteen, when it came time for my Confirmation, I chose "Roland" as my middle name. I remember the priest moving down a line of us kneeling at St. Jerome's. He was muttering deep in his throat the blessing he had issued a thousand times: "Domino, domino, Thomas. Domino, domino, Charles. Domino, domino, Frank. Domino, domino—Roland. Rolando? Roland? Hmmm. Rol*ahnd*?"

Even more fantastic for me was when I discovered that literature could move from the page to the stage. It was early in high school that I went to my first Broadway show, the guest of Dorothy Earl and her mother. It was Rodgers and Hart's *A Connecticut Yankee in King Arthur's Court*, and I was completely stunned by it. It was, in fact, one of the great experiences of my life: to see how words and images could come to life like that. I was instantly bitten bad by the Broadway bug, and whatever money I could scrape together I spent on tickets to shows. I also began to go in for dramatics at school and even appeared in the Erasmus Hall production of Gilbert and Sullivan's *H.M.S. Pinafore* at the prestigious Brooklyn Academy of Music. A teacher at Erasmus Hall recommended me to the American School of Dramatic Art, an idea I very much liked—until I discovered that you had to pay them $500 tuition. That put an end to that.

Much later, I would write two and a half plays myself—the finished ones are *The Two Faces of Janus* and *The Maid and the Martian*. I'm still working on the third, and I wish I could find time to write many more. When the *Who's Who* people asked me to list my "Fantasy Occupation," it was easy: playwright.

HIGH SCHOOL WAS A WONDERFUL TIME, a time of discovery and of dreams without limit, and Erasmus Hall was a great school, respected throughout the city. Even our football games attracted a crowd; 35,000 people came to Ebbets Field, home of the Brooklyn Dodgers, to watch a *high school* play football. In the fall, every Friday, we had dances, and some of them were very grand affairs. I remember one that took place in no fewer than five ballrooms, including the Waldorf-Astoria's. We just moved from ballroom to ballroom as the evening went on.

In my last year at Erasmus Hall, I was seduced by the notion of becoming a prizefighter. I say "seduced" deliberately, because, in those days, boxing was something very glamorous and romantic. You didn't see the bouts close-up on television, with the sweat and the blood, the splayed noses, and the cuts bursting open over the eyes, and you certainly didn't have Robert DeNiro movies like *Raging Bull*. You *listened* to fights on the radio, and a good announcer made it seem like a contest between gladiators. When a boy was given a pair of boxing gloves on Christmas or his birthday, it was like a young knight being presented with his spurs.

That last year, the school started a boxing class, and I eagerly enrolled. I used to box at school and spar with my friends in the backyard at home. Somehow we got hold of one of the early 8-millimeter movie cameras, and I still remember watching silent footage of myself imitating the high style of Al Singer, lightweight champion and my personal idol.

Meanwhile, at school, I fought six bouts and won them all. The seventh, for the lightweight championship of Erasmus Hall, was against a kid named Toomey. Now, Toomey was good, very good, and he knew it, and he liked it. He brought his entire family with him to the fight to witness my destruction.

The only thing was, that's not the way it turned out. Before the eyes of his entire family, I beat him, and I won a silver medal for it. (Later I learned that Toomey had gone on to the University of Pennsylvania, becoming lightweight champion of that school, and for years I anticipated a midnight knock at the door followed by Toomey's avenging fist in my face.)

Shortly after this victory, a man who introduced himself as Al Singer's manager came to see me. Singer, I had heard, was pulling down $125,000 a year.

"You're a good lightweight. I'd like to handle you," the manager said.

I couldn't believe it. Here were the twin prospects of life as a chivalric warrior and the opportunity to make even more money than my old man. Al Singer's manager went on, "Here's what I want you to do. I want you to train—road work every day. Then I want you to come down to Stillman's Gym in the city. I'll get you a sparring partner."

Roadwork—getting up before dawn and running until you are more than a little tired—fell short of what I pictured as the life of a noble warrior. But I kept at it, then, as I had been told, took the subway to Manhattan and Stillman's. At sixteen, I found myself inhaling the sweat-sharp air of the most famous training gym in the world of professional boxing. I stared. I gaped. There were five rings with fighters snorting, sniffing, punching, and pounding in each of them.

And in one—there . . . there was Al Singer, a fighter with a great body and fast hands, at the time lightweight champion of the world. I suddenly felt as if I were not in that gym at all. It was like I was watching a movie, and I was the camera. Now I panned down from Al

Singer to a clutch of elegantly attired men wearing blue suits that harmonized with their blue jowls, men with big cigars and pinkie rings. They were the managers.

And, just as suddenly, I *was* there, and I heard myself saying to myself: *I'm getting into this business at the wrong end.* With that, I turned around, walked out the door, and never thought about prizefighting again.

I GRADUATED EARLY, in three and a half rather than four years, and chose not to go to college. I had one uncle who became a professor of languages, and another who was a physician, but, even if I had been able to find the money to go to college, I had a girlfriend, the Juliet to my Romeo, whom I didn't want to leave for some college campus and for whose sake I was loath to postpone the making of money. Lots of money. The only question was: How?

History books will tell you that at the time of my graduation, 1928, America still had about a year and a half of prosperity left before the Wall Street crash of 1929. In reality things were not so tidy. Times were already very tough by 1928. The playing and dreaming of high school gave way all too soon to the terrifyingly stubborn fact that there were no jobs. One of my father's customers was associated with the Irving Trust bank, and through him my old man maneuvered a position for me at the bank's headquarters, at 1 Wall Street, corner of Broadway, directly across from Trinity Church in lower Manhattan.

I reported to a Mr. Dunbar, who took me down into the bowels of the building to a room labeled "Rack Department." No medieval torture chamber was ever more aptly named. Here about thirty men stood with adding machines—ancient and noisy devices of that prehistoric age before the advent of the silicon chip—totaling up incoming checks eight hours a day, every day. At prescribed intervals, each "racker" checked—*proved*, the procedure was called—his subtotal against a certain mystical figure. Recall that the nuns' rapture over my drawing ability at Holy Innocents meant that they I never learned the rudiments of arithmetic. I "racked" all day, but not once was I able to "prove" my totals, and the man in charge of the department always had to do my work over until he found what I had missed.

As punishment for my complete incompetence, I was offered a promotion. Having demonstrated my inability to add even simple columns of figures, I was given the choice of being an accountant or an assistant tax man in the Trust Department. I see now that to be fired would have been a blessing, but at the time, with most of my former classmates out of work, hungry, and desperate, I felt that I had no choice but to accept the promotion, and I elected to become an assistant tax man. The starting pay was sixteen dollars a week, and I got to work in an office with a view of Lower Broadway. From this vantage point, I watched any number of ticker tape parades. A number of aviators were periodically honored back then, and I remember in particular Balbo and his white-uniformed Italian fliers who were hailed for having circumnavigated the globe.

Me? Well, I could always dream of taking flight. Actually we couldn't even open the windows. Ours was a new building and the first in Manhattan to incorporate a new invention called air conditioning, which was so feeble that on stifling July days we would, against explicit orders, open our windows. In response, the building's management bolted them shut.

Of course, the worst thing about working as an assistant tax man is that I was still expected to work with numbers. My job consisted of adding up, filling out, and filing tax returns for some four hundred accounts held in trust. I believe that if the authorities in Washington were to undertake a full-scale investigation of the economic ills that currently afflict us, they would ultimately trace them back to the work I had mishandled in the course of six long, dark years at Irving Trust.

Not that I didn't try to fit in. I observed that my fellow inmates all behaved in an identical manner. They would begin by coming in at precisely nine o'clock in the morning. Now, in those days, nobody in New York, not even bank clerks, got to bed much before one or two in the morning. So these young men would troop in, faces gray and green with sleeplessness, liquor, caffeine, and tobacco, settle at their desks, light a cigarette, and, with great deliberation, open the *Wall Street Journal*.

I was willing to give it a try. But my difficulties began with coming in. Not once in six years did I make it into the office by nine on the dot. Under the cold eye and deep-set frown of a Mr. Zerkel, whose job it was to mark us in and out, I would skulk in at 9:01 or 9:02 or, on very good days, thirty seconds past nine. But never at nine sharp.

I was willing, too, to purchase a copy of the *Wall Street Journal*, but I could not master the use of a cigarette. To begin with, I had a strong aversion to tobacco, which had its origin in a Dodgers doubleheader at Ebbets Field Uncle Jim took me to many years before.

Jim was a rabid Dodgers fan. This was hardly unusual in Brooklyn. My mother, this little Italian lady born in a Sicilian country village a world apart from Brooklyn, New York, used to get into epic arguments with her brother over the merits of this player versus that or if, God forbid, she sensed even the slightest diminution in Jim's enthusiasm for the team. Even back then, as a little boy, I thought to myself, listening to the passion between them: *I don't believe what I'm hearing.*

It was a Sunday, and we had gone to Ebbets Field directly from church. A hot, humid, sun-soaked day in the bleachers, in my first long-pants suit, warm and woolen, little tie, little collar, watching Dazzy Vance pitch a doubleheader. And completely surrounded by raving Brooklynites with BVD tops stretched over great hemispherical stomachs. All of them smoked: cigarettes and nickel cigars, the smoke eddying around me, over me, past me, under me, all with the sun hammering down relentlessly.

Even after Mr. Drazian had dry cleaned it, I never wanted to wear that suit again. And I certainly had not acquired a yen for cigars or cigarettes. But, finding myself at this bank and looking for some way to convince myself that I fit in, I would sit back with the *Journal* and gamely light up—only to discover that, no matter where I held the cigarette, the smoke would curl up and hit me painfully in the eye. I abandoned smoking forever.

I was far more successful at another Trust Department ritual, which came at the end of every pre-tax day, when Rodman, the senior tax man, and I would get bombed after filing four hundred returns. But despite Rodman's good fellowship, I have to say, on balance, that I hated each and every minute of the six years I spent at the bank, and I started desperately looking for something that would get me through those deadly days. The lunch hour provided some escape, as I'd walk across the street to the pre-Revolutionary burial grounds adjacent to Trinity Church at the head of Wall Street where it joins Broadway. Back then, the burial grounds were open to the public, and temporarily paroled office workers like myself would perch on a convenient headstone, munch a sandwich, and read a book. In this way, I was captivated by the likes of Somerset Maugham's *Of Human Bondage* and Rudyard Kipling's *The Light That Failed*.

BUT I NEEDED MORE than a single stolen hour each day, and I returned to drawing. One day a friend of mine from Erasmus Hall asked me to do portraits of some priests for the St. John's University yearbook. Working from photographs, I produced a set of quite fine pencil portraits. When I accepted the assignment, I really had no idea that I could produce anything like that, and even more remarkable to me was the fact that I got five dollars apiece for the portraits.

At this time, too, I began drawing cartoons. I used to read all the magazines of the day, including *Redbook*, the *Saturday Evening Post*, and especially *Collier's*. All of these had cartoons—not comic strips, but single cartoons based on the kind of visual humor that always appealed to me. After having worked at the bank for some time, I had left my parents' house and rented an attic room in another Flatbush house. I'd get an idea, and I'd work it out, usually sketching up in my attic until two or three in the morning. After I had done a handful of cartoons I was satisfied with, I started submitting them to the magazines I was familiar with.

I'd mail my work to the *Post* in Philadelphia, but I'd go to *Redbook* and *Collier's*, located across Park Avenue from one another, in person.

It soon became a regular routine. Each Thursday, I'd watch the clock at the bank more closely than usual, waiting for twelve noon. Tick, tick, tick, then boom, I was gone—down the stairs and to my locker, where I'd pick up the drawings I'd brought with me. Then I'd continue to race downward, down to the subway station under the building, hop an uptown express, pass Fourteenth Street, Thirty-fourth Street, get out at Grand Central Terminal, race up the stairs at Grand Central and across its highly polished marble floor—a cacophony of clicking heels—out onto the broad expanse of Park Avenue and into 250 Park, where I bounded up to the fourth-floor offices of *Collier's*. There I would leave the new drawings and pick up the rejects.

There were always rejects.

These I would take across the street to *Redbook*, picking up the rejects their editors had left me. Mission accomplished, I dashed back into Grand Central, down to the subway, and made the trek back to 1 Wall Street, almost always timing my arrival (under the eyes of the dreaded Zerkel) to the stroke of one.

This went on for about two years. Reject, reject, and again reject. Why did I persist? Was it that I was convinced my destiny was to be a great cartoonist despite the blindness of any number of editors? Not really.

It was survival. It was staying alive. It was having something to look forward to—even if that was nothing more than drawing breath for a few moments in an office where people did something more than add, subtract, multiply, and divide. *Redbook* and *Collier's*—those offices were perfectly ordinary, and yet for me they exuded an atmosphere of creativity and the slimmest sliver of a possibility that I might be permitted to create something, too.

The bank, in the meantime, invaded my life further and launched me on a desperate course of deception. I was "directed" to attend classes at the American Banking Institute, one block below Broadway behind Trinity Church. I fared no better in banking class than I did in the bank job itself. Having earned an F in the course, I used my drawing skill to close the horizontal forks of the F and add a loop below, transforming the grade into a highly respectable B. Actually, no one ever checked on my grade.

At last, one blessed Saturday, I descended from my attic to collect the mail. There was a long envelope from *Collier's*. I opened it and took out a brief typewritten letter accepting one of my "comics" (as they called it) and pointing out that the rejected cartoons would arrive under separate cover. Accompanying the letter was a check for twenty-five dollars. It was a double check that folded over. I had never even seen a check like that, and, in any case, nobody had ever given me a check in my life. At the bank, they paid employees with an envelope containing cash. And here was a *double* check made out to me. It was an object of wonder.

WITHIN A SHORT TIME, I sold a total of four cartoons to *Collier's*. It was not that I now glimpsed a realistic alternative to the bank. I knew that a handful of cartoons were not going to put beans on the table. But those cartoons did *give* me something. They *made* me something, something more than a very bad assistant tax man. Maybe I *would* end up working at the bank the rest of my life, but, whatever happened, I would *still* have those cartoons, which I signed "J. Roland Barbera," using the name of the hero who had sacrificed his life to a code of chivalry and thereby achieved immortality in song and legend.

Now, just as I was beginning to sell cartoons to *Collier's*, I happened to see Walt Disney's groundbreaking "Skeleton Dance," a cartoon short set to Camille Saint-Saëns's "Danse Macabre." I was in the third balcony of the Roxy Theatre, as far up as you could get and still be under the roof, about seventy-two miles from the screen. But the impact on me was tremendous nevertheless. I saw these skeletons dancing in a row and in unison, and I asked myself: How do you *do* that? How do you make that happen?

To be honest, this event was not the birth of an animator. I did not go home determined to make animated cartoons. But what I had seen did excite me. As marvelous as literature was, a good story brought to the stage was even more compelling. As satisfying as it was to get a comic published in *Collier's*, the prospect of making drawings that *moved* on screen was far more exciting. And that is how I came to write my first and only fan letter.

I wrote to Walt Disney, enclosing a drawing I made of Mickey Mouse. To my surprise, Disney himself wrote back, thanking me for the sketch and informing me that he was coming to New York City and that he would call me. It was signed in his trademark script: *Walt Disney.*

As I mentioned at the end of the previous chapter, I still wake from time to time in a cold sweat, thinking about what would have happened had I failed to sell "The Flintstones." It gives me the shivers, too, to think what would have happened if Walt Disney had made good on his promise to call me. Historians of animation speak of the "Nine Old Men" of the Walt Disney Studio. I might have been the tenth. If Disney had called me—even if he had phoned me to say, *Look, kid, I can't see you. But if you want to come out to California on your own, well, we'll give you a try*, I would have quit the bank and hightailed it for Los Angeles. I would have become a painter, filling in the cels with color. I would have graduated to inker, tracing the characters' outlines on the cels. Finally, I might have become an animator—one more anonymous subject of Disney's empire. My work would have been seen by millions, but I would have remained as nameless as if I were still misfiling income tax forms at Irving Trust.

But Disney never did call me. And I humbly thank God for that providence.

IN THE MEANTIME, I became increasingly interested in the world of "high" art as yet another alternative to the bank. I started taking classes at the Art Students League on Fifty-seventh Street at the cost of fifty cents a lesson. My first class there was the first time I ever saw a live nude model, and I gaped with disbelief. The world of art was indeed wonderful—not that this particular lady would have won any award for her beauty. There she was, looking bored and weary, her vacant eyes unfocused upon the thirty or so student artists copying her form, just another struggling soul seeking to avoid total unemployment in the Great Depression that was now fully upon us.

As I had earnestly tried to fit in at the bank by imitating the actions of my fellow clerks, so I now set about absorbing the world of "high" art. After class, many of the students retired to the cafeteria, where a phonograph played some wild Russian music. I observed them as they attended to the music in various attitudes of pained concentration, which resembled nothing more strongly than acute constipation: hand to forehead, head down, eyes tightly shut. So I tried to listen in this manner as well.

As I became even more serious about formally studying art, I enrolled in evening classes at the Pratt Institute in Brooklyn. And while I was building my spirit there, I resolved to build my body as well and joined the YMCA. When quitting time came at the bank, I'd get to the Y as fast as I could, run around the track like a madman, jump in the pool for a few hasty laps, lift weights for a couple of minutes, dash into the shower, towel off, pull on my clothes, then take a subway train and a streetcar to Pratt. The idea was to achieve maximum health as quickly as possible, but what my schedule omitted was any time to eat. I developed an increasingly lean and hungry look and was always on the ragged edge of exhaustion.

At Pratt I met a wonderful teacher named Cimmiotti, to whom I mentioned my interest in animation. He suggested that I contact a former student of his, Willard Bowsky, an animator at the Fleischer Studios, whose major drawing card was Popeye the Sailorman. Cimmiotti arranged an introduction.

Diffidence has never been my way of dealing with the world, but Willard Bowsky was making $250 a week. Now, by this time, I was making twenty-five dollars at the bank—exactly one-tenth of Bowsky's salary. People like this were gods to people like me.

Bowsky received me very politely at the Fleischer Studios, which were located in what I think of as the Oliver Twist Hotel: a dim, dark sweatshop above the Wintergarden Theater in the Times Square area.

Bowsky was generous with his time and was very complimentary about my *Collier's* work. After the interview, I sent him a carton of cigarettes as a gift.

A short time later, I got a call at the bank. It was Willard Bowsky asking if I "would like to come up to the studio and try my hand at making cartoons." I worked up enough nerve to claim a two-week vacation from the bank with virtually no advance notice, and I reported to the Oliver Twist Hotel.

They started me at the bottom of the heap: the Painting Department. The least-skilled and most tedious job in traditional animation is applying color to the cels—the celluloid sheets on which the action characters are drawn. In those days of black-and-white cartoons, the only "colors" to apply were black and white, and you worked while wearing a white glove to keep your hand from sticking to the celluloid.

Oliver Twist? It was more like *A Christmas Carol*, with a roomful of Bob Cratchets presided over by Ebenezer Scrooge in the person of Frank Paiker. He managed the studio underlings, and, in fact, to compare him to Scrooge may be too generous. All he needed was to bare his chest, find a whip and a guy to beat a drum, and he would have made a highly creditable slave master in a Roman galley. He eventually came to work for the Hanna-Barbera studio. I remember catching a glimpse of the girl next to me reach under her drawing board to take a furtive bite of a sandwich, then thrust it back under the board.

My hope was to spend as little time in the Painting Department as possible, and, to that end, I brought with me my four *Collier's* cartoons on my first day at work. These were shown to Dave Fleischer, Max's brother, who promptly proposed to purchase gags from me.

"We'll give you a dollar for every gag we use," he said, which meant that I was free to labor over, say, fifty gags on spec and maybe make a buck for the single one they chose. If they chose even a single gag.

By my third day at the Fleischer Studio I was indeed promoted out of the Painting Department and became an inker. This job required considerably more skill as well as mind-numbing patience. An inker took the original drawing, put a cel on top of it, and traced the drawing in ink. Good inkers developed marvelous control over their line, mastering a demanding thick and thin technique.

At lunchtime on Thursday, my second day as an inker and my fourth day at the studio, I struck up a conversation with one of my colleagues. He was perhaps fifteen years older than I, about thirty-five.

"How long have you been inking?" I asked.

"Three years."

Three years of tracing over other people's work for what? Thirty-five dollars a week!

I knew that on Friday a friend of mine was about to sail to Bermuda on his honeymoon and was throwing a bon voyage party on board the *Queen of Bermuda*. The tale of the middle-aged inker was enough to convince me to go to the party. So I quit on Thursday, boarded the *Queen* on Friday, and cut short my vacation to return to the bank on Monday. I had washed my hands of the animation business.

(But Willard Bowsky had not washed his hands of me. Years later, during World War II, when I was making Tom and Jerry cartoons at MGM, Bowsky, whom I had known, really, all of four days, came to the studio to say hello. He was dressed in the uniform of a brand-new second lieutenant and had stopped by on his way to the Pacific. We talked about old times. He was killed almost immediately after he arrived on the front.)

FOR AMERICA AND THE WORLD, the Great Depression deepened and deepened. For me, it struck about three weeks after I had left the Fleischer Studio. Irving Trust decided to consolidate its marginal branches and brought in from these many senior employees, married men with families, to replace the young and unattached denizens of 1 Wall Street. I was laid off.

Much as I hated the bank, getting the boot was a shock. The world was cold and hungry, and I was without a job. But then, as I cleaned out my locker, collecting the drawings I had left there, afterwards emerging into the filtered sunlight of Wall Street's narrow canyon, my artwork under my arm, I suddenly felt free—freer than I had ever felt before.

On Tuesday of the week after I left the bank, I was walking up Broadway. At Fifty-second Street I ran into a fraternity brother from Omega Alpha Pi, the fraternity I had belonged to at Erasmus Hall.

"What are you doing these days?" he asked.

"I just got laid off from a bank job." And I told him about my brief career with Fleischer.

"What are you going to do?"

I had two friends who called themselves artists and who had invited me to join them in the vocation of starving in Greenwich Village. I said, "I'm going to Greenwich Village to starve."

My frat brother told me about a job at another animation studio, Van Beuren, and suggested I look into that before I embarked on a career of starvation. He said, "Just tell them you're an animator."

I was, of course, no such thing.

The sum total of my experience in the creation of animated cartoons consisted of two and a half days as a cel painter and a day and a half as an inker. But with my sights set on starving in Greenwich Village anyway, and armed with my four *Collier's* cartoons, I set sail for the United Artists Building, 729 Seventh Avenue, to offer my services as an animator.

Chapter Three

THE LEAST YOU'LL TAKE

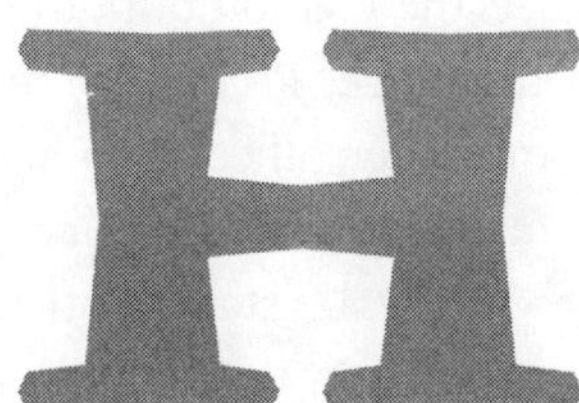

HERE I WAS, on the seventeenth floor of the dim, decrepit, and decaying United Artists building, passing myself off as an animator without having any more of an idea of how to make drawings move on screen than I had when I sat in the Roxy's highest balcony gaping at Disney's "Skeleton Dance." And yet never before (or since) had I felt more confident.

For one thing, I had my four wonder-working *Collier's* pieces, and when I walked into the Van Beuren Studio, I was introduced to Jack Bogle, who took the magazines away to show them to the guy in charge, Mr. Burt Gillette.

The Van Beuren Studio was an offshoot of Paul Terry's original studio—really, what was left after Terry moved in 1929 to New Rochelle in Westchester County to start a studio entirely his own. In the 1920s with Terry, Van Beuren had produced a successful series of silent cartoons called "Aesop's Film Fables." But once Terry decamped, Van Beuren, in the early years of sound, was . . . well, the polite term would be *struggling*. Actually, the studio was floundering, groping for some characters to hang a reputation on. Historians of animation might point out that one of Van Beuren's justly forgotten series featured a pair of characters named Tom and Jerry. This was the era of rubber-limbed animation—when, as far as movement was concerned, arms and legs might as well have been worms—and Van Beuren's Tom and Jerry, humanoid if not precisely human, bore a far closer resemblance to the funny papers' Mutt and Jeff than to the cat and mouse Bill Hanna and I would invent in 1940. Van Beuren did finally latch onto something promising with "The Toonerville Trolley," featuring the Powerful Katrinka (whom I used to animate, making her lift up the Trolley with her bare hands) and the Terrible-Tempered Mr. Bang, but this would hardly prove sufficient to sustain a studio. Burt Gillette had left Walt Disney and was assigned the mission of putting Van Beuren on the map. Now he was in his office, looking at my *Collier's* masterpieces, and I was sitting in the outer office, cool and uncaring as could be. If I had learned to smoke, I would have been casually indulging myself in a cigarette. After all, starvation in Greenwich Village was my principal objective, the trip to Van Beuren merely a detour along the way.

Jack Bogle came back out. "Follow me," he said, and led me into Gillette's sanctum sanctorum.

After some years in the cartoon business, I would learn that *everyone* who had ever been associated with Walt Disney either created "The Three Little Pigs" or *Snow White*. Burt Gillette claimed to have been responsible for both. But that was after we got to know one another. At this meeting, he was a man of few words. He was round, bald-headed, and hyper, as if he had glued himself in his deskchair but was always getting ready to rise, and his eyes blazed like coals.

He looked at my cartoons, then fixed me momentarily with a maniacal glance. The words shot out of him like rapid-fire cannonballs. "What's the least you'll take?"

My air of nonchalance deserted me. "Duh, dah, duh, well . . ." I'd better say something. "Thirty dollars?"

Reload and fire: "We'll let you know."

Bogle handed me back my cartoons, and I was out the door. As I walked back toward the subway, I started thinking. I had been making a salary of twenty-seven dollars a week when the bank let me go, and I had been living well enough: my own attic room, a membership at the Y, classes at Pratt, money to entertain my girlfriend, and something left over to send my mother. Now I began to lust after that additional three dollars. God, what *couldn't* I do with thirty dollars a week! Greenwich Village was all but forgotten. The only fly in this particular ointment was that the thirty-dollar figure had come from me, not Burt Gillette or anyone else at Van Beuren.

It was Memorial Day—Decoration Day, we called it back then—that I got a phone call from Jack Bogle.

"Can you start Monday?"

"Yeah, sure."

"We'll give you twenty-five dollars a week."

I swallowed my pride and modified my fantasy. Besides, maybe it wasn't such a bad deal. After all, it wasn't as if I really *knew* how to do animation.

So I showed up Monday and walked into a whole new world.

They gave me a desk and light board next to a guy at another light board, and they gave me what they called a "scene." This was a collection of drawings, like a flip book, only bigger. If you flipped through them, the characters would appear to move.

I sat looking at the "scene."

The man next to me introduced himself. "I'm Carlo Vinci." Then he looked at me looking at the stack of drawings on my board. "You don't know anything about it, do you?"

"I don't have the faintest idea."

So Carlo—who also would later come to work for Hanna-Barbera—got up from his board and explained the process to me. The scene, he said, consisted of drawings numbered 1, 3, 5, 7, and so on. My job, he explained, was to create the intermediate drawings, which were numbered 2, 4, 6, 8, and so on. You did this by putting drawings 1 and 3 on the light board, which was a drawing board that had a piece of frosted glass on it lit from underneath by an electric bulb. The animation paper had two holes punched in it at the top. These holes fit over two registration pins, or pegs, at the top of the board, keeping the drawings perfectly in place. So you put drawings 1 and 3 down over the lighted area, laid a blank piece of paper on top of this, then figured out how to bridge the positions in drawing 1 with those in drawing 3. That became drawing number 2.

Now, as painter and inker were the bottom and next-to-bottom rungs of the cartoon-making process as a whole, so "in-betweener" (that's what I was supposed to be) was the bottom rung of the more demanding animation phase of the process. To the uninitiated, the job of the in-betweener, supplying the drawing that goes between two other drawings, may seem timid and mechanical. But it demanded a keen understanding of movement, which no art class, not even the life classes at the Art Students League, teaches.

I began, then, doing the in-between drawings, and I became determined to learn animation, bottom to top. Carlo had been there to get me started, but in those days there really wasn't anybody around to teach me how to be an animator. So I bought my own light board and set out to learn on my own, working feverishly in my attic every night, practicing, practicing, and practicing—for all practical purposes, *inventing* (for myself)—the art and science of animation. After some months, I became good enough to ascend to the next rung on the animation ladder, an assistant.

The in-betweener gets drawings 1, 3, 5, and 7 to work with. The head animator—perched on the top rung—works from the original artist's drawings to create drawings 1 and 5 and 9. These drawings go to his assistant, who does the "breakdowns," supplying drawing number 3 to go between 1 and 5, and drawing number 7 to go between 5 and 9. Since it is a bigger leap from 1 to 5 than it is from 1 to 3, the breakdowns are more demanding than the in-betweens, requiring greater imagination, knowledge, and skill.

After a little while, my work was getting noticed, and, one day, one of the head animators, a man named Timmins, furtively poked his head out of his door. Looking first to the left, then to the right, he crooked his finger, motioning for me to come in.

"You're very good," he said, almost whispering. "I'd like to make you my assistant."

The next thing I knew, both Carlo Vinci and I were sitting next to Timmins's desk. Timmins would rough out—and I mean *rough*—the animation. Carlo and I would do the breakdowns and the in-betweens as well. We also had to clean up Timmins's roughs, making sure they were neat. Now, customarily the assistant animator also ensures that the animator's drawings conform to a model, but this assumes a rudimentary degree of organization and technical sophistication that Van Beuren, a most chaotic place, had failed ever to attain. The model sheet, which establishes the look, shape, and even dimensions for each character, and which is so essential to professional animation, was unknown at Van Beuren. This meant that even a simplistic, homely character like Gillette's real winner, Molly Moo Cow, given to thirteen animators, would emerge as thirteen different cows. Rubber-legged and amorphous to begin with, Molly would go through a most disquieting process of metamorphosis when the work of these thirteen animators was cut together into what was supposedly a singe five-minute cartoon. Novice though I was, I quickly began to feel that the whole Van Beuren studio was at most only a half-step ahead of me, and I was closing in fast.

In any case, Gillette was greatly pleased with the neat, clean work Timmins had been turning out as of late and gave him a nice fat raise. Carlo and I labored on, like mice turning a wheel in a cage.

With a staff of about 150, the organizational chaos at Van Beuren was a serious problem, but the worse fault was exemplified by the very idea of Molly Moo Cow herself. *This* was the best character they could come up with? I mean, what can you do with a cow? It isn't intelligent. It certainly isn't beautiful—except to a farmer or a bull. It is sedentary rather than lively, and, even with rubber legs, it doesn't move in interesting ways or in a way that allows much range or variety of action. As animated characters, cows do not work.

Well, what about birds? The subsequent history of animation would prove that birds could be successful characters. There were Tweetie Pie, Chilly Willy, Woody Woodpecker, even Road Runner. But the species Van Beuren tried was a cast of parrots, and they failed miserably. Probably the only asset a cartoon parrot's got is color. Take away color, and what you're left with is an annoying creature that, with its big hooked bill and reptilian claws, is downright ugly. What I realized, which nobody else at Van Beuren seemed to recognize, is that, all things being equal, a successful cartoon character needs to be something a kid can take to bed and cuddle. You can't really cuddle a cow—or, at least, you don't want to. And you can't cuddle a parrot, with its hard, sharp bill and scaly claws.

I began, then, to itch to contribute to the creative end of Van Beuren as much as I could. I wanted to get involved in inventing characters and writing stories. Gillette allowed me to participate in the so-called "creative meetings" we had once a week at the Blue Ribbon Cafe just off Broadway. The avowed purpose of these meetings was for us to get together and come up with cartoon ideas. That was the avowed purpose. The fact was that Van Beuren picked up the tab for our dinner and our Pabst Blue Ribbon (hence the name of the establishment), and what you had was a bunch of animators gnawing chops and swilling suds. To be sure, plenty of ideas came out of those creative meetings, but not one of them had anything to do with a cartoon.

It was clear to me—to most of us—that Van Beuren was not long for this world. And with that realization came the urge to have as much fun, as much silly, stupid, mindless fun as possible before the inevitable descent of the final curtain. For me, it was nothing more—

as a modern M.B.A. might say—than partaking of the prevailing corporate culture.

Mike Meyers, Van Beuren's wild storyboard man, pointed out an animator named Frank Amon. Mike used to call him "the Legionnaire" because Frank sported a toupee whose useful life had long since expired, and you could see bare canvas hanging down from the back of his head in an image reminiscent of *Beau Geste*. Now, Mike directed my attention to the intensity of concentration with which Frank habitually studied an "exposure sheet," a sheet of figures whereby the animator indicated timing. He seemed always to be poring over the sheet. Mike took me for a closer look.

Frank Amon, appearing deep in creative thought, was in fact sound asleep, leaning on his arm, the elbow of which rested on a chair, the exposure sheet carefully affixed to his thumb with tape. This, Mike said, was his routine—though, once, it is true, Frank fell asleep not upright in his chair, resting on his arm, but with his head down on his drawing board, the registration pins boring deep impressions into his brow.

Somnolence, it turned out, was epidemic at Van Beuren, perhaps a physiological defense against the prevailing chaos there. Four of us shared a corner cubbyhole in the studio. One of my cell mates, Andy Engman, who later became the head of personnel at Disney, was, like Frank Amon, inclined to take siestas and, also like Frank, favored cradling his head in his hand, his elbow propped on the arm of his chair.

Now, the plan that took shape in my mind was subtle, even rather gentle. What I intended to do was to tie a strong cord to one leg of Andy's chair and, without waking him, pull him, ever so slowly, outside of the cubbyhole and into the middle of the office floor. When he woke up, he would be shocked to find himself out in the open and exposed to universal scrutiny.

There was a lot of diabolical planning that went into the scheme, and I took infinite pains to tie the cord tightly, but work so quietly that Andy's slumber would remain undisturbed. I then positioned myself about six feet away at the other end of the cord and began pulling. Andy was a big, very heavyset individual, and, try as I might, the chair would not budge.

A lesser man would have given up the joke. But not me. I pulled harder. And harder. Now the way this chair was made, the arms hooked on to the back posts on either side. I pulled harder still, and fell backwards as the entire post separated from the chair. For a frozen moment, the office beheld a fat man sleeping on a three-legged chair. But the laws of physics dictated that the moment was not destined to last. Andy was leaning on his arm in the direction opposite the absent leg. So when the chair started to tip, it went slowly, and this big, round man eased over like some giant sequoia felled in a forest. I got to my feet as the chair picked up momentum.

Crash!

And Andy looked around far more surprised than I had intended him to be.

"What the hell happened?" And he looked at me, standing with the end of a rope in my hand.

WHEN ANIMATORS WEREN'T SLEEPING, they were drinking. At the top of the heap were men like George Rufle, who made three hundred dollars a week at a time when fourteen hundred dollars would buy a huge, top-of-the-line automobile like a Packard or a Hudson. Rufle greatly enjoyed his libation and made grandiose stabs at generally living it up by acquiring and doggedly attempting to enjoy some of the showier trappings of success.

He bought a boat. It sank. He left it. He bought a plane. It crashed. He left it.

That three hundred dollars a week put people like Rufle in a different universe from those of us earning thirty or thirty-five dollars a week. But liquor was a currency common to all, especially Mount Vernon rye, the drink of choice for Dan Gordon, a Van Beuren inmate and wild Irishman who, in addition to alcohol, thrived on tobacco, smoking cigarette after cigarette, but who could draw like crazy. He eventually came to work for Hanna-Barbera and drew the storyboards for the first "Flintstones."

Now I suppose I shouldn't talk since, at the time, I was going out with Dorothy Earl, whom I would subsequently marry, despite the fact that it was apparent to all and sundry that we were two very different people. But Dan, ebullient, full of energy, and always ready for a good drink, a good fight, and a good time, had somehow chosen to wed his exact opposite: a taciturn woman of whom we all saw very little.

One evening, Jack Zander (a Van Beuren cohort who would later come to MGM), Dot Earl, and I were having dinner. After a few drinks, we were moved by the realization that it was Dan Gordon's birthday and we should do something for him. We decided to surprise him with a cake, so we went out to a bakery, bought a cake, went to another store, bought some candles, got in the car, and put in the candles as we drove out to Dan's apartment in Forest Hills, Queens. We pulled up to the curb, piled out of the car, ascended the stairs to Gordon's door, and lit the candles on the landing. I rang the bell.

No answer.

I rang the bell again. And again.

At length, the door opened a few inches, and the worried face of Dan Gordon peeked out.

"Surprise! Happy birthday! Surprise!" we all yelled.

Dan, now looking frankly terrified, reached out, grabbed the cake, and shut the door. End of party.

The next day, I posted on the studio wall a drawing depicting a cake with candles melting, the wax dripping to the floor, and the cake itself drooping, about to implode, all above the legend HAPPY BIRTHDAY!

IT WAS NO JOKE to be stuck in the middle of the Great Depression, acutely aware that the company you're working for is doomed. To assuage the angst, Jack Zander and I tried taking out on a date two sisters who worked at the studio. We took them to dinner and up to Jack's apartment afterward.

The time I put in at Van Beuren taught me how to be animator, taught me how not to make a successful cartoon, and taught me two surefire methods a woman can use to fend off amorous advances. The sister in whom Jack was interested giggled. Her weapon was giggling, and she wielded it unmercifully. Jack would lean over to kiss her, and she would giggle. He would offer her a drink, and she would giggle. He'd try to touch her arm, and she would giggle. Observing Jack, I learned that there is nothing you can do with a giggling girl.

For myself, I decided it was time to make a move on the other sister and, toward this end, had encouraged her liberal indulgence in cordial libation. Just as the situation was beginning to look promising, she excused herself. Then disappeared utterly. At length, I decided it was time to investigate, and, against a background soundtrack of incessant giggling, first knocked upon, then opened the bathroom door. There she was, draped around the toilet bowl, passed out cold. And that is the second foolproof means of foiling a would-be Romeo.

As the studio likewise drifted into coma, the pace and frequency of the creative meetings increased, which meant that the consumption of free food and liquor increased proportionately. It was at this time that I discovered the Rob Roy—essentially a Manhattan made with scotch instead of bourbon—and, much as Neanderthals carried coals from one campsite to another, my destiny was to transport this drink to the West Coast, where, before my arrival, it had been unknown.

The culmination of each year at Van Beuren was the studio Christmas party, an experience entirely new to me. At Irving Trust, come Christmas, no one even shook your hand, let alone threw a party. But, as the end loomed larger at Van Beuren, the Christmas parties became wilder and more desperate. Men were chasing girls amid wild shrieks, and the girls were chasing the men as well. But mostly there was drinking, drinking as if there would be no tomorrow—at least as if there would be no free drinks tomorrow. Animators were staggering into the men's room to throw up, and the women staggered in right after them.

Confronted by so many signs of the apocalypse, Dorothy Earl and I suddenly decided to get married. I took a Friday off, we tied the knot, and set off by cab for our honeymoon at the Waldorf-Astoria. On the way, we passed the Transluxe Newsreel Theatre—a movie house that showed only short subjects, newsreels, Frank Buck shorts, and Charlie Chaplin films. The marquee proclaimed a Chaplin short, and, as Charlie Chaplin was my great delight, I stopped the cab and dragged Dorothy into the movie, postponing our honeymoon to see my favorite comic actor. I suppose we both should have taken warning from that detour and stopped to think: *Are we doing the right thing?* But we saw the film (I, at least, laughed), emerged from the Transluxe, went to the Waldorf, and, after a weekend there, it was back to the *Götterdammerung* at Van Beuren on Monday.

When the end of the studio finally came, it was a stunning anticlimax. The studio manager, doubtlessly burdened with everyone's problems, had gone across the street to the Transluxe to take in a newsreel. It turned out to be a real eye-opener. One of the news stories showed Walt Disney signing with RKO to distribute his cartoons. The thing was, RKO was Van Beuren's distributor, and now that Disney was on board, it meant just one thing. Van Beuren was out of business.

The sword hanging over us fell at last, and the layoffs began. Some of the more experienced people were able to get jobs at Paul Terry's studio in New Rochelle. Me? I had bought a slightly used 1936 Ford roadster, a neat little car in great condition, $150 down and monthly payments, and I decided to drive it to California, where I would knock on Walt Disney's door.

BEFORE I EMBARKED ON THE LONG JOURNEY, I decided to take a shorter one to New Rochelle, to say good-bye to my Van Beuren cronies, including Dan Gordon and Jack Zander, who had found refuge at the Paul Terry studio. At lunchtime, Terry was standing by the water cooler, teeth clenching the unlit cigar that was a fixture of his face as permanent as his nose. Looking at him, all I could think of was Sidney Greenstreet: barrel chest sloping out to a gut of truly massive proportions.

One of the boys introduced me. "This is Joe Barbera. He's on his way to the Coast to work for Disney."

Terry glared down at me. "Hummmph." It was a guttural sound that was barely recognizable as human. Paul Terry hated Walt Disney, who had been hiring away his best animators one by one. "You're going to California—to work for Disney?" he breathed out. He even *sounded* like Sidney Greenstreet.

"Yes," I answered weakly.

"I'll give you forty-five dollars a week to work for me."

And in this way I got a job, for a second time evaded the oblivion of a career with Disney, and Terry was able to savor an opportunity to spite the father of Mickey Mouse.

Paul Terry had been a news photographer and a syndicated Hearst cartoonist before he got into animation on its ground floor in 1915. He pioneered many of the techniques that became standard, and, all in all, his Terrytoons were a quantum leap beyond Van Beuren if for no other reason than Paul Terry was in business and Van Beuren wasn't. Terry did not command an empire, but he was making a modest fortune from his operation. Later, after I had gone, he would create two important properties: Mighty Mouse and Heckle and Jeckle, a pair of diabolical crows who should be added to my short list of birds that made for successful animated characters. By 1955, when he decided to retire, Terry was able to sell his studio and characters to CBS for three million dollars, which was a steal on account of Mighty Mouse alone. But in 1936, when I started with him, his bread and butter were the Terrytoons. These were not exactly the products of a burning desire to make great art. Terry's creative philosophy consisted chiefly of his pledge to grind out a new cartoon every two weeks.

"Making cartoons," he said, "is like delivering milk. People expect the bottles at the door every morning. If you miss a morning, people get upset. I see to it that we don't miss a morning and nobody gets upset."

It is true that *60 Minutes* would one day call Hanna-Barbera

Productions the "General Motors of animation" (and me the "Sultan of Saturday Morning," no less) and that at one point we were responsible for something like 70 percent of all the cartoons on television. But key to this volume of output is devising shortcuts in the production and animation process that do not visibly compromise the creative quality of the characters and the stories. In contrast, to meet the production quota he had set for himself, Terry cut each and every available corner, and we turned out some pretty dreadful stuff. Does anyone remember Farmer Alfalfa? Or Kiko the Kangaroo?

I was working for Terry as an animator, but, as at Van Beuren, what I longed to get into was creating stories. As cartoon characters go, Kiko the Kangaroo was just terrible, but he had more promise than any of the others, and I decided to take him home with me. Working on my own time, I drew up a Kiko storyboard, putting the kangaroo in an anthropomorphic biplane for a coast-to-coast air race against a handlebar-mustachioed version of Baron von Richtofen I called Dirty Doug—suggesting as another option, Dirty Dog. In true melodrama villain fashion, Dirty Doug/Dog twirled his mustache, which, however, spun like a propeller. The race quickly turned into comic aerial combat featuring a great deal of machine gun fire that whittled the aircraft down to virtually nothing.

I completed the storyboards and brought them in to Manny Davis, the director. He liked them enough to let me hang them up and present the story to Paul Terry. I did so, Terry looked and listened, and, after a particularly sepulchral *huuumph*, sent me out the door.

I was, quite honestly, not in the least disappointed. I had proven to myself that I could do a storyboard, and I had gained the experience of presenting it. For now, that was enough. (This storyboard may have failed to impress Terry, but it withstood the test of time. Somehow, my mother got a hold of it and gave it to my nephew, who has preserved it, pencil on yellowing animation paper, to this day.)

MANY OF US AT THE TERRY STUDIO were chronic grumblers. We were restless, and we wanted to do better work, to be something more than a corps of cinematic milkmen. Each day at noon we animators would meet in a bar across from the studio and talk about how unhappy we were. On one occasion, a little guy named George Canatta joined us. He had been out to the Coast and had come back.

"Gee," he told us, "you can't believe what it's like out in California. In the morning, the sun is shining, and the air is so fresh. Palm trees everywhere."

And on subsequent days, he would repeat the story, weaving in new details of this paradise on the Pacific. We were all spellbound, but I was captivated more thoroughly than anyone else. Since the age of fifteen, when we moved into my grandparents' house, I had never been really warm in the winter. My room was at the end of the steam line, and the old boiler barely pushed enough heat into my radiator to keep it from frosting over. I craved sun, and in the summer would climb up a black iron ladder to the flat roof of the building, spread a pathetically thin towel over the sharp gravel embedded in the tar of the roof, and soak up as much of the feeble Brooklyn sun as I could. My vista was not ocean waves and bathing beauties, but a crooked forest of chimneys and ventilator pipes. So it is no wonder that, at odd moments, I found myself whispering, moaning under my breath, "Oh, California."

In the meantime, a few of us—Jack Zander, Dan Gordon, and I—would meet at night to work on story ideas. One we came up with was about a goat who ate everything, including the fenders of an automobile. He'd eat over the fender, down along the running board, and up over the rear fender. And there was another cartoon that revolved around pink elephants. We worked over Paul Terry until, beaten into submission, he let us do the cartoons. He certainly didn't cheer us on. He didn't even actively support us. But he didn't stop us from doing them, either, and they were the first cartoons I had a hand in actually creating from the beginning.

We thought we were shaking up the world with our goat and elephants, creating something to rival Disney himself. To tell you the truth, beyond the goat gag and the color of the pachyderms, I can't remember anything more about these cartoons today.

I had been working at the Terry studio for about seven months, feeling a restless mixture of dissatisfaction over the bulk of what we did and yet a sense of excitement about the few stories to which I had contributed. The two hardest drinkers in the studio were two of my good friends, Dan Gordon and Tom Kelly, both partisans of Mount Vernon rye, neat, which they consumed until the moment (and that moment always came) when Kelly would hit the floor.

Gordon was brilliant but impulsive, and went on to work for Hanna-Barbera, where he created the first "Flintstones" storyboards. In contrast, Tom Kelly was a journeyman destined to be an assistant animator throughout his career in cartoons. That career did not last long, however, because Kelly decided to undertake the rigors—some seven to nine years of study and devotion—required to become a Jesuit priest. I always liked Tom, and I was thrilled, years after we both left New Rochelle, to attend his first mass, which he celebrated in a church in Hollywood. I was kneeling with the other communicants, and Father Tom passed down the line, laying hands on each while intoning the Latin blessing. He reached me, laid his hands on my shoulders, and said: "Where the hell have you been?"

It was in 1937 that Tom Kelly was contacted by a Disney man named Ted Sears. Out in California, MGM had put Fred Quimby, a former theater owner and Pathé executive, in charge of organizing a cartoon studio, and Quimby's first step was to find artists, animators, and story men. He casually asked Sears, who was taking a trip east anyway, to poke around for talent. Kelly spread the word to us, touching off a series of clandestine nocturnal meetings among Terry staffers.

"Are you going to California?"

"Are you?"

"Are you going?"

The result was that Quimby, through Sears, and Sears, through Kelly, ended up recruiting seven or eight of us. Over the next several weeks, one by one they left, leaving me—very much on the verge of leaving myself—in New Rochelle.

The prospect was an enticing one. First of all, there was the promise of California itself—land of eternal sunshine, balmy breezes, a life of fantasy in the fresh air. And then there was the salary. Quimby was offering $87.50 and a one-year contract. I had risen sufficiently in Terry's estimation to be earning fifty-five dollars a week.

Finally, after a year of marriage—or, more precisely, a year of fighting punctuated by random moments of marriage—Dorothy and I had separated. She went back to her parents, who were just as happy that their Irish daughter was no longer living with the son of a Sicilian barber, and I returned to my mother's house, where I ate better than I had in a very long time. Strange but true, the time Dorothy and I spent apart were the halcyon days of our lives together. I would come calling on Dorothy in my Ford roadster, we'd go out, have a good time, and then we'd both return to our respective homes. The bottom line was that, although I was still married, I was essentially free to get into my car, point its nose west, and head for MGM.

Terry must have realized that I was poised on the starting line. I ran into him at the water cooler one day. He fixed me with his gaze, adjusted his unlit cigar between his teeth, and said in his best Greenstreet voice, "I'm taking care of you."

That was all. He withdrew into his office, closing the door behind him.

I can't say that I was comforted by this utterance. I knew how Sidney Greenstreet might "take care of" me, and I didn't much like the thought of it.

The next day was payday, and I was sitting at my desk working on an animation scene, when Bill Weiss, Terry's accountant, a man with a heavy black beard and dark, hairy arms, handed me my check. I looked at it. Sixty-five dollars. A ten-dollar raise! Now, I stared at the figures on the check, weighing the difference between $87.50 and $65 and wondering if it was worth uprooting myself from the East (and my mother's home-cooked meals) to move out to the opposite end of the country, leaving a known quantity for one unknown, especially when the defection of so many others was inevitably making more room for my upward mobility right here in New Rochelle.

All this consumed about a second and a half before my mental deliberations were interrupted by a second intrusion of Sam Weiss's hairy arm into my cubicle. He seized the check from between my fingers. "Made a mistake," he muttered.

So then I thought: What could this be? Maybe I was getting a bigger raise, and not only a raise, but a promotion to some titled position—vice president perhaps.

The hairy arm returned a third time, proffering a new check, which I took with delighted anticipation. Then I looked at it. Sixty dollars.

I stared at the check, waiting for the figures to rearrange themselves. I was not so much disappointed as I was utterly baffled. If Paul Terry's animators were slipping away from him, and if he wanted to "take care of me," why would he give me a ten-dollar raise one second only to take back five dollars of it the next?

Well, then, I would go to California.

Chapter Four

INTO THE LION'S DEN

SEPARATED, living with our respective parents, Dorothy and I were getting along better than we ever had before. Also, having rediscovered the incredible home cooking I had shunned as a teenager—thinking back then that it savored too much of the old, square, backward world of my Sicilian ancestors—I was not eager to leave my mother's kitchen.

But Paul Terry's idea of "taking care of me" left no alternative. Besides, I had a '36 Ford roadster, shiny, practically new, and pointed westward. Someone—I forget who—recommended a young man—and I forget who he was, too—to drive out to the Coast with me. The two of us laid out a trip we figured would consume three luxurious weeks. We'd get some maps. We'd take our time. We'd learn about and savor the country, and whenever we saw a beautiful lake or a crystal stream, we'd pull over, put our trunks on, dive in, and stay two or three days, lying out in the sun.

The first day we got as far as Lancaster County, Pennsylvania—Amish country and a beautiful place. But what we managed to find there was a ratty motor court with rooms held together chiefly by cobwebs, which were regularly traversed by an impressive assortment of spiders, some, no doubt, poisonous. The bed was a rack fit for a dungeon, with a mattress that reminded me of very thinly sliced white bread, except that it had long ago ceased to be white.

After spending the night there, we got in the car, now thoroughly disgusted but with a very long way yet to go. In a single dreamless night, our dreams of drifting at our ease to golden California congealed into a dogged determination to *get this thing over with as fast as possible*. Accordingly, we drove like Furies all day long, heading out at six A.M. and pushing on until nightfall.

We crossed the Mississippi at Ottumwa, Iowa, and were promptly pursued by a tornado—a black funnel bearing down on us out of a sky the sickly color of a hard-boiled egg yolk. Through the endless, barren landscape of the entire state of Wyoming, we drove with the top down, the onrushing wind scraping at whatever facial flesh was left by the time the sun got through with us.

As I recall the geography of that trek, Utah came after Wyoming and seemed to my eastern eyes like a more reasonable place. I mean, at least there were traces of green. We spent the night in an Ogden YMCA, then hit the road again. Top down, rolling along, I saw something blocking the road, looming larger and blacker as we got nearer. It was a bull, tail twitching and head pointed in the direction of what now seemed to me my ludicrously flimsy roadster. That head was lowered, the eyes raised as if to challenge our headlights. I've since, on occasion, received many such stares from studio executives. Except for that nervous tail, he was not moving. And we weren't going anyplace either.

At length, weary of the standoff, I eased the car into reverse, slowly let in the clutch, and inched the car back. For every foot we retreated, the bull stepped closer, until, as if he had finally decided that two petrified Easterners in a second-hand Ford weren't worth bothering with, he turned slowly and, slowly, walked off.

After this, we no longer wanted to stop for anything. When the intense scenic beauty of the Great West beckoned overwhelmingly, we would yield only to the extent of pulling to the side of the road, motor always running, doors left open, getting out, grudgingly taking in this vista or that valley, and hopping back in until we were ambushed by the next annoying view. I recall that Bryce Canyon had a lot of tunnels with large windows cut out of them at intervals so that tourists could gape at the spectacular scenes. We'd skid up to these vantage points, jump out, gape, jump back in, and be on our way again before the images had even registered on our retinas.

The Glitter Gulch of Las Vegas was a thing of the distant future when we pulled into that dusty little gambling town after midnight one evening. As to California, it made a remarkably slight impression when we crossed the state line.

But downtown Los Angeles, when we finally reached it, did make quite an impression. It was an impression of failure, of disappointment, of despair, and of oddly makeshift lives.

This *is California*? I thought.

The city looked like just another bled-out Depression community—even more ramshackle and down-at-the-heels than most. Paul Gaugin had dreamed of finding a paradise in Tahiti and found there instead poverty and degradation. George Cannatta and others had charged me with visions of a paradise on the Pacific, but what I found were ugly streets lined with squat buildings under a blue sky perpetually stained with rust-colored smog. A slow wave of homesickness washed over me. It would be the first of many.

SOME OF US WHO HAD FOUND JOBS at MGM were staying at the Mark Twain Hotel on Wilcox a half block off Hollywood

Boulevard. I don't know if its famous namesake had ever came to Hollywood, but he did write a very good book called *Roughing It*, and that would have been reason enough to name the hotel after him. Its principal architectural feature was a long corridor lined with rooms on either side, as if designed on the model of a not particularly enlightened penitentiary. Cells at the Mark Twain went for ten bucks a week, for which you got a bed, shower, toilet, and reasonably clean linen.

While most of us lived in Hollywood, MGM was out in Culver City, a lengthy drive that seemed all the longer because you went through a distinct climatic change getting there. You'd start out on one of those sunny L.A. mornings, with the eternally blue sky mocking you, deepening your dominant sense of doom and depression, and by the time you reached Pico Boulevard you'd be enveloped in a dirty gray mist through which the sun still shone, but feebly, a poor ghost of itself.

MGM did not build us facilities on the studio proper, but instead bought or leased a rundown bungalow behind Lot 2. This house, which must have once sheltered some hopeful and (I thought) utterly doomed family, was now the abode of a collection of artists, animators, story men, directors, and producers. It was, in essence, an empty house, whose few bare furnishings—a table and some chairs—made it seem even more forlorn.

My first day of work started with an interview with Fred Quimby, nominally in charge of the embryonic cartoon unit, and a guy named Maxwell. I sat down. My nose was painfully burned and split down the middle, the result of having heedlessly driven three thousand miles in an open car.

Maxwell pondered, then asked, "The cartoons—can you make them funny?"

"Well, you can make anything funny," I responded.

Quimby and Maxwell nodded in solemn agreement. I was definitely in.

But at the time all I really wanted was *out*. Homesickness, when you've got it bad, is unmistakably a *sickness*. You feel sick and depressed, but not just depressed—physically ill. Hoping to snap me out of it, my fellow inmates at the Mark Twain would take me, arm in arm, and walk me up and down Hollywood Boulevard as if they were trying to sober up a drunken stumblebum. So I'd survive another night, get up the next morning, greet the sun with a curse, drive into the region of gray mist, pull up to the bungalow, pour a mug of coffee, sit on a chair with a bunch of other guys holding coffee mugs and sitting on chairs, and spend the day talking aimlessly about what our next step should be.

The only thing that must have been clear to everyone assembled in that melancholy little house was that none of us had any idea of what we were doing or what we should be doing. Nor could we look to Fred Quimby for direction. Quimby had come to MGM in 1926 to head its short-feature department, and since cartoons are short, the studio brass judged Quimby sufficiently qualified to create our department. A Bostonian, Quimby was more refined than the typical movie executive, and he was certainly better dressed than any of us. He always wore beautifully tailored double-breasted suits, yet did not impress one as dapper so much as old beyond his years. In 1937 Quimby was fifty-one and looked like he was in his sixties. Moreover, the effect of his Brahmin accent was severely compromised by ill-fitting dentures and an abundance of loose jowl.

Quimby presided over weeks of research in an effort to find just the right vessel in which the MGM cartoon studio might make its maiden voyage. Hours of painful thought were followed by more hours of tedious deliberation and discussion in that empty bungalow. At length, the inaugural project emerged. It would be an animated version of the "Katzenjammer Kids" newspaper comic strip—also called "The Captain and the Kids."

I was a newcomer to Hollywood, so the monumental stupidity of this decision, the product of very deliberate, very time-consuming thought, came to me as a terrific shock. True, "The Katzenjammer Kids"—or "Captain and the Kids"—had been popular in the funny papers for a very long time. But it was one thing to read about and look at drawings of this basically unattractive family with its two insufferable offspring, and quite another to endure a five-minute ordeal of watching them all in action. Much worse, it was one thing to *read* the vaudeville-German dialect in a comic-strip balloon ("Vas? Das? Nicht? Nein? Zoh?") and quite another to *listen* to it. This was late in 1937. At this time, I can tell you, a German accent seemed anything but funny. How, I said to myself, can you make a cartoon about the very characters who are in the process of conquering and despoiling the civilized world? *Vas? Das? Nicht? Nein? Zoh?* It was insanity or stupidity or both.

More depressed than ever, I called Dorothy in Brooklyn and told her I was coming home. "Don't you dare," she answered. "I'm coming out there. I miss you." Which meant that we would try living together again, and, lonely as I was, that sounded good to me, despite our year of misadventure back east.

So I stayed. And there *were* compensations. In the late 1930s, MGM—except for our tiny corner of it—was a bustling, exciting place, producing fifty-two pictures a year and bursting with stars, most of whom sooner or later showed up at the commissary, where, informally and unofficially but nevertheless rigidly, stars sat with other stars, cinematographers with other cinematographers, writers with other writers, cartoon people with other cartoon people, and so on. But all conversation and shoveling of food stopped whenever the likes of Gable or Hepburn would walk in. (Another benefit of eating at the commissary was the availability of absolutely fresh and delicious chicken soup each and every day, pursuant to an edict of Louis B. Mayer, who craved the stuff and believed—I think with considerable validity—we would all likewise benefit from a daily bowl of it.) Somewhere among all the bewilderment, misdirection, and tawdry surroundings of Hollywood, there *was* real magic, and I was hardly immune to it.

In fact, I was bound and determined to *make* that magic happen. Remembering my efforts to capture a few minutes in the sun atop a

Brooklyn rooftop, I often dashed out to my car at lunchtime, drove like hell straight down Washington Avenue to the gray, dreary beach that was Culver City's feeble claim on the Pacific coast. There was often less sunlight than shone down on Brooklyn, and lying on the beach, its stone-strewn sand much coarser than Jones Beach back in New York, was about as gravely an experience as stretching out on the rooftops of home. However, it was, after all, Golden California, and I really meant to try my best to enjoy it.

But the time inevitably came to go back to the bungalow, where the situation deteriorated daily. Not only did we lack good material, we were plagued by personality conflicts, beginning with a basic geographical-cultural incompatibility between the Westerners and the Easterners. Quimby, directly or through Ted Sears, had recruited at least eight of us from New York. Within a few months, one by one, they all returned east—except for me.

In the meantime, the situation on the home front wasn't exactly terrific, either. Dorothy had made the trek west, we set up housekeeping, and, ever hopeful, endured one another for four weeks before deciding to call it quits once and for all. Dorothy was preparing to return to New York when she realized that she was pregnant. The combination of our upbringing, the prevailing mores of the late 1930s, and biological fact kept us together for the next twenty-three years.

AMONG THE WESTERNERS at the MGM cartoon studio was Bill Hanna, who had been hired as a writer and director. Bill came from a background about as different from mine as it is possible to get. While I had been born in a tenement on the Lower East Side and raised on the bustling streets of Flatbush, Bill was born in a place called Melrose, New Mexico. His father worked for the Santa Fe railroad, supervising the construction of stations and other structures throughout the West, so the family moved from one remote place to another, including Baker, Oregon; Logan, Utah; and San Pedro, California, before finally settling in Los Angeles when Bill was twelve.

By this time, Bill developed two lifelong passions: music and Boy

Scouting, in which he is still very active. By the time Bill entered high school, the family had moved to Compton, California, and after graduation he enrolled in the local junior college, majoring in journalism and engineering. Bill excelled in math as thoroughly as I was deficient in it, and it is no accident that one of Bill's greatest strengths in creating cartoons is his uncanny genius for timing.

WITH THE COLLAPSE of Wall Street in 1929, Bill left college and went forth into the world as an apprentice structural engineer with the gang who were building the Pantages Theatre in Hollywood. When he realized that this was not the work he wanted to devote his life to, he started looking for something else. His brother-in-law told him about the animation studio two artists associated with Walt Disney's early years, Hugh Harman and Rudy Ising, had started in L.A.

Bill began at the bottom with Harman-Ising, washing cels in the tiny studio, located above a dress shop. (In those days, the expensive celluloid was routinely reused and, in this way, untold millions of original images were literally flushed down the drain—a cultural catastrophe that has, however, greatly enriched modern gallery owners who have reaped the rewards of selling the few surviving original cels as well as special limited-edition cels created expressly for the market.) He graduated to cel painter, then became head of the tracing and painting department. Soon Bill started contributing gags and stories as well. Making good use of his musical training, he contributed tunes and lyrics to many Harman-Ising cartoons.

The Harman-Ising Studio had been financed by Leon Schlesinger, with whom Harman and Ising broke in 1933. Bill, an intensely loyal man, stayed with the men who had hired him, and Harman-Ising—with Bill on board, writing and directing—went on to do a good deal of contract work for MGM. In 1937, when MGM started up its own studio, Fred Quimby persuaded Bill to leave Harman-Ising and join MGM as a writer and director.

To his horror, Bill—and another director, Bob Allen—were immediately saddled with "The Captain and the Kids." One by one, they turned out the cartoons, and, one by one, they flopped.

Now, within a few weeks of my starting at MGM as an animator, I became a story man working under Friz Freleng, whom Quimby had also hired away from Leon Schlesinger's studio. Freleng tried to explain to Quimby that "The Captain and the Kids" would never—*could* never—work, but instead of acknowledging the lunacy of squandering substantial talent and good money on doomed material, the studio demoted Bill and Bob Allen from directors to story men. At the same time, the brass called in Milt Gross, a brilliant comic artist and writer who did a hilarious newspaper column called "Nize Baby."

Originally, the studio was interested in having Gross develop a character from his column, "JR," as an animated character, but the cigar-chomping New Yorker was soon pressed into service beyond this and was called upon to rescue the drowning studio. Unfortunately, like many would-be rescuers, Milt ended up getting pulled under himself. That he was enormously talented and hilariously funny was beyond question, but he was not cut out to manage a studio. He would, for example, start out with the intention of giving direction to an artist or an animator in order to refine a character, but he would soon end up asking the man to stand "for a few minutes" while he redrew the character himself painstakingly from scratch.

IT DOESN'T TAKE A SIX-FIGURE management consultant to tell you that if you try to do everybody's job for them, you'll soon be buried under a ton of work, you'll alienate everyone around you, and you'll drive yourself crazy in the process. Milt, who had a heart condition, would joke uneasily about the strain he had put himself under, declaring in the cadences of a streetwise New Yorker: "Yeah, someday a waiter will find my head in the soup. Pick my head up by the hair and say, 'He's had enough.' "

What failed Milt Gross, however, was not his heart, but his mind. He *did* drive himself crazy, becoming increasingly paranoid with each passing day. His office was located directly above Fred Quimby's, and Milt soon discovered a grillwork heat register against which he would put his ear in a struggling effort to make out what (if anything) was going on in Quimby's office.

Milt started spending more and more of each day listening at the register. We all knew when he had come out of an especially protracted spell of eavesdropping because the criss-cross pattern of the register would be engraved on the side of his face from jaw to temple. From time to time, he would emerge from his office, thus imprinted, loudly muttering over and over: "Can't hear the cocksucker. Can't hear what he's saying. Can't hear the cocksucker."

I returned from a rare vacation one evening to a frantic phone call from Dan Gordon, who told me that Milt had finally popped his cork and was going through the studio firing everybody. In context, that really wasn't such a crazy thing to do, although he should have started at the top.

MILT GROSS WAS SOON REPLACED by Harry Hershfield, another newspaper cartoonist and a Manhattan raconteur, who was hired *over* Quimby (much to the latter's chagrin) and from the very beginning was explicitly charged with running the studio. While Hershfield was certainly a wittier and more sophisticated man than Fred Quimby, he knew no more about animated cartoons than Fred. Quimby was quick to seize upon the loud grumbling he heard among us in a successful bid to engineer Hershfield's ouster. He arranged a showdown meeting with Hershfield, himself, the studio brass, and us, the "creative people." It was one of those brutal events you read about as typical of Hollywood's "Golden Age." Quimby went around the room, demanding from each of us a recitation of grievances. The result was Hershfield's removal, the crystallization of a fresh batch of hard feelings, and our deliverance wholly into the hands of Fred Quimby—at least until MGM brought in the pair who had served the studio so brilliantly as contractors, Hugh Harman and Rudy Ising.

At the request of Harman and Ising, Friz Freleng relinquished me to their unit, and I began working under them.

With their help, MGM did turn out a few very good cartoons, and, in particular, Rudy created Barney Bear, a lumbering, drawling creature obviously modeled on MGM's own Wallace Beery, but (equally obvious to all who knew him) also struck from the mold of Ising himself, who was affectionately nicknamed the Sleepy Bear. Like Barney, Ising drawled and spoke with great and gradual deliberation. Working on his own, he would stay up to all hours and was extremely creative, but, when he was working with others, he seemed acutely afflicted with an inability to make a decision. The result was that when you walked into Rudy Ising's office you wandered into another dimension in which, as in some science fiction movie, time seemed to stand still.

You'd come in with a drawing and show it to him, and he would lay it down on his desk, lean back, pat himself slowly, methodically, in search of a pack of cigarettes, locate the pack, pull it from his pocket, withdraw a cigarette, bring it gingerly to his lips, then start patting himself in search of his matches. Once these were secured, he'd strike a match, apply it to the cigarette, take a long, slow drag, remove the cigarette from between his lips, exhale, and begin to speak: "Yeahhhhhhh-uppp. Waaaal, thaaaat's nice."

But it wasn't over. Not by a long shot. He'd take another contemplative drag. "Maybe you should make him—rounder. Yes? Try him—oh, waaaal—rounder."

And you'd go out and redraw the character. After a day or two, you'd return. Following the ritual of the cigarette, Rudy would look and nod. "Maybe . . . taller. Try him—taller. Yes, taller"

The languorous pace under Rudy's direction gave me time to develop a cartoon idea I had about a tomato and a worm. Normally, when I had an idea, I'd just sketch something up, but in Rudy's realm I found the time to work and rework my tomato, applying gorgeous red color and a carefully crafted highlight so that the thing finally *breathed*.

Friz Freleng saw what I had done and remarked, "I didn't know you could draw like that." In point of fact, neither did I. He whispered, "I want you to come back and work for me." But Friz would soon give up on MGM and return to Warner Bros., where he remained until their cartoon studio closed in 1963.

It was obvious to me that the MGM cartoon studio could not survive on the kind of schedules we had under Rudy Ising: six months just to get through a storyboard that should have taken two weeks at most, and that was before final approval.

This gargantuan pace was one form of commercial suicide. "The Captain and the Kids" had been another. And Hugh Harman managed to come up with yet a third.

Hugh was a handsome man with a Clark Gable mustache and a genuine ambition to raise cartoons to loftier heights. At MGM, this ambition became a peculiar passion to animate Thomas Gray's "Elegy Written in a Country Churchyard":

The curfew tolls the knell of parting day,
The lowing herd wind slowly o'er the lea,
The ploughman homeward plods his weary way,
And leaves the world to darkness and to me.

And so on. The poem, which earned Gray the title of father of the "Graveyard School" of poets, is very beautiful, and I, who ate my lunch on the headstones of Wall Street's Trinity churchyard, had absolutely nothing against country churchyards. But it is not what any of us had hoped for from the co-creator of "Merrie Melodies" and "Looney Tunes."

The really crazy thing is, Harmon actually began working on the project. Some six months were consumed in creating artwork and working up storyboards, all of which were beautiful and none of which could be used to make a cartoon. (In fairness to Harman, who was sincere, high-minded, and very talented, he was to create an extraordinary, wholly original cartoon with his 1939 "Peace on Earth," which took as its theme something even less promising for animation than the possibilities presented by Gray's "Elegy." It was a beautifully realized cartoon depicting the aftermath of a world war that had annihilated humankind, leaving only the animals to rebuild civilization. Nominated for an Academy Award, it was also cited by the Nobel Peace Prize committee—I assume the only cartoon ever to earn that distinction. Bill Hanna and I thought enough of "Peace on Earth" to remake it in a 1955 CinemaScope version as "Good Will to Men.")

TAKE QUIMBY, A FAMILY OF ANIMATED HUNS, our own real-life version of Barney Bear, Gray's cheerful little "Elegy," and the parade of pretenders and paranoids who marched in and out of the studio—take these, add them up, and what you get is two very worried guys: Bill Hanna and me.

Convinced that the studio was foundering and about to go down by the bow, I said to Bill: "Why don't we do a cartoon on our own?" And he enthusiastically agreed. He knew that we had to do *something,* whether it had much chance of working or not.

When I let on to the others in the studio, including Harman and Ising, that Bill and I were developing a cat-and-mouse cartoon, we were greeted with a universal chorus of jeers and raspberries. A cat and a mouse! How *unoriginal* can you get? And how much variety can you milk out of such a hackneyed, shopworn idea? How many cat-and-mouse cartoons can you make?

Well, they all had a point. In fact, the very thing I liked about doing a cat-and-mouse story *was* its obviousness. Once you settled on a cat and a mouse, half the story was written before you even put pencil to paper. You have a cat and you have a mouse, ergo, you have the cat chasing the mouse, and the mouse doing his damndest to keep from getting caught.

Now I can't honestly say that Bill and I thought we were going to make the world sit up and take notice with "Puss Gets the Boot," as we called our first cartoon. What we *were* sure of, though, is that we wouldn't do any worse than anyone else at the studio, and one good thing about working under a man like Fred Quimby is that he didn't know enough to interfere. Technically, we were answerable to Rudy Ising, who was supposed to be supervising the cartoon. In fact, he didn't want anything to do with it, figuring we could go down the drain very nicely on our own, thank you. If we weren't given any positive support, neither were we stopped.

As I had back during my years at Irving Trust, I worked late into the night developing the story as well as sketch after sketch, bypassing storyboards and going directly to full-size layouts, because we didn't have a layout man assigned to us. These I'd turn over to Bill, who timed them, then turned them over to an animator.

Bill and I decided that we couldn't afford to go it completely alone. We needed some kind of support, but in order to get that support we had to prove what we could do. We wanted to present something more than a storyboard, but less, of course, than a finished cartoon. So we invented what we came to call "limited animation" in order to produce a demonstration film of the cartoon. I laid the cartoon out as I wrote it, and Bill shot my full-size layouts directly. The technique used far fewer individual drawings than a fully finished cartoon—fewer than 1,800—but these were shot to length so that the film produced by means of limited animation would run as long as the final product, resulting in a preview of the picture before it went into full production.

We used various shortcuts to get as much movement out of the technique as possible. For example, instead of using a lot of drawings to animate walking legs, I would take two drawings and alternately reverse the legs to give the impression of movement. We'd use zooms and pans to suggest other kinds of movement, and if we needed to indicate the effect of a head-on collision, Bill would just whack the side of the camera.

"Puss Gets the Boot" was not the first of the Tom and Jerry cartoons, but it was an immediate ancestor to them. The Tom of this cartoon was called Jasper, and Jerry didn't even have a name yet. We also had a ways to go in developing the look of the cat and the mouse. Jasper was proportioned more like a kitten than a full-grown cat, yet he was not as cute or expressive as Tom would become. He had something of a Cheshire cat grin, which verged on looking downright wicked. The unnamed mouse, leaner than Jerry, looked more like a real mouse than his cuddly descendent—and he did not sport the bow tie Jerry often wore. But the basic elements of Tom and Jerry were unmistakably present, and the limited animation demo was a success, provoking laughter—howls, even—from an MGM executive corps that was not known for its sense of humor and that was none too well disposed toward the faltering cartoon department. We were given the green light to make the full cartoon, which was completed in 1940.

Bill and I were disappointed by the in-house reception accorded the finished cartoon. To begin with, Rudy Ising, who had deliberately removed himself from involvement in the film, got sole producer credit, while we got no on-screen credit at all. And while the demonstration version had gone over very nicely with the studio big shots, Quimby and other executives greeted the finished cartoon with a resounding round of utter indifference. Nor was the release of "Puss Gets the Boot" treated as anything special. It was just dumped in the theaters.

Then the public got a hold of it, and "Puss Gets the Boot" proved wildly popular, running at some theaters for weeks. An Academy Award nomination followed, and it was far and away the most successful cartoon MGM had yet released.

Were we hailed as heroes and saviors? No, not quite.

Quimby summoned Bill and me into his office. "I don't want you to make anymore pictures with the cat and the mouse," he said.

You spend enough time in a Hollywood studio, and you figure you're well beyond ever being surprised by anything said or done there. Then something like this comes along.

"Why?" one of us managed to ask.

"We don't want to put all our eggs in one basket," came the reply.

Of course, Fred Quimby had failed to acknowledge that, before "Puss Gets the Boot," MGM hadn't a single good egg to put into any basket. But, with that remark, we were sent off to work on a variety of totally unpromising characters around whom we made a couple of terrible cartoons. The first of which, called "Swing Social," featured a cast of catfish in blackface doing black songs. Now, like all cows and at least most birds, fish don't work in cartoons: zero, exclamation point. They float suspended in space, which makes for singularly boring animation, they are ugly, and you wouldn't think of cuddling up to one. Even worse is what we tried to do with the black dialect in this picture. There was an all-black musical in town—with a terrific cast—whom we hired for the voices. Unfortunately, Bill wrote the black dialect in the way a white man thinks a black man talks, and the actors strained to read and sing the lines in that stilted Stepin Fetchit manner. This disaster was followed by another, called "Galloping Gals," which featured horses.

We might have made fish pictures, horse pictures, and any number of other failures, continuing on the studio's infernal tangent to nowhere until some executive would finally have the decency to put the cartoon department out of its misery. But then a single, miraculous letter that appeared in Fred Quimby's mail. It was from a leading Texas exhibitor named Besa Short. "When are we going to see more of those charming cat-and-mouse cartoons?" the letter pleaded. Instantly, we were directed to make more.

If we were to make them, we needed a name for the mouse and a better name for the cat. Neither Bill nor I came up with "Tom" or "Jerry," but, like so much of what I have found myself involved in, we left the choice of names to chance. We invited studio personnel to write down pairs of names on pieces of paper and toss them into a hat. We shook the hat and drew "Tom and Jerry," which had been submitted by an animator named John Carr. He won fifty dollars. As for us, well, the names failed to set off any bells and sirens, but we stuck with them, and I've come to the conclusion that the simpler the name, the easier it is to remember. Tom would chase Jerry for the next seventeen years.

FOR THE FIRST TIME IN MY CAREER—maybe in my life—I felt that I was really in control and the master of my fate. Bill and I were pretty much left alone to create the cartoons we wanted to make the way we wanted to make them—which meant that they were beautifully drawn and painstakingly crafted. Backgrounds ranged from domestic settings rendered in great detail, to Manhattan streetscapes (which even included the view—so familiar to me from my days at Irving Trust—looking west down Wall Street toward Trinity Church), to the seventeenth-century France of "The Two Mouseketeers." Action was both broad—some have even said violent—and yet subtle as well; we made Tom and Jerry come alive by giving them a genuine vocabulary of what today would be called body language, especially where the faces were concerned. Cartoon character faces are often little more than masks with hinged jaws and sliding eyelids. In contrast, the faces of Tom and Jerry were capable of expressing a whole spectrum of emotion.

As much as we devoted ourselves to the art and the animation, we also emphasized story. Sure, the basic plot was always inherent in the characters—a cat plus a mouse equals a chase—but, working from this premise, we introduced twists, turns, and nuances that endowed this *particular* cat and this *particular* mouse with individual, recognizable, three-dimensional personalities. We all know that a cat and a mouse are destined to have a certain kind of relationship—that of predator and prey—but we added something human to that relationship, something more complex, so that the audience always got the idea that Tom, determined as he was, never *really* wanted to catch Jerry, and Jerry, far from being the cowering victim, was exuberant in his evasiveness, at times diabolical, at times merely bemused.

Without the high level of the art and the animation, and without genuine personalities, the MGM jeering section would have been right, and we would have made a single cat-and-mouse cartoon, soon forgotten, and no more. There are a lot of cartoons in the world, but only a handful of real, honest-to-goodness cartoon *characters*, characters who can sustain a long-running series. I'll leave it to the reader to make his own list, but I can assure you that list will be a short one. Just take Disney, for example. Donald Duck and Goofy are characters capable of carrying a series. But what about Mickey Mouse?

Disney tried very hard to make him a star, but what he really succeeded in doing is making him a corporate logo—and, as such, Mickey is probably among the most universally recognized images of all time. But that's just the point. Mickey Mouse is more of a symbol than a real character.

Making cartoons means very hard work at every step of the way, but creating a successful cartoon character—I mean one that will carry cartoon after cartoon after cartoon—is the hardest work of all. It's a lot like the task Dr. Frankenstein set for himself: nothing less than the creation of life or, at least, a reasonable facsimile thereof.

Where does it all come from?

Like anything else creative, it comes from one's own life. Now, I don't want to start psychologizing here, but I can tell you that, more often than I care to remember, I have found myself in the position of Jerry Mouse. The cartoon industry, like any other intensely creative endeavor that becomes a big business with potential for great profit and even more disastrous loss, is full of predator-prey relationships. The studio fat cats are always ready to get a little fatter—on you—and, as the Depression drove home to me and to anyone who came of age during that decade, the proverbial wolf is always hovering at the door. By and by, Bill and I would also learn about the feeding habits of another kind of cat. It was a lion, and it roared at the start of every motion picture our studio produced.

But, for now, the beast had his claws retracted, and we—Bill and I—began to enjoy a period not of celebrity and adulation, to be sure, but of benign neglect.

As I have said, as the studio was structured at the time, Bill and I were, in theory, supervised by Rudy Ising, toward whom Bill felt intense loyalty. Shortly after we got the go-ahead to make more Tom and Jerry cartoons, I took a short vacation and returned to discover that Bill, troubled by his conscience, had gone to Quimby to tell him that we would be willing to work under Rudy Ising. This was not something Quimby wanted to hear. His objective was to develop production units independent from Harman and Ising, with whom he was constantly at odds. He called Bill and me into a meeting.

"Bill said that you would both be willing to work under Rudy."

I answered, "I don't know why we would do that, because Rudy never even came into the room when we were doing 'Puss.' "

Quimby, realizing now that Rudy Ising had taken producer credit for a film in which he had not been involved, worked himself up into a loose-dentured rage tinged with no little glee. "Are you telling me that Rudy never came into the room?"

"Yes."

"Is that right, Bill?"

"Yes, it is."

"Well, then, I'm not about to give him credit for these pictures. You just keep going along the way you are."

And so Tom and Jerry were born, and my half-century-plus partnership with Bill Hanna began in earnest.

Chapter Five

CAT AND MOUSE GAMES

WITH TOM AND JERRY LAUNCHED and Bill and I assured of our position at the helm, I was savoring the thrill of having at long last gotten hold of something real. Then the phone rang. It was Friz Freleng, who had left MGM to work again with Leon Schlesinger, who was now running the cartoon department at Warner Bros. "Joe, I'd like to talk to you. Can you come over to a meeting at the studio this Sunday?"

Even slave-driving studios take Sundays off, so, I figured, a meeting on the Sabbath must be a very important meeting. I showed up, and Friz laid down a proposition: If I would come over to Warner's, I could be an animator, a story man, a director—whatever I wanted to be—and they would beat my current salary at MGM.

If the offer had come before "Puss," I'd have been out MGM's door and through Warner's before Fred Quimby could twitch a jowl. But I had started something at MGM now, and I found myself desperately groping for an excuse not to sign on the dotted line. "Well, gee, Friz, I don't know if it's legal to sign anything on Sunday," I said, and by the end of the meeting, I had managed to talk my way out of a perfectly good job as a full-fledged director and at a better salary than I was currently making.

By Monday, Quimby had heard about the meeting. "Is it true?" he asked.

And I told him that it was.

"I'll match their offer," Quimby said.

MGM was paying me a hundred dollars a week, and Friz had offered $125. So I agreed, and Quimby and I shook on it. Before I left his office, he motioned for me to remain in my seat as he picked up the phone and dialed Schlesinger. He wanted me to hear this. Leon Schlesinger was quite literally one of the heavyweights of animation. He was a big, gross, crude man, who larded his conversation liberally with four-letter words. Quimby, phone to ear, sat erect at his desk, gave his necktie a tug, cleared his throat and began what he proposed to be a thorough dressing down. It started with a challenge: "Well, what do you mean by trying to steal my people?"

To which Schlesinger replied, "Fuck you," and hung up.

End of phone call. Only Quimby still had the receiver to his ear, his jowls quivering. I should point out that it took me more than six months of continual needling to get the raise he had promised me.

From time to time, Fred Quimby liked to mount the high horse of righteous indignation, whether or not the occasion struck anyone else as particularly relevant or consequential. One person who could always be counted on to turn Quimby livid was Tex Avery. Now, Quimby's task in opening up the MGM cartoon department was to find people he could depend on to produce hits consistently. He found us, and he also found Tex.

Those of us who make cartoons consider Tex Avery one of the greats. Chuck Jones, Friz Freleng, and Bob McKimson all acknowledge a big debt to him, and although Bill and I didn't work directly with him at MGM—he headed up another unit—his irreverence, daring, timing, headlong pacing, and total originality certainly inspired us in what we did with Tom and Jerry. Admirers have called Tex "anarchic," "free-wheeling," and "surreal." As far as Quimby was concerned, however, Tex Avery was a thorn in his side and a royal pain ninety degrees south of that. He stubbornly refused to pay any attention to schedules, and he insisted on doing his own thing. This drove Quimby crazy. Then, when Tex came up with a very sexy girl character and put her in "Red Hot Riding Hood" and "Wild and Wolfy," Quimby was outraged by what he deemed a display of vulgarity and bad taste. He didn't want to do the cartoons, but as usual Tex was able to get his way, and the films with Tex's sexy girl not only captured the racy, streetwise, smart-alecky spirit of the period, but proved to be among the studio's biggest hits—a fact that irritated Quimby even more.

I remember how he raved when Tex used a spinach gag, having a character eat spinach and thereby gain instant strength. The source of the gag was as obvious as its humor, and all of us thought it was damn funny. But Fred just didn't get it.

"This is just terrible," he sputtered to us. "You know what this is like? This is just like sneaking into a man's house, going into his safe, and taking everything he's got! That's what it's like!"

There are two ironies at work here. First, as the Oscars began rolling in—and Tom and Jerry cartoons would win seven of them before we were through—Quimby, not Bill and I, appeared on the Academy stage to lay exclusive claim to each. And it wasn't as if we stood by waiting for Quimby to show us some generosity. We implored, we cajoled, we begged him to give us at least co-producer credit so that we would be eligible for an Oscar. No, he replied, his hands were tied. Eddie Mannix—MGM vice president and general manager of the studio—"wouldn't like it." The second irony came when MGM rereleased our cartoons. Quimby reprinted them, inserting his name, full screen, as producer of each and relegating us to director-writer credit. He did precisely what he had condemned Rudy Ising for doing.

Well, I would be lying if I did not admit that, for me, such injustices were bitter pills that went down very, very hard. On the other hand, the meeting with Quimby early in the Tom and Jerry series gained us our creative independence from Rudy Ising—who soon left MGM—and made us answerable to Fred Quimby alone.

What did that mean? Blessedly, very little.

In his way, Fred was the most dependable human being I have ever met. He would come in every morning at ten, settle into his office, and read the trade papers. Then, at eleven, he would get into his car and drive to the studio barber shop for a straight-razor shave followed by a liberal application of talc. Next came a leisurely lunch, after which he would return to our studio, go into his office, lie down on his couch, and take a nap. At three o'clock, he would get into his car and drive home. The routine was as inevitable as death and taxes, and everybody knew it well.

One day, Bill and I approached Quimby's secretary, Virginia Kenwood, and asked to see her boss. "Is Mr. Quimby back from lunch?"

"You know, I didn't see him come in. Let me check."

She got up, knocked quietly on his door, and, hearing no response, opened the door and peered in. She didn't see him, so she walked to his closet to see if his suitcoat was hanging there.

Suddenly a groggy voice rumbled out through loose dentures and wattles: "Are you looking for me in the closet? Do you think you'll find me in the closet?"

Virginia shrieked and leaped backward out the office door.

What had happened was that, instead of lying north-to-south on his couch, as he always did, Quimby had oriented himself south-to-north, so that his feet, encased in their big black shoes, were where his head had been for as many years as Virginia had worked as his secretary. Not seeing what she had always seen when she looked into his office, she simply failed to notice Quimby lying there at all.

But Fred Quimby was, after all, our boss, and Bill and I persisted in truly heroic efforts to talk to him about what we were doing. On one occasion, I went into an extended spiel about the Tom and Jerry then in progress, reeling off the gags, and dancing around to indicate some of the action. I was working right in Quimby's face, maybe a foot away from him at most, when, oblivious of my creative calisthenics, he said, "You know something, I think this Nixon is a horse's ass."

What made us finally give up even the pretense of talking to him about what we were doing was the time he stopped me in mid-sentence with, "You don't have to tell me anything. I know what you're thinking before you even tell me." And with that claim to clairvoyance, he neatly absolved himself of the responsibility of ever having to listen to us again.

On occasion, Fred would escort visitors—usually major exhibitors—through the cartoon department to show us off. Routinely, I would launch into whatever we happened to be working on at the time, showing storyboards, doing the sound effects, acting out the chases. It must have dawned on Quimby that, sooner or later, if he brought enough visitors through, someone upstairs would figure out where everything in the studio was really coming from. Quimby took Bill and me aside.

"You know something, you fellows are too important to be disturbed like this. I'm not going to bother you with any more visitors."

In this manner, we achieved a state of splendid creative isolation. On balance, that was a blessing conducive to creativity. But it was also—well—lonely, never seeing anyone from the outside world, and it was, if I let myself think too much about it, infuriating. Jerry was a mouse, but, pursued though he was, he was nevertheless a free mouse. Bill and I? We were mice in a cage, making that little wheel spin and spin. On the other hand, we were also—by the standards of the time—very well paid mice.

I never gave it much thought back then, but I guess nobody other than the studio brass knew how much Bill and I were getting. Since we were locked away in our cage, the general belief was that we were being financially exploited as well. This erupted into a labor dispute of minor proportions when Bill Hanna was informed that animators had started complaining to their union that we were taking a low salary and thereby hurting the industry, making things bad for everyone else. An irate group of animators demanded a meeting at a local bar.

Bill, always more cautious and thoughtful than I, feared a full-blown dispute, even the kind of major strike that had hit Disney, and he walked into the bar with trepidation, eager to placate. They looked at us up and down as we entered. One of them, who was actually drumming his fingers on the table, announced that he intended to speak bluntly, and he laid it out: We were working for low wages, and that was bringing everybody's salaries down.

Bill made some conciliatory remarks. Then it came to me. Well, I tried.

"Listen, I understand that you're upset about the inequity of salaries. But, actually, you don't know what I'm making, and if you want to know what I'm making," I said, working up to a crescendo, "it's none of your goddamn business," and walked out the door.

That little exchange left a few hard feelings, but, remarkably, that was as violent as it ever got—if you don't, of course, count touch football and the two major wars we fought.

AMONG THE GREAT GLORIES of the MGM lot were the vast outdoor sets that had been constructed over the years. You'd walk a few yards in one direction and you were on the streets of Manhattan. Another few yards would put you in a Roman village, or a town in the Wild West, and so on. There was also a vast expanse of beautifully kept lawn, which we in the animation studio claimed at lunchtime for titanic touch football matches. I was a respectable broken-field runner, but Bill Littlejohn, a very big man, was a fierce competitor, and Harvey Eisenberg could throw a forward pass at least forty miles straight and true. I remember one game when a huge cast of extras, all dressed in World War I uniforms and brandishing weapons, gathered to watch us play. Harvey laid a long forward pass squarely into my hands, and I took off like hell with it—until I became aware of Bill Littlejohn bearing down on me, his teeth gritted, determined to stop me or kill me, and I went down with a charley horse in each leg. I fell short of the touchdown, but I was at least saved from the wrath of Littlejohn. However, I could hardly walk, and Quimby, seeing me in this condition, muttered his usual admonition to his studio staff: "Goddamn stupid high school kids."

The next morning, Eddie Mannix himself issued an edict forbidding touch football games—not, however, because of the risk of injury to his talented personnel, but because of the damage being done to the lawn.

In the meantime, Tex Avery had scouted out a new form of lunchtime amusement for us. He found a comfortable nook behind one of the great facades that made up, as I recall, a Manhattan streetscape, and he put together a crap game, which soon became a respected lunchtime institution—albeit a short-lived one. Hearing about it, Quimby issued a proclamation forbidding gambling on the lot.

Unlike football and craps, our two wars were indoor activities. The first broke out almost immediately after I arrived at MGM, when I was working with Friz Freleng. It began when one of us discovered the aerodynamic properties of the pushpin—a discovery (I'm told) that had also been made independently at the Disney studio. Animators use a lot of pushpins to tack sketches, drawings, model sheets, and storyboards to the wall. If you hold a pushpin just so and throw it just right, it sails like a dart and penetrates its target almost as effectively.

At first, we just had contests, often for money, throwing at inanimate targets, including the little hole that was drilled at the back of each animator's desk for the electric cords. But within a short time, as each day neared its end, we began to throw these missiles not at inanimate targets, but at one another. It was really an art, and I was considered one of the best pushpin throwers. Friz and I fought many such duels, and I delighted in making him dance, hurling pushpins at his feet like a Western gunfighter. If Friz weren't quick enough, the pushpin would penetrate his shoe, producing some highly interesting linguistic innovations. And dancing—you never saw such dancing in your life. I remember an occasion when one of my pushpins hit him in the leg, stuck there, and he limped around the studio like a cavalryman pierced by an Apache's arrow.

The Pushpin Wars eventually yielded to the Water Wars. I can't explain the fatal attraction between cartoon people and water. It's not enough that we use it in animated gags, we also seem to be unable to resist using a lot of it on each other. For me, the water mania started back when I was at the Paul Terry studio in New Rochelle. It was a hot, hot August day, and I went over to the water cooler to get a drink. It was by the window, and I leaned out in an effort to get a breath of air. At that very moment, ten floors below me, I saw five of our guys walking out into the alley, across to a little diner there. One of them was story man Mike Meyers, and the other was Dan Gordon. I pulled back from the window and looked down at the base of the water cooler. Somebody, breaking for lunch, had left a rag mop in a bucket filled with dirty water. Seeing this, naturally, I pulled out the mop, lifted the bucket, and hurled the dirty water out the open window, carefully calculating the trajectory so that the water would splash down right in front of Dan Gordon and company.

Funny thing about water thrown from ten stories up. It doesn't come out in a stream, but in a *piece*, so that what I watched flying out of the bucket was a solid hunk of water, which sailed in an arc out and over and then, to my horror, back, so that it splatted squarely on the top of Dan Gordon's head.

I was petrified. A hunk of water dropped from that height—it must hit you with velocity of a rock. Had I just murdered Dan Gordon?

I tore down the stairs, into the alley, and across to the diner. I opened the door, trying to look as innocent as possible, and there I beheld five frowning, grumbling men, their hair plastered down on their heads. Dan, cautiously sniffing at the air and at the shoulder of his shirt, was still dripping brown drops of filthy water.

"What happened?" I asked, eyes wide.

"If I ever catch the sonofabitch that did this," Dan said, "I will dismember him." And the others expressed similar sentiments—with which, of course, I could only agree and commiserate before backing out the door.

Now, you would think that I had learned my lesson, but I have to confess that, not only did the New Rochelle incident fail to reform me, I became, in fact, the instigator of the MGM Water Wars. They began with little enough inspiration. I took a paper cup, filled it with water, and placed it above an office doorway. When the victim opened the door, the cup would tip, fall, and douse him with water. From this modest beginning, I graduated to brilliant feats of genuine engineering. I tied one end of a string to my desk fan, ran the string up and over the pipe for the sprinkler system, which ran overhead, then tied the other end to a two-handled trophy cup I had, which I filled with water. I plugged the fan into the socket for the animator's light board, so that when he turned on his lightboard, the fan would start instead, wind up the string, upset the trophy cup, and, once again, douse the animator.

This technique rarely yielded a direct hit, though it did soak the desk, eliciting very satisfying screams and curses from the victim. It also incited others to join the ongoing combat. A particularly intense rivalry developed between Harvey Eisenberg, a layout man, and Irven—Irv—Spence, an animator. This escalated rapidly until one would take the entire bottle off the water cooler and use it against his foe as heavy artillery. Thus attacked, Irv, taking note of a hole in the back of Harvey's shirt, stuck his finger in it and pulled down sharply, ripping his shirt from near the collar all the way to the tails. By way of retaliation, Harvey tore off the breast pocket of Irv's shirt. Irv then ripped off Harvey's. Before the two of them were through, they were both drenched, and their shirts hung down from their belts like hula skirts. Harvey then grabbed the water cooler bottle under one arm, climbed to the top of his desk, took hold of the overhead sprinkler pipe with his free hand, and started swinging from it like an ape.

At this juncture, Fred Quimby, who had been utterly unaware of our battles, walked in. The mouth opened. The jowls drooped. "Jeeez-us. A bunch of goddamn high school kids." And he turned and walked out.

This hardly ended the wars. Irv Spence devised what he considered a brilliant defensive strategy. He brought into his office a pile of empty film cans, which he stacked precariously on the edge of his desk. He attached string to them, and ran it to the doorknob, so that nobody could come into his office without triggering a very loud booby trap.

At lunchtime I secured a ladder and a drill. I set up the ladder outside in the corridor and drilled through the plywood wall of Irv's office right over where his head would be. We all waited for Irv to come back from lunch. He went into his office and set up his defensive booby trap. With Irv behind his closed door, I brought back the ladder, set it up, took a big mouthful of water, climbed the ladder, put one end of the straw in my mouth and the other end through the hole I had drilled. Then I let loose with the water.

Now, we had timed all this, and we had studied the trajectories involved. The stream must have hit Irv squarely on the head. He let out a scream, and unable to figure out where the water was coming from, thoughtlessly pulled open his office door, triggering his own booby trap of some twenty empty metal film cans. It sounded like the end of the world. Of course it wasn't. But while we were throwing pushpins and developing the weapons of a water war, Europe and Asia were erupting in a very real war we all wondered how long we could stay out of.

AFTER DOROTHY HAD DISCOVERED that she was pregnant and we decided that we would stay together, we rented a tiny house in Westwood for forty dollars a month, which included a garage filled with wild cobwebs that looked as if they had been spun by a badly deranged spider. I showed them to a friend.

"You've got black widows," he said.

Well, what do you want for forty dollars a month? So, whenever I ventured into the garage, I took a flashlight and a long taper, sought out each of the arachnids, and got them before they could get me. By and by the nice old German spinster sisters who owned the house offered to sell it to me for four thousand dollars. It was tempting, but I couldn't get those black widows out of my mind, and I spoke to a contractor friend of mine who told me that I could buy a vacant lot in Brentwood for $1,850, and, once I had that, I could secure an FHA loan to build a brand-new house.

I had two little children at the time and exactly two thousand dollars in the bank. The $1,850 expenditure left me with reserves of $150, and the total cost of the house—$7,200—seemed like a formidable sum back then. But I went ahead and built the house.

Proud homeowner and playing the role of dutiful suburban *pater familias*, I was on my hands and knees on my front lawn searching for and destroying weeds one beautiful L.A. winter Sunday morning. I had the window open so that I could hear the radio playing—and that's when the announcement came, as it came to most all of us, while we were engaged in this or that perfectly ordinary, mundane, homely activity, an activity forever after etched in memory, washing a car, preparing a meal, or ripping up an offending weed by its roots: THE JAPANESE HAVE ATTACKED PEARL HARBOR . . . HEAVY CASUALTIES . . . FLEET SUNK . . . ACT OF WAR . . .

So you sit there on your bought-but-by-no-means-paid-for lawn, a hank of grass and weed in your fist, and you stare at it and at the quiet little cul-de-sac of a street you live on, and you say to yourself: *What does this mean? What do I do now?*

As a father with two children at the start of the war, I was not drafted. Besides, MGM quickly turned over many of its resources to the war effort, and even our department was assigned to create animated training films while we were still turning out the Tom and Jerrys. So, as far as the Draft Board was concerned, I was working in a vital war-related industry. I remember making films about PT boats, showing how they were maneuvered and illustrating the fine points of their tactical deployment, and I recall a picture titled "Lighter Than Air," which was about dirigibles. Those of us at the studio also had charge of a flock of handsome second lieutenants who were assigned to us to learn aspects of animation and film making.

Unlike me, my brothers were eager to get into the shooting. Ted, my kid brother, was not yet eighteen when the war broke out, but he had read a magazine article about fighter pilots, and he decided that a fighter pilot is what he would be. One of my uncles talked my mother into signing a form granting permission for her underage youngest to enlist. He enrolled in a grueling training program at Randolph Field, near Chicago, entering as one of a class of four hundred young men and graduating as one of the forty who made the final cut. Commissioned as a second lieutenant, Ted came out to visit me at the studio on his way to his assignment at Fort Hamilton in Anchorage, Alaska. I could not get over the fact that so many other men in uniform saluted him—Ted—my kid brother. Clark Gable, himself in a U.S. Army Air Force uniform, shook his hand.

He served with distinction in a little-celebrated and very dangerous theater of the war. The Aleutian Islands of Alaska were the site of Japan's only invasion of our territory, but the enemy up there was as much the weather as it was the Japanese. Ted, who quickly rose to the rank of first lieutenant and then captain, was full of stories of pilots who took off, became fog bound or snow bound, and simply vanished without a trace. The scenes he'd paint of life in the officers' club seemed to come straight out of *Dawn Patrol*. The pilots would get together, throw their wallets in a heap upon the table, and drink until their pooled resources ran out. I became a war profiteer to the extent that Ted was able to get me Johnnie Walker Red Label scotch for two dollars a bottle. It was virtually impossible for unconnected civilians to get it at any price, and the bottles were treated like gold. Not that I talked to my brother much about price. He learned a lot about the cost of things. Before the war was over, all but two of his squadron had been lost to the weather.

I was very proud of Ted Barbera, but not really all that surprised by his heroism. The one who stunned me was my older brother, Larry. He was the last person on the face of the earth I'd ever figure would volunteer for anything, let alone an opportunity to get shot at. You see, Larry was a born salesman—if you want to be polite about it. He was, in fact, a born con man, and he could have become a great actor, or a great bunko artist, or a great Electrolux gas refrigerator salesman—which is what he chose to do for a living. His greatest coup was selling refrigerators to a huge Manhattan apartment complex, a deal that set him up like royalty at the Taft Hotel.

Yet he was almost always strapped, and whenever he was broke he would show up at my mother's. I remember his coming through the door one afternoon and, seeing my mother on her hands and knees scrubbing the floor with a brush, feigning absolute horror. "My God, what are you doing? No mother of mine scrubs floors! Here, you sit, and give that brush to me."

And he gave the floor a few licks. That was enough. Without either of them saying a word about money, Larry knew what to do. My mother would leave some bills under a lamp. At the end of his visit, Larry would go to the lamp, lift it, pocket the money, and we wouldn't see him again until his next financial crisis.

The histrionics were nothing new. Back when we were kids, one of the horrors of civilization was getting a toothache. The pain in and of itself was bad enough, but the cure was even worse. My mother would send us to a dentist on the corner of Bedford Avenue and Clarendon Road, a big, burly man with hairy arms, whose instruments were medieval, and for whom anesthesia consisted of a whack on the side of the head. He'd drill, dig, and pull, and I'd yell or jump—then, wham: "Don't move!"

Faced with the choice of enduring a toothache or going to the dentist, we generally tried to ride out the bad tooth. My method was to put a pillow on a rocking chair, lay my head on the pillow, and rock until the pain went away. Now, Larry would deal with a toothache by falling to his knees, gazing up at heaven, and screaming, "God, why, God, why are you doing this to me!" So you can imagine my shock when I heard that Larry had enlisted, and I was even more stunned—and proud—when I heard that he had distinguished himself in the American landing at Sicily.

Me? I just kept working at the studio. By the time they were calling up fathers with two children, I had a third. Of course, those of us on the home front endured our share of hardships. Many commodities were being rationed, including gasoline, and, as a patriot, I made it my business to operate a carpool, regularly giving a lift to five young women who worked at the studio and whom I would pick up at various corners. It was a lot of fun at first, but I soon discovered that you couldn't put the same five girls in the same car every day of the week. Spontaneous enmities and downright hatreds developed. I could never figure out just what the sources of conflict were, and it didn't seem to matter. The meat eaters just naturally hated the cheese eaters, the front seat just naturally refused to talk to the back seat, and so on. With all the racket every morning, I had no opportunity to think, let alone find romance.

THERE WAS ONE GREAT-LOOKING GIRL at the studio named Doris, who would sachet down the corridor, pulling in her wake the heads of a couple of dozen animators, who would peer out of their office doorways. In that most politically incorrect era, this went on for some time—a silent ritual among us—until one day Heck Allen called out, "It's a bird! It's a dame! It's Supercan!" And it was super, too.

Among our group was a terrific animator, who shall remain nameless here, and a very pretty young woman. In the course of things, the two became a kind of lunchtime item. There was gossip and speculation of all kinds, since the young lady was married, and her husband was in the service. Finally, one day at lunchtime, a car drove up, and a man in uniform emerged, asking for her. It was, of course, her husband. Word of his presence shot through the whole studio.

"Oh God," came the whispers. "Do you know who's out there?"

Soon, everyone had assembled at the window—about fifty faces peering out at the car and the soldier just across the street.

Then the animator and the girl drive up, back from lunch. They push each other and giggle. Suddenly, they freeze.

The soldier yells something to her from across the street, and she runs to the car. She gets in, he slams the door, and he swings the car in a u-turn to the our side of the street. Opening his door, he peers over the top of the car, fixes the animator with a steely stare, and says: "The next time we meet, one of us shall fall!" With that, he drives away, and the studio had a phrase that was savored and repeated on every possible occasion.

As was the case at the moribund Van Beuren studio, the annual Christmas parties were the real apogee of excess among us. If there's one thing that *most* cartoon people have in common, it's an affection for drink. And if there is one thing that *all* cartoon people have in common, it's an affection for free drinks. I saw this demonstrated in 1943, when we won our first Oscar, for "Yankee Doodle Mouse." Quimby, of course, took the award for himself, but Bill and I decided to throw a party for the people who worked on it. Getting word of this, Quimby stepped in.

"Look here, the studio will pick up the tab for the party," he said, and who were we to argue? So it was free drinks at the Beverly Hills Hotel, with the byword being, "Make it a double."

The Christmas parties were likewise orgies of drinking and singing and groping and pawing. In an effort to regulate the consumption of liquor, the studio sent invitations announcing that a turkey dinner and a full bar would be provided after eleven o'clock. This actually induced the cartoon staffers to invest their own money in preparatory liquor, which they'd start consuming in the privacy of their offices at about eight, so that by the time eleven rolled around they were already very well primed.

There was one young man who worked with us—very religious, a bachelor, who lived with his mother—but, come the Christmas party and a few drinks, it was like Jekyll and Hyde. He became a raving lunatic running up and down the halls, grabbing girls and kissing them.

Then there was a mousy young woman, not very attractive, quiet and demure year round, until the Christmas party, when she'd set herself immovably under a sprig of mistletoe, strong-arming anyone who passed and planting upon them a big, wet, and generally unwelcome kiss.

I was walking toward the door, saw the trap, and skidded—cartoon fashion—to a stop. She looked at me. I looked at her.

"Uh-huh. I just remembered. I gotta make a phone call," and turned on my heel.

"You son of a bitch."

BUT THERE WAS ONE tremendous difference between the revelry at Van Beuren and at MGM. At Van Beuren, the horseplay and the parties were born of despair and desperation. At MGM, they were the byproducts of good feelings, of feelings of accomplishment and the knowledge that we had created the hardest-working, highest-quality studio in the business.

To me it makes little sense to talk about the cartoons we did. The way to appreciate them is to see them. Our cartoons were nominated eleven times for Oscars, and we won seven times—which, I believe, is a record. We did just about everything you can do with a cat chasing a mouse—and we did quite a bit more than that. The artwork and animation for "Mouse in Manhattan," which reproduced the New York of 1944 in loving detail; for "The Cat and the Mermouse," an underwater fantasy from 1949; and for "Mice Follies," a mouse-size version of the Ice Follies, made in 1954, explored wholly original directions. In "The Two Mousketeers," which won an Academy Award in 1951, we created a historically accurate cartoon version of seventeenth-century France against which Tom, Jerry, and Jerry's fellow Mousketeer, Nibbles (also called Tuffy), played out their hilarious brand of swashbuckling. We even introduced dialogue—*French* dialogue, spoken exclusively by Nibbles (and voiced by a real live six-year-old French girl).

The Tom and Jerry cartoons were not our only field for innovation.

In 1944, Gene Kelly approached Bill and me with what was at the time a very unique request. He wanted to dance with a mouse—not a live mouse, but a cartoon mouse. The story was that, being Gene Kelly, he really wanted as his dancing partner the world's most famous mouse, Mickey, but Walt Disney turned him down flat. So he came back to his own studio, MGM, and to us. If he couldn't have Mickey, Jerry would have to do.

The problem was that Fred Quimby told him he couldn't have Jerry, either. Fred did not want to take us away from the dependably lucrative Tom and Jerry to work on the technically formidable project of integrating an animated mouse into a live-action film. Kelly, who was called by admirers and detractors alike the "Smiling Killer," was a powerful MGM star and a monumentally determined man. He returned to Bill and me literally behind Quimby's back, using the back entrance and stairs of our offices.

For our part, we were always excited by the prospect of doing something new. We had invented the "limited animation" technique to provide a full preview of each and every Tom and Jerry cartoon we did—something entirely unique to our studio. We had brought full animation to unsurpassed technical heights. We had endowed two perfectly ordinary characters, a cat and a mouse, with a most extraordinary range of expression and emotion. Now, we decided, we would indeed make a cartoon mouse dance with a live man—who happened to be one of the two greatest film dancers the world had ever seen.

The film was George Sidney's 1945 *Anchors Aweigh*, and our painstaking task was to animate and create art for more than ten thousand frames. Quimby's concerns over the amount of time the job would consume were amply justified. The project consumed two intensive months. As with any other cartoon, we began by working up storyboards. Next, Kelly's dance was filmed, with Kelly having to behave as if he were teaching Jerry (a melancholy Mouse King who has banned music from his realm) to dance. Of course, at this point, King Jerry existed in storyboards only. Finally, we used a device Max Fleischer had invented, now outmoded, called a rotoscope. This enabled the animator to trace over the live-action footage *frame by frame*. Tedious? You bet. Demanding? Harder than building a big ship in a very small bottle.

When the film was premiered in Glendale, the audience went crazy over the sequence. Director Sidney admitted that the bit "stole the movie." Much to my disappointment, Kelly, who received an Oscar nomination for *Anchors Aweigh*, was no more generous than Fred Quimby in sharing the critical kudos with Bill, me, and the animators.

We worked with George Sidney one more time, providing animated opening credits for his 1946 *Holiday in Mexico*, and we created another live action/animated sequence for *Dangerous When Wet*, a 1953 film directed by Charles Walters and starring Esther Williams, one of the sweetest, most considerate, and unassuming stars I have ever worked with. For her, we developed an underwater ballet featuring Esther, Jerry, and Tom.

We worked with Kelly again on his directorial debut, *Invitation to the Dance*, a highly innovative feature-length movie based entirely on music and dance and totally without dialogue. The film consisted of numerous individual sequences, and the one we worked on was called "Sinbad the Sailor." This involved far more than getting a mouse to dance with a man. It called for creating an entire animated *world*, in which the live action takes place. Against cartoon backgrounds, Kelly and another dancer, David Kasaday, dance with a whole array of fantastic animated characters, including ornately turbaned palace guards, a bejeweled harem girl, and—most difficult of all to animate—a giant serpent.

Completed in 1953, *Invitation to the Dance* was held back by totally baffled studio brass until 1958, when it was dumped on the market and attracted disappointingly few moviegoers. In Europe, however, the movie drew critical raves, and Kelly was presented with the Grand Prize at the West Berlin Film Festival. As with *Anchors Aweigh*, our unit received no credit.

I NEVER GOT TIRED of Tom and Jerry, but I did have a dream of doing more with my life than making cartoons. Since I had seen my first Broadway musical back in high school, I couldn't get rid of the theater virus, and I wrote a play I called The Two Faces of Janus. It was a romantic comedy about a mother and a daughter. The daughter is set to marry the young man of her dreams, but must first pass muster with the boy's mother. The trouble is that the girl comes down with the measles prior to the meeting—which cannot be postponed because the young man's mother is leaving on a long trip to Europe—and her mother decides to stand in for her own daughter. The situation, unlikely as it seems in synopsis, came from my own experience when, as a high schooler, I used to go to parties given by a beautiful girl named Dot Wynn, whose mother was every bit the knockout she was—and she knew it.

I was stunned one Sunday to get a call from Gene Kelly. He had read the play and now offered to coproduce it. I couldn't believe it.

And I shouldn't have, because that was the last I heard of it from him. I subsequently heard that his agent at William Morris talked him out of it. But, in the meantime, I got a call from a New York producer named Lena Abarbanel, who was associated with the Dwight Deere Wyman Company. Wyman's middle name was the clue to his fortune, which derived from the John Deere tractor manufacturing enterprise, and he headed the only theatrical company in New York that financed its own plays. His daughter, Ana Wyman, had read The Two Faces of Janus and was interested in staging it. Accompanied by Lena Abarbanel, she came out to visit me in L.A., and a dialogue began, which fitfully spanned many aimless weeks before it came to nothing at all.

I put away The Two Faces of Janus and pursued another extracurricular activity, which was producing a series of comic books. One of the writers contributing material to these was a brilliant woman named Bea Sparks. I remarked to her one day that I had an idea for a play, and I started telling her about it.

"Why don't we do it?" she said. And we drew up a solemn pact. We agreed that we would set aside two days a week to work on the play. We would work in Bea's house in Malibu, and we would never break a work date, because I realized right then that it would be like taking medicine. You had to do it regularly or it wouldn't do any good.

Twice a week I would leave the MGM studio in Culver City, drive into Hollywood for a steam bath at the Hollywood Athletic Club, then drive out to Malibu, where I would arrive about seven in the evening. I never *wrote* a word during these sessions. Instead, I would dictate to Bea, who not only took down what I said, but acted as critic, and audience, and sounding board. The result was that the dialogue was very natural, because I could hear it as I was inventing it. Sometimes, after a two- or three-hour session, we'd have two or three lines, sometimes three or four pages. It didn't matter, because I soon discovered that I had the knack of picking up at the next session exactly—to the word—where I had left off at the previous one. After six or seven months, we had a complete first draft. After another month of revision and polishing, the play I first called *Down to Earth* was finished, then retitled *The Maid and the Martian*.

It was *finished*, yet I had very little idea what to do with it. I found a literary agent who shopped it around, but to no avail. I was at length resigned to putting it away with *The Two Faces of Janus* when, while I was on a trip to New York, my agent sent me a telegram: CELEBRATE STOP JUST SOLD THE SHOW TO RKO STOP $25,000 OPTION STOP.

Speechless, I stared at the telegram as if I expected the words to rearrange themselves on the page.

When I got back to L.A., I discovered there was one minor catch. All such deals had to be initialed by Howard Hughes.

"Well," I said to my agent, "isn't that a job for somebody at RKO?"

"Apparently not."

"How do you find Howard Hughes?" I asked.

"I don't know. Nobody knows."

Some catch. How was I—a mere insect in this pond called Hollywood—going to get to Howard Hughes?

A short time later, I was telling this story to my masseur. Now, I'm a person who certainly was not born wealthy, but I learned early on that the best investment you can make is in service. I believe in paying for service. In the film *Blue Heaven*, Steve Martin delivers his character's philosophy of life: "I believe in tipping. Actually, I believe in over-tipping." Pretty much the same thing has worked for me, and my masseur was willing to volunteer a very valuable piece of information. First, Hughes was a client of his. Second, he lived in a bungalow at the Beverly Hills Hotel.

There are a lot of bungalows at the Beverly Hills Hotel, but a member of an amateur theatrical group consisting of RKO employees tipped me off to which bungalow was his.

Armed with this information, I could now do—what?

I simply couldn't imagine myself tiptoeing up to Hughes's door, knocking on it, and thrusting a piece of paper at him for his initials. So the deal—and the play—just sat until Gordon Hunt, who was directing cartoons with us at MGM and who was involved in a little theater called the Gallery Stage, phoned me. He had a musical scheduled for production, it fell through, and, having read my play, he wanted to know if he could do *The Maid and the Martian*—on a mere five days' notice at that.

I can't say I was very excited. The Gallery Stage was a semi-amateur or semi-professional company—depending how you chose to look at it—but I was tired of trying to do anything else with the play, and I said, sure, go ahead, why not.

The Maid and the Martian is about a small group of people—a broker and his wife; Jessica, the wife's apparently virginal farm girl niece; Mitchie Chase, the couple's wisecracking, love-hungry friend, a thirty-one-year-old divorcée; and an obtuse college professor drafted as Mitchie's date—who spend a weekend together in a remote mountain cabin, where they are visited by a Martian whose saucer crash lands nearby. Though Mitchie is more than willing to do the job, it becomes Jessica's mission to seduce the Martian—literally a test-tube baby who has never seen a woman before—in order to save planet earth from invasion. I hasten to add that we're talking farce here, not Eugene O'Neill.

After I agreed to let Gordon stage the show, I was filled with second, third, and fourth thoughts and racked with self-doubt throughout the next five days. *Why did I ever allow this to happen? What if it is a dreadful bomb?* It wasn't as if my livelihood depended on a good review, but to be universally panned would be a tremendous embarrassment.

My heart sank on opening night when I entered the theater and saw that it was packed, jammed, and that every newspaper in town, including the trades, was represented. But then the thing got under way, and there was one laugh, then another, then a roar, then more roars. At one point, a squat gentleman in the front row actually rolled off his seat and onto the stage. The Gallery cast, whose day jobs ranged from professional bit actor to professional shoe salesman, had rehearsed for only five days, yet delivered my deathless prose with conviction and energy, copping all the laughs I had intended—and then some. The dreaded opening night ended with a standing ovation and my being dragged onstage for a bow.

THEN CAME THE REVIEWS. On October 16, 1952, the *Los Angeles Daily News* said the play had "tremendous potentialities," and the *Los Angeles Herald and Express* judged it "a hilarious two hours." On October 17th, the *Hollywood Reporter* called it a "racy hit," the *Los Angeles Examiner* reported that the "audience roared with laughter," and even a dour *Daily Variety* reviewer allowed that "it might stand a chance on Broadway" ("with extensive revision"), as did the commentator for the *Los Angeles Times*.

Even Fred Quimby, it turned out, read some of these newspapers, and shortly after opening night he called me into his office.

"What is all this?" he asked.

"It's just a hobby," I said.

"Well, I can't say that I'm happy about it. You have a full-time job here."

I was in no financial position to tell Fred Quimby that what I really wanted to do was quit my full-time job, quit everything, and just write plays. In the flush of opening night, I said to Dorothy, who had been about as thrilled with my play writing as Quimby was, "Hey, we might be going to Broadway!" That meant new clothes, a new hairdo, and a new set of friends, and—for a brief moment—the prospect transformed her perception of me.

As far as I was concerned, the greatest thing I could ever achieve would be to have a play open on Broadway. I mentioned to a few people that I was thinking of quitting my job at MGM—which was probably paying me close to six hundred 1952 dollars a week—and setting up as a playwright full-time.

"You'll starve," they all said. "Do you know what playwrights do? They starve."

While *The Maid and the Martian* was playing at the Gallery, I got a call from Ingo Preminger, who told me that he and Laslo Benedek, who had directed Frank Sinatra's film premiere, *The Kissing Bandit*, and the MGM film version of Arthur Miller's *Death of a Salesman*, had passed by the Gallery the night before, wandered in, and thought the play was hilarious.

"I'd like to represent it," Ingo Preminger said. As usual, nothing came of this, but the call was flattering enough to keep alive in me thoughts of writing more plays, and when a man named Dick Charlton called—he ran the Sombrero Playhouse in Arizona—and said that he had just read the reviews and wanted to option the play, I jumped. The money wasn't big, but it was paid out over quarterly installments for the life of the option.

And therein, I learned to my regret, lay the rub. It proved to be the Option that Would Not Die. Charlton held it for three years, during which time I was approached by several other groups, who either wanted to perform the play or option the play, and I had no choice but to turn them down.

Dick Charlton was married to a woman whom I understood was "The Former Mrs. Winston Guest." At one point during the life of his immortal option, Dick summoned me to the former Guest estate on Syosset, Long Island, to discuss the play. I came in from New York on the Long Island Rail Road, and Dick picked me up in his yellow Cadillac convertible. After driving up to the estate, I was ushered into a great hall, where the butler and the housekeeper took my luggage. Later, when I went up to my room, I discovered that they had unpacked everything and laid it out, including some veteran underwear with a hole or two and a toothbrush that, seen in the marble context of the Guest guest bathroom, looked like some disreputable article excavated from the tomb of a pharaoh.

The centerpiece of this visit was a glittering barbecue on the lawn of the vast property, where I was set upon a folding chair, a flute of champagne in one hand and a plate of barbecued ribs and caviar balanced on my knee, to hold court before some of the toniest people on Long Island. All of these people—anyone of whom could buy and sell me a dozen times over—were gathered around me, sitting on blankets, staring at me, asking: "Do you see Clark Gable?" "Do you know Lana Turner?" "What is Spencer Tracy like?" "What about Judy Garland?"

For New Yorkers, no matter how sophisticated, Hollywood held magic. For me, now a citizen of Hollywood, Broadway was the elusive Mecca. And so it has remained. Nothing more came of *The Maid and the Martian*. I started a third play shortly after its premiere more than forty years ago, and I fully intend to finish it very soon.

EARLY IN 1956, Fred Quimby called a meeting of all the studio personnel and announced that he was retiring because of ill health. Bill Hanna and I were put in full charge of the studio now, and the first thing we did was to double production. We were, not to mince words, at the top of the heap. I was drawing a salary of seven hundred dollars a week, a figure I wouldn't even have dreamed of not very many years before. More important, we were doing great cartoons, innovative cartoons, which earned more Oscar nominations and wins than Warner's or Disney.

Beating out Disney, I must admit, was a kick, and not just because Walt had failed to call on me in New York, as he said he would, back when I was serving my Irving Trust sentence. No, Walt Disney had nothing but contempt for other cartoon studios and for any and all writers, directors, artists, and animators who didn't work for him. For that reason, each Oscar we earned was a notch up on him.

During this time, I did have one occasion to talk to Walt Disney when I was invited to a gathering of animation professionals he hosted at Disneyland. Disney was wearing a checked Western-style shirt and a bandanna, and, scotch in hand, he was chatting with a group of us, talking about various features of his theme park. One of the secrets he let us in on was the existence of his very private office overlooking "Main Street," right near the entrance to Disneyland.

Later on, as we milled around, waiting for the buffet to be opened, I again found myself next to Disney, who was clutching a fresh scotch. Lacking for conversation, I remarked to him, "Gee, Mr. Disney, it must be great to have a hideaway office you can get away to . . ."

Looking up from his glass, he flared out at me: "*Who told you that*?"

I opened and closed my mouth a few times like the wooden Pinnochio and managed to stammer, "W-why, you did."

That was my first and last face-to-face meeting with Walt Disney. I had it in my mind to tell him about the fan letter I had written—and he had answered—so many years ago. ("Walt! You were supposed to call me. What happened?") But this alcohol-charged exchange made that impossible.

I CAN'T SAY THAT I BASKED in the glory of our cat and mouse after all these years. You never relax in this business. But I did feel more secure, more in control than I ever had reason to feel before.

To be sure, there were plenty of tensions at home. Once Bill and I took over and doubled production, a "day at the studio" became more demanding than ever, and I'd go home feeling drained. Dorothy, who had had a full day herself with three kids to manage, figured I had spent my time passing pleasant hours in La-La Land and, as I walked in the door, she would get up from the kitchen table, at which she was feeding our children, and summarily announce: "Here. You take over."

Dinners at our house were not the Ward-and-June-Cleaver love feasts that were just then making their way onto television. When I walked in, Dorothy would step out for a breather, and I would be left to argue with my offspring about finishing their food and drinking all their milk. Inevitably, a half-inch of milk would be left in each glass, and, just as inevitably, one or more of the children would knock a glass over.

What I still cannot fathom to this day is how, in my particular household alone among the many households that populate this universe of ours, how Lavoisier's law of conservation of mass could be so consistently violated. Because—somehow—this half-inch of milk would spread out across the entire kitchen, finding its way into every crack, each crevice, every irregularity on whatever surface presented itself. It was a veritable flood, which, had we been the *Queen Mary*, would have scuttled us. And all from a half-inch of milk.

Each spill sent me into a frenzy of damage control, mopping up here, blotting up there. It was a little thing, of course, but it was compounded by stress and fatigue. Then add to the spilled milk, the evil and nefarious sabotage committed by our canary, who occupied a cage in a corner of the kitchen. That little yellow bastard could outperform the milk catastrophe with a collection of pin feathers and seed husks that he managed to broadcast through a radius of ten, maybe twenty feet in every direction, including up. The husks and feathers would adhere to our tile ceiling as well as to the walls and the floor. Like Sylvester's nemesis Tweetie Pie, he never even looked guilty over what he was doing.

It was during such an episode of spilled milk and canary floppings that I got the first asthma attack of my life. I thought it would be my last; for it was a terrible, terrifying thing made all the worse by the memory of an aunt who had died of an asthma attack at the age of thirty-four. Suddenly, I simply could not breathe. In those days, they didn't have the inhalers and sprays we have now. Instead, you called the doctor, who came over with a shot of epinephrine, which brought you back from the brink.

Not everything at home was so dire, and even when one of my kids would try and try my patience, I had to love them. I had learned very well from my own father how *not* to raise a child, and I didn't believe in ranting, raving, and belt wielding as a form of discipline. I do remember one occasion when my middle child, Lynn, managed to drive me out of my mind. With a flair for the dramatic, I sat her down in a little wooden chair, took a length of strong bakery twine, and tied her around the middle to the chair.

"Now you sit there and don't you move."

With that, I went into the kitchen to have a cup of coffee with Dorothy. Before long, my fatherly ear picked up something that sounded like Lynn's voice among a welter of children's voices out on the quiet Brentwood cul de sac where our house was. I went to the door, looked down the street, and saw Lynn laughing, talking, and playing—with the chair still securely tied to her backside, and neither she nor anyone else paying the least attention to it. I started laughing so hard that I couldn't call her back in—and I didn't have the heart to do it anyway.

My children, Jayne, Lynn, and Neal, were pretty casual about having a cartoonist for a father. They liked for me to draw Tom and Jerry for their friends—a lot of these were done on paper napkins at birthday parties—though I don't ever remember any of them gasping in awe at such demonstrations of obvious genius.

More than drawing, my kids liked me to tell them stories. Most parents, if they don't just prop their kid up in front of the television set, get away with reading aloud from a book at bedtime. Not me. My children insisted that I make up a story, and it had to be a new story every night. So I started telling them about a character named Billy, a cowboy who got involved in chasing horses or chasing bad guys, and that evolved into a never-ending bedtime serial. It taught me something about how to keep a character consistent even as you dream up new adventures for him, and it was a lot of fun, though the pressure was high. If I didn't come up with a new Billy story, the kids would refuse to go to sleep that night.

Living with a story-telling cartoonist doesn't seem to have been all bad for my children. Each of them grew to love the cartoon business and, as adults, worked in the industry. Jayne was senior vice president with Hanna-Barbera for twenty-eight years and still works in the business. Lynn does free-lance coloring at home, for our studio and others. Neal has worked for Hanna-Barbera as a story man and a story editor. He is also a writer, who has had, to date, three scripts produced.

Then there was Christmastime. When I was a kid, in a household more often than not missing a father, Christmas was a repeated disappointment, and, however else my job might keep me from being as good a father as I wanted to be, I swore that, for my children, Christmas would be nothing less than magic time.

We didn't talk about Christmas, we didn't let on that we had bought presents, we didn't decorate the house or put up the tree. All of this just suddenly materialized on Christmas morning. On Christmas eve, there was nothing. On Christmas morning, there were stockings tacked to the mantle, a wreath on the door, a fully decorated, lighted tree, with about a hundred and fifty presents heaped around the bottom—and a father near death because, truth to tell, none of this had really appeared by magic.

I had the major job of buying a tree and hiding it, as well as hiding all of the presents. Then, on Christmas eve, I would undertake the monumental task of getting the children to bed, warning them that Santa Claus would not come if he discovered even one of them awake. It was important to get them to sleep as early as possible, because I was in for a long night, and that long night would come on top of a very long day featuring the studio Christmas party—a paler version of the wild parties we had in the studio's earliest days, but lubricated with a significant quantity of alcohol nevertheless.

The last thing I felt like doing on a night like this was erecting and trimming a tree, but the first thing I had to do was go outside, set my extension ladder against the side of the house, and climb up near my children's window to shake a string of sleigh bells. One Christmas, I tried to heighten the sleigh-on-the-rooftop effect by climbing up through the trap door in our second-floor ceiling and crawling above their rooms, but I hit my head on so many rafters that I'm afraid my kids' dreams were punctuated less by the silvery sounds of sleigh bells than a series of very un-Santa-like oaths and exclamations.

Still, it was worth it, come Christmas morning, to see their faces when they beheld the transformation. It was a moment of undiluted innocence—but a moment only, soon displaced by a wild-animal frenzy of six little hands, thirty pared claws, tearing into the heap of lovingly wrapped treasures that lay before them, briefly inspecting one, casting it aside, groping for another, tearing into that, looking, casting, tearing, thoughtless—as children should be—of the sweat, the worry, the worn emotions that such a display of plenty represented.

AS THE GREEK TRAGEDIANS have told us, it is precisely when you get to the top of the heap, that the ax is destined to fall.

I mentioned in the first chapter of this book that the bad news came not to Bill and me, who were running the studio, but to the business manager. A phone rang, a bookkeeper answered, and the message was: "Close the studio! Lay everybody off!"

We had built what by rights should have been an impregnable fortress, an unassailable monument to success. But Arthur Loew, Sr., heeded the advice of his financial people, who told him that the old Tom and Jerry cartoons could be rereleased at will, and each would bring in 90 percent of the revenue that a brand-new cartoon would produce—without having to spend the thirty thousand, forty-five thousand, even sixty thousand dollars each new cartoon cost the studio. In 1957, Hollywood was under siege by a one-eyed box that had not only pushed the radio out of the living room, but that was keeping people on their sofas and out of the movie theaters. Every studio, MGM included, was looking desperately to save cash.

If I had been Hugh Harman, maybe I would have seized on the catastrophe to animate, say, *Oedipus Rex*. Instead, Bill and I, who still had several months left on our contracts, tramped from studio to studio and agency to agency, hoping that, as the creators of Tom and Jerry, we'd be a very hot commodity indeed.

We were wrong.

Everyone we saw agreed: Cartoons were just too expensive.

We were out. And, at forty-six, I was not eager to learn a new trade—didn't want to sell insurance, or open up a chicken stand, or wash cars. I had two daughters and a son. We were all at a Little League game, and I was watching them play and laugh, and all I could think was: *Go ahead, laugh. Two weeks from today you'll be starving.* How was I going to feed, clothe, and shelter these kids?

Well, I did have one idea.

Chapter Six

ROUGH BUT READY

MY LAST DAYS AT MGM were like the fall of the Roman Empire run in fast motion. Every day, it seemed, some big star left the lot—Tracy, Gable, Lana Turner—all the glamorous icons my friends and family back East continually asked me about. For Bill, me, and the cartoon staff, the end was very sudden: a single phone call. And for everybody else, it certainly *seemed* sudden. But the decline had begun almost a decade before, in 1948, when the practice of block booking was declared an illegal unfair trade practice. Block booking had required an exhibitor to buy, sight unseen, a certain number of films (some good, many not, most cheap) in order to secure the one or two major features that really interested him. It was hard on the exhibitor, but a great deal for the studio, which was assured of the cash flow needed to bankroll fifty-two films a year and maintain a stable—MGM liked to call it their "heaven"—of more than a hundred of Hollywood's biggest stars.

By the mid-1950s, however, Hollywood in general and MGM in particular seemed less interested in aggressively facing the economic realities of life after block booking than in pinning their financial woes on the single convenient scapegoat they found in the eerie glow of a Cyclops-eyed appliance that was masquerading as a singularly ugly piece of furniture in the living rooms, dens, and even the bedrooms of America.

It was true enough: Television was cutting deeply into the picture business, as people were spending more time glued to their sets and investing less in the Saturday afternoon or Friday evening ritual of "taking in a movie." In part, MGM responded intelligently to the crisis. Early in 1956, the studio acquired a 25 percent interest in the *Los Angeles Times*'s KTTV television operation in exchange for a long-term lease of more than seven hundred MGM features made before 1949. The studio made a number of stock ownership swaps in order to acquire more TV stations, and by the end of 1956, MGM had gained stock ownership in seven stations and had released a staggering 2,700 features to the medium.

So much for the financial side of the picture. On the creative side, instead of adopting the strategy of joining what you can't beat, most of the Hollywood studios, MGM included, directed all the hatred and contempt they could muster at TV, as if doing so could will the monster away, even as their own companies were investing a lot of cash and older properties in the medium.

During this seizure of schizophrenia on the MGM lot, it was downright dangerous even to mention television. Bill and I did not, however, join in the mass burial of heads in the sand. We did get a taste of TV, even while we were still turning out the Tom and Jerrys. I had a friend at the advertising agency that was handling Pall Mall cigarettes. He approached us, in confidence, to talk about our doing animated commercials for his client's product. At the time, this seemed like an impossibility, but, a little while later, we arranged with an outside artist, Gene Hazelton, to do—anonymously—three or four animated promo spots for the enormously popular "I Love Lucy" show.

At about this time, one of the Big Three at MGM, L. K. Sidney, a man with a good deal more vision than most of his colleagues, quietly assigned us the task of developing two one-minute animated commercials for television to promote two big pictures, *Scaramouche* and *Pat and Mike*. Sidney showed our work, which was in black-and-white, at an exhibitor's convention as an example of how the annoying new medium could actually be used to sell movie tickets. Sidney and the exhibitors were delighted with what we had done, but nothing more came of it.

In the meantime, Quimby, nearing retirement, called Bill and me into his office one day for a rare discussion and, fixing us with his knowing gaze, said: "If you fellas really want to see how to handle TV for advertising, you should take a good look at the promos for 'I Love Lucy.' *That's* the way this thing should be done!"

I don't know about Bill, but I had all I could do to keep from jumping up and saying, "We did it! It was us! We did it!" But that would only have gotten us canned, sued, or, even worse, lectured at.

So when the end came at last in 1957, we had had the merest taste of television, but we had no real leads—aside from a few individuals who told us they might give us business if we went free-lance. You can't build a future on "might" and "maybe."

Now that I look back at it, I suppose that what I *did* have was slim enough at that. It was nothing more than an idea for a television cartoon series based on a dog and a cat. I readily confess that there was no particular spark of genius in this combination of characters. Bill and I had just spent seventeen years making cartoons about a cat and a mouse. So why not a dog and a cat?

There was, however, one very crucial conceptual difference

between the Tom and Jerry and the Ruff and Reddy cartoons. The Tom and Jerrys were made for the theater in the tradition of the classic theatrical short subject as my idol Charlie Chaplin might have handled it. The cartoons had no dialogue. Instead, they were based on wild variations of the chase situation naturally inherent in the combination of a cat with a mouse. But I did not think that the slapstick chase approach would work on the small screen. Somehow I felt that the basis of these television cartoons would have to be *story*, not *chase*, and a story would require dialogue—something I had not touched (except for my forays into play writing) for the past seventeen years.

I did the first "Ruff and Reddy" storyboard at home, and my daughter Jayne, twelve years old at the time, colored the art in. With this little clump of artwork, then, Bill and I went to the only studio operation that, at the time, was serious about television. Screen Gems was the television production arm of Columbia Pictures—though "arm" is rather too grandiose a description. "Stump" might be a better word for it. Columbia was going into television, but they were doing so grudgingly, and their niggardly attitude showed in the crackerbox facilities they had provided for Screen Gems behind the main studio lot. Bill and I had come a long way from the forlorn bungalow we'd started in at MGM, and now we were calling at a place that looked even less promising.

FORTUNATELY FOR COLUMBIA and for us, Screen Gems had a terrific vice president in charge of sales named John H. Mitchell, who had joined the company in its infancy in 1952 after having been director of television for United Artists and having developed radio and television stations in Rochester, New York. When nobody thought cartoons could be made to work on the kind of budgets available for television in those days, Mitchell was determined to *make* them work. When we called on Screen Gems, they were already working with a cartoonist named Al Singer—no relation to the lightweight boxer I had emulated in high school—who was developing a crude series revolving around a character named Pow Wow the Indian Boy. By necessity, Singer's cartoons were cheap—and they looked it. On a meager television production budget, Singer operated out of a cavernous loft space, which he tried to make look more impressive by deploying his handful of animators across the entire available space: a desk here, another here, about a mile away, another a few more miles in the distance. His operation looked like a very small archipelago lost in a very big sea.

Well, how could it have been any other way? It cost between forty thousand and sixty-five thousand dollars to make a single Tom and Jerry cartoon. Screen Gems was offering the sum of $2,700 for five minutes. No wonder Pow Wow the Indian Boy looked like hell and Screen Gems was unhappy with it.

Could we do better? Mitchell wanted to know.

Yes, we said, we could do better.

Our secret weapon was the "limited" or "planned" animation technique we had developed when we were working on the Tom and Jerry pictures. We had used the technique to create full-length trial runs of each cartoon we did. Instead of the twenty or thirty thousand drawings that went into a fully realized Tom and Jerry, the limited animation test required only about 1,800. For television, we needed to refine and perfect the technique, and we developed working procedures that used about three thousand drawings for a five-minute cartoon—still a lot more economical than creating ten times that number.

We had another inestimable advantage. MGM had fired a complete animation studio—and the best in the business at that. All we needed to do was make a few phone calls, and we would have, ready made, a highly seasoned staff who knew all the shortcuts.

There was one curve in the road, when Bill was approached with another job offer. That might have ended our partnership right then and there. It was difficult for a family man to turn down a sure thing, but Bill had enough faith in himself, in me, and in the two of us to turn the offer down. On the strength of our deal with John Mitchell, we scouted locations for our plant and ended up renting space at a studio on Highland Avenue.

It was a tiny space, but it had two big pluses. First, the rent was dirt cheap—and that we couldn't have any other way. We were operating on our own meager capital, an advance from Screen Gems, and a modest investment from George Sidney, who had directed *Anchors Aweigh* (the film for which we furnished Jerry Mouse as a dancing partner for Gene Kelly), *Scaramouche* (for which we had created the experimental animated television commercial), and many other major MGM pictures.

The second plus was, for me, downright magical. The LaBrea Studio on Highland was known as the Charlie Chaplin studio. It was the very place that the Little Tramp had made some of his best films. Chaplin was, of course, very much alive in 1957, but, to me, it was as if the studio were happily haunted by his creative ghost. I hoped he would bless our endeavor.

John Mitchell was not your average customer or client. He didn't make a deal or order a show and then sit back waiting for it to be delivered. While we were working on "Ruff and Reddy," he urged—goaded, really—us to develop more. Although he was officially head of sales for Screen Gems, John rapidly developed into our de facto agent, frontman, and promoter.

While we were in the middle of "Ruff and Reddy," John called to give me the absolutely terrifying news that no less a figure than Harry Cohn, head of Columbia, wanted to check up on us, to see just where his munificent $2,700 was going. It had taken all of John Mitchell's formidable powers of persuasion to talk Cohn into financing the creation of new cartoons for television. All Cohn had wanted to do is rerelease venerable theatricals, which could be had for even less than what he was paying us to produce new ones. But Mitchell managed to sell him on the idea of mixing in new material, created expressly for the tube, with the old. There would, then, be nothing so ambitious as a "Ruff and Reddy Show," but, instead, a package of theatrical cartoons with a new "Ruff and Reddy" inserted at either end.

I had made contact with some tough men at MGM, including Louis

B. Mayer, but Harry Cohn, who had transformed Columbia Pictures from a collection of shanties on Hollywood's so-called Poverty Row into the powerhouse studio it became, ruled his kingdom as an absolute despot—and by no means a benevolent one. The son of an immigrant tailor, he had little formal education, but was naturally shrewd, ruthless, even predatory. It was known that he spied on his staff through an elaborate system of stool pigeons and hidden microphones. He hired and fired at will and at whim, courting the strong and gleefully preying upon the weak. Early on, they called him "Harry the Horror," until the great screenwriter Ben Hecht gave him the moniker that stuck: White Fang.

All we had to show Mr. Cohn at this point were pencil tests, which, even at their best, are never very impressive to the uninitiated. There's no sound track, and the colorless outline drawings move across the screen like so many chicken scratches.

We took the film to the suffocatingly hot little screening room at Screen Gems and set it up. There was no question of my being introduced to Harry Cohn. He had neither the time nor the inclination to grant such courtesies. The mogul and his lieutenants just walked in, sat down, and we ran the pencil test—all four or five minutes of it. Without punctuation, let alone ceremony, the lights came up again, and White Fang, accompanied by his entourage, left the room without uttering a word or cracking a smile. All that was left for me was to pack up and go back to the Chaplin studio, where I waited within reach of the phone as long as I could stand to wait, then finally dialed John Mitchell myself.

"What did he say, John?"

"He said: 'Get rid of 'em.' "

Well, our career with Screen Gems—which meant our career in television—was over before we had even finished a single cartoon. It was not a happy day.

AGAIN WE WERE DESTINED to be saved by the slimmest of threads. A man in New York named Roger Muir, who had a children's

TV show on NBC, heard about "Ruff and Reddy" and wanted to use the cartoons much as we had originally planned—as bookends between which the hoary theatricals would be run. Muir's offer kept us alive, and Screen Gems went ahead with the deal.

Now we had to swing into production full tilt. As I mentioned, this was made possible in large part because MGM had, in effect, presented us with a studio staff made to order. We would not have survived the kind of floundering MGM itself had endured back in the 1930s, when Fred Quimby was desperately scrambling for talent. However, as I have mentioned, the television cartoons were also radically different from what I had been doing for almost the last two decades in that they revolved around stories rather than variations on a simple chase, and they therefore required dialogue. One of the great glories of Tom and Jerry was, of course, the lushness of the art and animation. Without this quality—which was impossible on a television budget—the sustaining power of the new cartoons had to come from something else. Furthermore, whereas Tom and Jerry were eternal antagonists, Ruff and Reddy were friends, which is fine and dandy, but not very dramatic. So, much of the interest of the new series would have to come from an elaborate cast of adversaries, including the Chicken-hearted Chickasauraus, Scary Harry Safari, Killer and Diller, the Goon of Glocca Morra, and the Mastermind from the planet Muni-Mula—a truly exotic extraterrestrial name that is really nothing more than "aluminum" spelled backwards.

What was needed to make Ruff, Reddy, and the other characters come alive were great voices. I very quickly learned the one lesson about making cartoons that I had not had to learn when I was working on Tom and Jerry: If you don't have the right voices, you don't have a cartoon.

Voices make or break any cartoon that relies heavily on character and dialogue, and this is especially true of cartoons made for television, which is as much a verbal as it is a visual medium. More gradually, I also learned that it does not take a complex process of analysis to cast the right voices. What you do is hand an actor a script, fill him in on the character and the situation, and then let him take it from there while you sit back, *close your eyes*, and listen. If you smile, chances are very good that you've found the right voice. If not, you have to keep looking. Simple? Yes. But exhausting. Casting a single character frequently meant auditioning sixty, seventy, even eighty voices.

Fortunately, in casting "Ruff and Reddy," we immediately discovered two great voice actors, Daws Butler and Don Messick. I say "actors" deliberately, because they looked on their assignments as acting projects, and they developed the characters just as fully as any actor would. If you watched them before the recording mike, you saw actors going through the physical motions and facial contortions of the parts they played. The audiences who saw the finished cartoons thought they were just getting voices. What they were really getting were *characters*.

Hanna-Barbera's relationship with these actors began in 1957 and proved to be an enduring and very satisfying one. Daws ended up working with Bill and me until his death in 1988, and Don still voices many of our characters.

Another major lesson about making cartoons for television was not long in coming. It was this: You're never done working. No sooner do you sell a project than you've got to do everything needed to deliver it while simultaneously getting to work on inventing a new project.

We were just beginning to turn out "Ruff and Reddy" when John Mitchell took me to Chicago to talk to the people at the Leo Burnett agency, who were handling television advertising for Kellogg's. The world of the advertising agency, a world populated by brilliant men and women as sharp as they were hard, was entirely new to me. At MGM, I never had to sell anything. In fact, after Fred Quimby decided that Bill and I were "too valuable" to waste our time being "bothered" by studio visitors, I rarely even *talked* to anybody other than the people I worked with every day. Now, without any formal, deliberate decision among Bill, John, me, or anyone else, I suddenly emerged as our company's spokesman and sole delegate to the agencies. That's how it started, and that's how it's always been.

Ever since we began turning out Tom and Jerry cartoons, Bill and I have called ourselves partners. When we moved into the Chaplin studio and started our own company, George Sidney served as president to begin with, then Bill and I alternated annually in that post until we sold the company to Taft Broadcasting in 1967. At that time I became president, and Bill assumed the title of senior vice president. After we were acquired by Turner Broadcasting in 1991, Bill and I were each dubbed co-founder and co-chairman. But, the fact is, we never argued about titles or responsibilities. The division of labor came naturally and automatically. When we started the Tom and Jerry series, it was entirely natural that I would do the initial character art and create the storyboards and that Bill would time the scenes and hand out the work to the animators. When we broke into television, a similar division of labor came about—again, naturally. I came up with the characters and created or supervised the creation of the storyboards. Then I directed the recording of the track. Once this was done, I handed the track and storyboards to Bill, who timed the scenes and distributed them, complete with track and model charts, to the animators. Bill, who loves music, also emerged as the composer of some of the themes and generally managed our personnel resources while juggling orders and budgets. In the meantime, I developed new characters, new stories, and undertook what I thought of as the epic task of selling them.

I am frequently asked to account for the longevity of our partnership, which has lasted more than half a century now. Gee whiz and golly, people say, you two must be great friends!

The fact is, we hardly ever talk to one another. Indeed, over the past fifty years, we have hardly ever gotten together socially. We have almost nothing in common. Bill loves the outdoors—hiking, camping, fishing. As a kid, he joined the Boy Scouts, became an Eagle Scout, and has remained very active in scouting ever since. Recently, the Scouts honored him by naming him a Distinguished Eagle Scout.

Me? I hate fishing, and I can't even imagine why anyone would want to hike when you can get in a car and drive. I enjoyed camping in the Catskills with my Uncle Jim when I was a kid, but, with the onset of adulthood, well, I'd sooner go in for a round of root canal work than pitch a tent and lie down under it. What I like is to stretch out in the sun on a sandy beach, close to a great hotel, and in reasonable proximity to liquor and a really good meal. That is not Bill's idea of a good time. I used to visit a masseur regularly, two or three times a week, and once convinced Bill to try a massage. That was a lot of years ago. He's not been back since.

In the workplace, too, we were always less of a "team" than we were opposite, but equal, ends of a remarkably smooth production continuum. Bill's job began precisely where mine left off. As the pace continually intensified very early on during the television years, we didn't even sit down to discuss characters or story ideas. There was no time. I came up with the characters and the stories, and Bill just took them from there, as completely confident that I had done my job as I was certain he would do his.

We never—ever—got in each other's way.

Friends don't necessarily make good business or creative partners. What we had—what we have—goes beyond affection and even beyond simple respect. We have worked in the same quarters for more than half a century, and yet days and weeks will go by in which we neither talk to one another nor even see one another. Nevertheless, we have literally entrusted our careers, our futures, and the welfare of our families to one another. Bill knows that he can depend on me absolutely, and I know that I can depend absolutely on Bill. There has never been any need for debate, scolding, praise, congratulations, handshakes, or hand holding. Which is a very lucky thing, since there has never been time for any of that.

Maybe people are disappointed by the reality of our partnership. They expect us to be bosom buddies, like Yogi and Boo Boo or Fred and Barney, or even alter egos: When one catches a cold, the other sneezes. Or maybe they like to think that we secretly hate each other.

The fact is, ours is a partnership no different from the handful of other creative partnerships that have endured and actually succeeded. Gilbert and Sullivan had nothing in common. Neither did Rodgers and Hammerstein. And I don't believe Mr. Sears was even on speaking terms with Mr. Roebuck. But, like these, our partnership worked, and that's the way it was from the very start.

In any event, without discussion or debate, I found myself deep in a Chicago winter at the offices of Leo Burnett. John Mitchell led me, open-mouthed, from office to office and introduced me as the co-creator of Tom and Jerry who was now making cartoons for television destined to serve as the chariots on which the Kellogg product would fly into the breakfast bowls of untold millions of American children, including generations yet unborn.

I didn't have anything specific to show the Leo Burnett people beyond a sketch or two, but on the strength of John's suave hype and the credibility afforded by Tom and Jerry, I was encouraged to develop new characters.

HUCKLEBERRY HOUND, Yogi and Boo Boo Bear, and the "meeces" Pixie and Dixie versus Mr. Jinx the cat (who hated "meeces to pieces") all emerged at about the same time. Huck was the first to go into development, but his name was almost bestowed upon one of a pair of bears. I had drawn two itinerant bears—hobo bears, really (for Jellystone Park had not yet come into existence)—and we made up a list of about eighty names. Among these was Bumpkin Bear, Barney Bear—the name Rudy Ising had given his MGM character—Huckleberry Bear, and Yogi Bear. Huckleberry Bear sounded pretty good to us, but Yogi seemed even better. I've often been asked if "Yogi Bear" was a deliberate reference to the irrepressible Yogi Berra ("It's deja vu all over again!"). My answer is that no deliberate reference was intended—Yogi Bear doesn't play baseball, and Yogi Berra was not passionate about pic-a-nic baskets—but, undoubtedly, the sound of the name was awash in our collective unconscious at a time when Yogi Berra was a very popular figure. As a matter of fact Yogi Berra's first name was actually Lawrence.

Now, "Huckleberry Bear" certainly isn't a bad name either, but "Huckleberry Hound" is much better. Why? In a word, *alliteration*. Mickey Mouse, Donald Duck, Daffy Duck, Bugs Bunny, Huckleberry Hound. Not that the name or character sprung from purely linguistic inspiration. Huck developed from a combination of my recollections of Tex Avery's great MGM character Droopy—a deadpan, droop-jowled basset hound who would greet his public with "Hello, you happy people" uttered in a forlorn monotone—and Daws Butler's remarkable range of southern dialects.

One day, I innocently asked Daws to do a southern accent.

"From what part of the South?" he replied.

"Huh?"

"Well, there's at least ten distinct dialects I know. There's South Carolina and there's North Carolina. There's Tidewater, Piedmont, and Hill Country. There's the Georgia cracker dialect and the Florida swamp country accent. In Louisiana, you get the Creole influence . . ."

From the welter of Daws's erudition emerged Huck's inimitable drawl. As to the color of the hound dog, that was an easy choice. Huck's blue hue was born of one of the very few things I knew about the South, which is that folks down there like to name their hunting dogs "Blue": "Hey, Blue, you good dog, you," as the old song goes. Of greater significance is the fact that we were concerned about color at all. The first cartoons we did were sold into the black-and-white world of television's so-called Golden Age, and we could have saved good money by drawing them in black-and-white to begin with. But Bill and I figured that color television would eventually catch on and that ultimately the demand for color product would greatly extend the shelf life of what we were doing.

"Ruff and Reddy" made their debut on NBC in 1957, and John Mitchell sold "The Huckleberry Hound Show"—over the phone, no less—to Kellogg's in 1958. Among the cast of characters on that show were Yogi Bear and his little friend (who, in dramatic terms, served as the voice of the errant Yogi's conscience) Boo Boo. Two years later, Yogi and Boo Boo would get their own show. With "Huck" barely in production, we started "Pixie and Dixie," a team of "meeces" perpetually pursued by Jinx the cat. And I started looking forward to "Augie Doggie and Doggie Daddy," "Quick Draw McGraw," and "Snooper and Blabber."

JOHN HAD SOLD KELLOGG'S on Huck, but he was anxious to move on to other shows in order to develop a long-term relationship with the cereal giant. So, while I was drowning in development and production, he hauled me back to the Leo Burnett agency to show the Kellogg's people what I had in the works. I took with me a very funny piece of film featuring a character called Judo Jack. This was a mouse, even smaller than Pixie and Dixie, on whom the two meeces had called for aid in their ongoing battle with Mr. Jinx. The diminutive Jack, attired in a black-belted judo outfit, handily disposes of Jinx, who, thanks to Daws Butler, remarks in a voice inspired by a young Marlon Brando: "Like, uh, did anyone get the license number of that truck?" I also had some terrific footage of what was then going to be a featured "Huckleberry Hound Show" character, Yogi Bear.

In what would become my many travels in quest of sales, I was destined never to see the Windy City in spring, summer, or fall. This trip to Leo Burnett, like the previous one, was made in the depths of a midwestern winter—as would be the trips I would make through many more years, show after show, pitch after pitch. I was shivering with a combination of the cold and utter terror as I entered the agency's meeting room. The ways of a high-powered agency were entirely foreign to me, and, on my way in, I was greeted by a corps of men in virtually identical Brooks Brothers suits who darted stares as icy as the frozen whitecaps on Lake Michigan.

I was ushered into the conference room, and two particularly sharp young agency types in button-down white shirts and super-thin black neckties took the film from me to set it up.

"Now, you understand," I said, "this is film and track—separate. This film goes with that track, and this . . ."

One of the black ties cut me off with a wave of his hand. "Don't worry. We'll handle it. All *you've* got to do is press this button under the table here, and that will start the film."

The pair retired to the projection booth, and I was left to survey the empty conference room—paneled walls, polished table—until Roy Lang, the head of Burnett's art department, burst in like Paul Revere.

"We're running late," he panted. "The Kellogg's people will be here in a minute. But we're running late, and they've had no lunch, and, worse, they've had nothing to drink. They're getting cranky. In fact, they're getting ugly. I advise you to keep it short."

Open-mouthed once again, I stared blankly at Roy Lang, then plastered myself up against the wall to make way for a battalion of forty-two hungry, thirsty executives, who were loudly and collectively grumbling, mumbling, and making what struck my ear as distinctly animal noises.

John Mitchell, flashing me a sadly anemic version of his customary super-salesman's smile, turned to the horde and introduced me as the co-creator of Tom and Jerry.

That piece of news was met with overwhelming indifference. John might as well have been speaking to an array of headstones—except that these guys had teeth and were (it seemed) continually murmuring oaths and threats.

Then, out of the blue, one of the assemblage yells out like a cannon shot: "Have you got any children?"

I have—and had then—*three* children. But, at the time, I simply could not answer the question, not even yes or no, let alone how many and who. I just stared at the questioner and said absolutely nothing until, after what seemed an eternal moment, one of the young black ties emerged from the projection booth and nodded to me.

"Well, I said, let's start the picture, shall we?" With that, I reached under the table, groped for the button during a prolonged interval of augmented panic, found it at last, pressed it, and on came Pixie, Dixie, Judo Jack, and Jinx—all talking in the voices of Yogi, Boo Boo Bear, and Ranger Smith.

Uncomprehending, the black tie gazed in my direction.

"Wrong track," I said to him in a grit-toothed groan that carried across the room. He ducked back into the projection booth.

For the next fifteen minutes, as the pair fumbled with the machinery inside the booth, I found myself ad libbing, spewing out one story idea after another to an audience now snarling, snapping, and growling.

At last, the black tie reemerged and nodded. I pressed the button, and Judo Jack did his thing.

I mean he *really* did his thing.

The room was transformed as if by magic. Where there had been forty-two barely restrained beasts in suits and ties, there were now forty-two belly-laughing children in suits and ties. After the "Pixie and Dixie" piece, I ran Yogi, then staggered out of the room, into the permafrost of Michigan Avenue, hopped a cab, and buried myself in my room at the Ambassador East. Within a few minutes, Lee Bland, Leo Burnett's executive in charge of the Kellogg's account, rang me up.

"Go down to the Pump Room and get drunk. You've sold the show."

I thought I was fully and painfully aware of how close I had come to not selling the show. But, as it turns out, at the time, I did not know the whole story.

It seems that I was actually competing against myself. MGM had released twenty-six Tom and Jerry cartoons for television play and approached Kellogg's with them. After my presentation, those Kellogg's executives made the gutsy decision to identify their product with something brand new but untested rather than with something tried and true, but merely recycled for television.

My elation over the sale was short-lived. After I got back to L.A., I received a panicked phone call from Kellogg's.

"We can't use the bear."

What was I going to say, "No refunds or exchanges"? So all I said was, "Huh?"

"Another cereal company has Honey Bear on their box. The industry doesn't have room for two bears."

Alas, poor Yogi. Bill and I endured two or three days of hand wringing and had resigned ourselves to coming up with another show for Kellogg's when another phone call came through. The company had decided that Yogi was sufficiently distinct from Honey Bear—who was, after all, only a logo, not a television star—to identify with Kellogg's. The show was on again.

Even without the Honey Bear conflict, Kellogg's made a bold gamble buying "Yogi Bear," and it paid off—for Hanna-Barbera as well as for the cereal giant. A few years later, when "The Yogi Bear Show," sponsored by Kellogg's, was a big hit, the folks from Battle Creek launched a door-to-door survey in which they showed families and children a picture of Yogi and Boo Boo and asked, "What does this make you think of?" Overwhelmingly, the response was "Kellogg's Corn Flakes."

WHAT STARTED IN WINTRY CHICAGO was a warm relationship—with Kellogg's and the Leo Burnett agency. The pack of snarling executives became a creative family in a tremendously profitable association that endured for a decade. They were delighted with "Huckleberry Hound," which proved popular not only with children, but quickly accumulated a cult audience among college students. Bill and I learned that in one San Francisco bar favored by the college crowd, the barkeep would ring a bell at six on the evening when the show was aired and direct the patrons' attention to a sign that announced: NO TINKLING OF GLASSES OR NOISE DURING THE HUCKLEBERRY HOUND SHOW.

The biggest kick of all came in 1959 when "Huckleberry Hound" became the first cartoon show on television to win an Emmy for distinguished children's programming. In those days, the awards program was a modest affair, held in a studio, not in a big auditorium, and it was hosted that year by an up-and-coming Bob Newhart, who did one of his hilarious telephone routines. Sir Walter Raleigh was phoning the king of England long distance to explain that he had discovered tobacco.

"Uh. Th-that's right. It's a leaf. What do you *do* with it? Well, you roll it up, see, and then you smoke it."

After Tom and Jerry cartoons earned seven Oscars—every one of them claimed by Fred Quimby—it felt damn good to win again *and* be allowed to walk up on a stage to receive the statuette. Bill was so excited that, in the car on the way home, he put his Emmy next to him on the seat, it rolled off, and broke a wing. Fortunately, although I am a Sicilian, I put stock in good omens only. Besides, one trip to a jeweler, and the statuette was as good as new.

Not that there was any time to sit and admire it.

Basking in the success of Huck, Kellogg's ordered "Quick Draw McGraw," "Augie," and "Snooper and Blabber." We had so much business that we were able to hire back those of the MGM cartoon staff we had not yet employed. But even with a growing, committed, creative, and highly seasoned staff, the pace was grueling. At MGM, we had worked hard to produce about forty minutes of animation each year. Now we were moving toward turning out an unheard of—indeed, an insane—two and a half hours of animation a week. It was crazy to think about something like this and even more ridiculous to talk about it, but here we were *doing* it.

The days I put in were fifteen or sixteen hours long. Each and every day I worked on storyboards in the morning, looked at film in the afternoon, then recorded a picture every night, five nights a week, often working until midnight. As if that weren't enough, I had a briefcase—it was about twenty years old then, fifty now—and each night I stuffed it with scripts and storyboards that had to be read and revised before the next morning. I swear, some nights that case stared at me, its mouth open, groaning, growling, baring its teeth.

Then there were the Leo Burnett and the Kellogg's execs. They were all bright, lively, very decent, certainly generous, stimulating, always forward-looking—and very, very hard-drinking. When they came to town, you dropped everything to entertain them. Was a schedule hanging by a frayed thread? It didn't matter. You made dinner reservations and met them for drinks before and after. Out of morbid curiosity, I once kept score on an agency man I entertained from six P.M. until after one in the morning. During that period he consumed sixteen scotch and sodas, often ordering them thusly: "Give me a scotch and soda on the rocks; hold the soda and the rocks." Yet it had no visible effect on him. I really liked these people, but, after nights like that, you wondered if they were even human.

Once you got home, well, you were pretty much used up. These cartoons—and everything you had to do to develop them, to sell them, then to deliver them—became your life, elbowing out whatever warm thoughts and affections you used to bring home. You'd lie down, waiting fruitlessly for sleep while staring up at the ceiling, thinking: There's no way we're going to get this show out. No way. We're finished. Finito. Doomed. In big trouble.

My marriage to Dorothy had been impulsive. It was an understandable impulse; she was a strong and very attractive person, and she proved to be a terrific mother to our three children. But, in truth, that marriage should have been short-lived, a matter of weeks at most instead of the twenty-three years it spanned.

The marriage had withstood the initial shock of the closing of the MGM cartoon operation, but, it seemed, as my relations with Screen Gems and Kellogg's grew closer and stronger, Dorothy and I moved further and further apart. The unrelenting demands of television finally snapped what frayed and fragile cords remained between us, and we separated, then divorced.

The divorce did not destroy us. Our children remained with their mother, and I supported them all financially and, I like to think, emotionally as well. We have all gone on to make our own lives, yet we have tried to remain as much of a family as possible. Still, it was a hard time and a cruel lesson. The world I had entered when my career at MGM ended was exciting, challenging, and ripe with potential for creativity and for profit. But the price, I now realized, was very, very steep.

Chapter Seven

BALANCING ACT

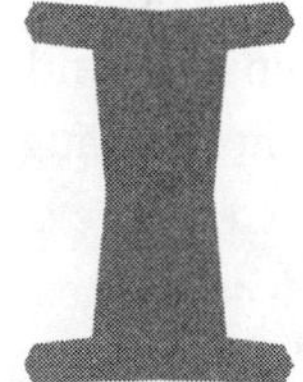

HAVE SPENT A LOT OF YEARS on the outside looking in: when I was a little boy, watching Mr. Drazian fit my old man for a suit; when I was chained to tax forms at Irving Trust, sitting among the headstones in the Trinity churchyard, peering over my copy of *Of Human Bondage* at the procession of men in homburgs, velvet-collared overcoats, and spats; when I raced racing through the subway like mad on my way to pick up rejected cartoons at the offices of *Collier's* and *Red Book*; when I shivered in Brooklyn and pictured the sun and surf of Southern California; when I finally got to Hollywood and, like everybody else, gawked at Gable walking into the MGM commissary. And, even nowadays, I often wonder what my world might have been had I chucked Tom and Jerry and headed to Broadway as the playwright I dreamed of being.

When you're outside, of course, all you can think about is how great it must be inside. What a kick it must be, you think, to give interviews and have reporters ask you all kinds of questions. I would be lying if I claimed that I had no interest in the spotlight, no desire for acclaim. When I let myself think about it, I am still plenty sore that Fred Quimby didn't share the seven Tom and Jerry Oscars. But, after more than thirty years of making cartoons for television, I have to tell you that the publicity gets more than a little tiring. You want it, you crave it, you need it, and you're scared as hell when it stops. But you find yourself answering pretty much the same questions a hundred times with pretty much the same answers while trying to make the interviewer feel like he's the first person on the face of the earth who has ever had the brilliance and imagination to ask that particular question in that particular way.

Today, my biggest kick comes from the individual fans I run into: folks who tell me that they grew up with Snagglepuss and Huck and Yogi, middle-aged men who ask me when we're going to do more Jonny Quest cartoons, people who tell me that something Bill and I have created has made them feel good or has given them a laugh when they really needed one. I am thrilled when I make an appearance at an art gallery and autograph animation cels for a stream of fans from all walks of life who willingly part with five hundred, eight hundred, even twelve hundred hard-earned dollars just to take home a piece of the little world we have made. The fact that it all means so much to them means a great deal to me.

I also get a good many children visiting the studio from time to time. They walk around my office wide-eyed, looking at all the characters, mostly stuffed animals and other doodads I have stashed away here. Quite often, I ask them if they ever got an Emmy. When they say no, I pose them with one of mine—some of the younger kids, beaming, can barely lift the statuette—and a parent snaps a picture. But I don't let the kids off with that. I usually ask them to make an acceptance speech, and I'm always amazed at how quickly and naturally they get the hang of it. "Well, I want to thank my mom and dad for all their help and inspiration . . ." I mentioned to one young man that, seized by the devil during a particular Emmy ceremony, I had it on the tip of my tongue to say, "I want to thank my wife, who had absolutely nothing to do with this," but then I saw her sitting out there in the audience and realized I'd be a doomed man before I got off the stage. I was tempted, and it would have been refreshing for the audience, but discretion was, in that case, the better part of valor—proven by the fact that I am still here to tell the tale.

Then there are the more casual encounters, which are equally delightful. Recently, I was in Manhattan at the hundred-plus-story World Trade Center, where I had just accepted an award from LIMA, a licensing industry trade association. I was coming down from the top floor, where the award had been presented, riding in one of the building's cavernous elevators, which was like a moving room. One of my fellow passengers, a young woman, looks over at me and says, "Yabba-dabba-doo!" Next, a spiffily dressed and expensively coiffed button-down lawyer type starts humming, then singing "The Flintstones" theme song.

That was when another one of my devils—unaccountably—seized me.

"Hold it a minute. I'll give you a hundred dollars if you can sing all of 'The Flintstones' theme song."

Without so much as loosening his gold collar bar, he sang it, sang all of it, and sang it with gusto, beginning to end. In fact, by the time we reached the lobby floor, the entire elevator was singing it—Armani-clad men, Chanel-suited women—out the door, into the lobby, and, I like to imagine, arm-in-arm, out onto the streets of Lower Manhattan.

It was the most satisfying hundred dollars I've ever spent. Though I'm just as glad I hadn't offered a thousand.

BUT THIRTY-PLUS YEARS AGO, back in 1961, it was the big publicity splashes that excited me. Media attention was a brand-new thing for me, and when the *Saturday Evening Post* did a feature on Hanna-Barbera that year—"TV's Most Unexpected Hit"—I was flabbergasted.

"Four years ago," the *Post* story ran, "they were has-beens, bounced out of the movie business with no prospect for future employment. This year, as owners of four fantastically successful television shows, plus a major contender, they will gross an estimated $9,000,000. . . . 'The Flintstones' finished the 1960–61 season with an audience of 13,882,000 homes, according to Nielsen figures." Three-year-old "Huckleberry Hound" ("the Barrymore of the bunch") "appears weekly on some 180 independent stations. . . . On another midweek evening, same time, same station, Quick Draw McGraw stalks his man. . . . On still a third evening during TV's kiddie hour, Yogi Bear cavorts around Jellystone Park in a pork-pie hat telling all comers that he is 'smarter than the average bear.' . . . Last, but by no means least in Hanna and Barbera's economic expectations, is a new half hour, 'Top Cat' . . ."

The *Post* was kind enough to point out that Bill and I were middle-aged—fifty years old—observing further (to my no little satisfaction, though I must have *tried* to disguise it at the time) that "Joe Barbera looks fifteen years younger than Hanna." The story went on:

Darkly handsome in the Valentino manner, Barbera lives beside a swimming pool in fashionable Bel Air, comes to work in open-neck shirts and Hollywood sport coats. He talks at teletype speed and likes to work on three things at once. He can argue business with an agent on the phone, read a script which awaits his approval and simultaneously make notes on a story which pops into his head.

I like to think there is truth in this description—particularly the Valentino part—but the writer made it sound like I *enjoyed* doing a dozen things at once and did these dozen things simultaneously on purpose. The fact is, I had no choice.

Really, the most accurate feature of the *Post* article was the illustration we provided for the opening spread, which showed Bill and me on opposite ends of a painter's scaffold, in the process of sketching our cast of characters—Betty, Wilma, Dino, Pixie, Dixie, Fred, Barney, Snagglepuss, Yogi, Boo Boo, Top Cat, Huck, Augie Doggie, Doggie Daddy, Hokey Wolf, and so on—while Quick Draw McGraw, looking in a hand mirror, practices a trick over-the-shoulder shot, which passes through Baba Louey's sombrero and cuts through the rope on my side of the scaffold. Bill is shown leaning over backwards, losing his balance, while I, hands and feet splayed, eyes and mouth wide with terror, have already slipped off and am on my way down.

That pretty much expresses what it was like and how it felt in those days: a highly hazardous balancing act.

True enough, Hanna-Barbera was grossing nine million dollars—that year and then . . . tomorrow? Tomorrow, it could all be over.

At MGM, Bill and I had deceived ourselves into thinking that what we had created would last forever. It's the same kind of thinking that motivated the builders of the *Titanic*. This thing, they said, is unsinkable, absolutely, 100 percent guaranteed. Bon voyage!

After what had happened at MGM, I was always looking over my shoulder, waiting for the bubble to burst, and in this condition I was always driven to generate new ideas even while Bill and I were running on a high-speed treadmill just to keep up production on what we had already sold.

Were we keyed up?

You bet.

Typically, we had three to five shows going. On any particular day, one story was in development, another at the storyboard stage, yet another in layout. Meantime, I kept developing new ideas and would get on a plane to pitch a show in development, sipping a scotch en route and sketching, blocking out action on sheets of animation paper for a show currently in production. At the end of a round trip, if I were lucky, I would not only have sold a new show, but would be able to hand two complete storyboards to a layout man, who would clean them up, render them into full-size layouts, and give them to Bill for timing and distribution to the animators. At night, I'd go over to the sound studio to direct the voices in the cartoon.

Despite the pace, we ran our shop in the kind of loose, anti-corporate, no-bullshit way we knew animators respected and under which they did their best, most imaginative work. We had no time clocks to punch or sign-in sheets to initial. Our artists and animators came and went as they wished. We paid them by the foot. For each foot of film an animator produced, he received so much. In those days, a good animator—if he were lucky enough even to find work—made between $175 to $225 a week. Paying by the foot gave our animators incentive to work at a blazing pace, using all the effective shortcuts their expertise commanded, and they made as much as fourteen hundred dollars a week. No one ever complained to me about making fourteen hundred dollars a week in the early 1960s, but union intervention soon forced us—and our animators—to cut back on the hours. We hired more animators and sliced the pie more thinly among them.

Given this pace, you can appreciate how costly were those eight solid weeks it took me to sell "The Flintstones" in New York. But getting into the virgin territory of adult prime time meant a chance to keep our balance for one more season or one more year or, if we were unbelievably lucky, even longer.

THE FIRST TWO "FLINTSTONES" were the work of Dan Gordon and myself; I controlled the content, and Dan did the storyboards. Despite the half-hour sitcom format, we didn't hire prime-time writers at first, but did everything ourselves, drawing the characters and creating the storyboards as we wrote the script.

After the show was sold and became a hit, I was talked into hiring an ex-"Honeymooners" staff writer and made a three-script deal at an unheard of three thousand dollars per script—a fee so high for cartoon writing in those days that, even as I signed on the dotted line, I couldn't believe I was agreeing to it.

It was a big mistake. Coming from a sitcom writer, the scripts were all dialogue. There were no cartoon gags, and, without them, I knew the story wouldn't work—even on prime time. We junked the scripts, ate the money, and learned a lesson.

The demands of the show were such that we began to pick up and try out various cartoon writers in Hollywood, most of whom simply could not make the transition from the five- or seven-minute format to the half-hour. Thank goodness we had an in-house writer, Warren Foster, who was an incredible genius and ended up doing no fewer than thirty-one "Flintstones" in a row. Warren didn't *write* his scripts; he *drew* them, sitting at his desk, drawing and laughing out loud as he worked. And he did this for fifteen weeks straight, laying the foundation of a show that lasted six years in its original run. (During that run—over 166 half-hours—we had scripts from many other terrific writers, including Michael Maltese, R. Allen Saffian, Barry Blitzer, Tony Benedict, Herb Finn, Jack Raymond, Sydney Zelinka, Arthur Phillips, and Joanna Lee.)

At lunchtime, a bunch of us from the studio would often eat at one of my favorite restaurants in the world, Musso Frank's on Hollywood Boulevard. The interior, cool, dark, and inviting as a Viking's mead hall, hadn't (and hasn't) changed since the restaurant opened its doors in 1919, and neither had the menu. The waiter brought out your martini on a tray holding an empty glass, a half-dozen olives, and a little flask that looked like it came from a child's chemistry set. It held enough dry martini for two drinks—so each martini you ordered was, de facto, a double. And it's the only restaurant in Hollywood, to my vast knowledge of these matters, where you could—still can—get real rice pudding for desert.

For me, however, these pleasures were not the only attractions of Musso Frank's. Sheila Holden was the daughter of a British army colonel and had left England to come to the United States in 1960. She was a kid and had no job and no experience, but Mr. Musso, the man who had started the restaurant back in 1919, offered to break her into the business. It's no wonder he did, because Sheila, tall, blonde, big eyes highlighted with lavender eye shadow, bright, witty, and disarmingly frank, was impossible to resist.

By the time I became a regular at Musso Frank's, Sheila was keeping the restaurant's books and spent much of her time out of sight in the upstairs office. But, during the lunchtime crush, she would come down to the dining room and sail by my table on her way to take over at the cash register.

It was like the whole place came to attention when she passed—and this was in Hollywood, where, at least in those days, people were accustomed to seeing beautiful women. Every guy in town was after her. I remember how Broderick Crawford, a grumpy, argumentative, thoroughly sour regular at Musso Frank's bar, would suddenly brighten—almost—to a smile when Sheila walked by.

There was a phone booth, one of those old, dark, folding metal-door kind you see nowadays only in old Ray Milland movies, near the back entrance of the restaurant. I was sitting in it one afternoon, making a call, when Sheila walked by.

I slid the door open with my foot, shot my hand out of the booth, took her by the wrist, and said into the receiver, "I'll call you back." Those are the last words I actually remember, but I'm confident I started saying all sorts of clever things to this blonde beauty many years my junior. Because, somehow, the net result was a date—the first of many.

Years after this, I went to my tailor's on LaCienega Boulevard. He was fitting a man I recognized as Mr. Gelson, who owned a chain of exclusive high-end import grocery stores and who had been a regular at Musso Frank's.

The tailor looked up at me.

"I'll be with you in a minute, Mr. Barbera."

"Barbera!" Mr. Gelson said. "Are you the guy—you were going with that beautiful girl at Musso Frank's?"

I said, "Yeah."

"You were going with her?"

I said, "I married her."

"Ohhhhhh," he moaned. "He *married* her! Can you believe that? Can you believe that? He *married* her!"

The man was actually pissed off—and I can't say I blame him.

Yes, in 1963 I talked Sheila into marrying me. I made her a single promise. "I'll never say no to you," I told her, but I was careful to make sure that she understood just what she was getting into. That *Saturday Evening Post* story had put it bluntly: "Barbera's marriage would seem to be the first victim of the partners' television success. . . Joe and Dorothy Barbera separated quietly . . ." And I warned Sheila that my hours were long and often unpredictable.

She understood, she said, and one of the things I most love and admire about Sheila is how she has not only endured my creative life—which continues to eat up time as voraciously as the gluttons consigned to a circle in Dante's hell—but has actively participated in it as a brilliant hostess and a source of great ideas. It was Sheila, for example, who suggested, midway through the "Flintstones" years, that Fred and Wilma have a baby, an addition to their animated family that greatly extended the life of the show and created as-yet unexhausted spin-off possibilities.

Only once, after one too many dinner-hour phone interruptions from a script writer, did Sheila complain. "Can't they even let you have your dinner in peace?"

"Sheila," I said quietly, "they're only trying to make a living."

Well, like me, Sheila knows what that's all about, and she has accepted untold numbers of interrupted dinners—not to mention disrupted weekends and a million other demands—ever since.

That idea of hers—to give the Flintstones a baby—set off two days of uncharacteristically rancorous meetings at the studio debating the sex of the offspring. After much collective hair pulling, we decided: It's a boy!

Relieved at having reached a decision at last, I turned to other matters. A few days later, I took a phone call from Ed Justin, our merchandising man in New York.

"I hear the Flintstones are having a baby."

"That's right," I said.

"Boy or girl?"

I leaned back in my chair.

"It's a boy! Fred, Jr.—a chip off the old rock!"

"That's too bad," he said. "I've got the vice president of Ideal Toy here, and the only dolls they're doing are girls. We could have had a hell of a deal if it had been a girl."

"It *is* a girl," I said. "Her name is . . . Pebbles. A pebble off the old rock."

Some ideas develop after days of meetings. Others are born in the flash of a dollar sign set off by a single phone call.

NO QUESTION THAT "The Flintstones" has meant a great deal to Hanna-Barbera creatively and financially, but I learned just how much more the show meant when, one evening, I was at Sheila's apartment (we weren't married yet), watching TV, but paying no particular attention to it until I heard, "We interrupt this program to bring you a special bulletin."

And the voice went on to say that Mel Blanc had been critically injured in a terrible automobile accident. I hadn't been working with Mel for long, but long enough to realize that he was indispensable as the voice of Barney and Dino on "The Flintstones" and, even more importantly, long enough to come to the conclusion that he was not only a genius but a great guy who was rapidly becoming a good friend.

The accident, we learned, had happened on a particularly treacherous curve near UCLA. It was poorly engineered, banked the wrong way, so that if you took it with any speed, especially on a wet night—which this was—you had very little control over your car. Mel's was the sixth serious accident on this curve in a short period. He slammed head-on into another car. Mel was in his little Aston-Martin, a super-lightweight aluminum-bodied sports car he loved and I envied.

Nobody expected him to live, or, if he did live, nobody expected there to be much left of him.

During his long hospitalization, we had the show to think about. The always-remarkable Daws Butler quickly worked up a convincing imitation of Mel doing Barney, and, thanks to Daws, we were able to continue production.

When Mel was finally released from the hospital, he went home to what promised to be a long and painful convalescence. I was stunned when he called me right away to say that he wanted to get back on the show.

"Of course you will." I assured him. "Just give it time."

"No. I mean now," he said.

We set up an entire sound studio in Mel's bedroom. That would not be too big a deal today, in this era of microchips and subminiaturization, but in the early 1960s, the equipment was only halfway toward becoming portable.

Mel was swathed in bandages from head to toe. There were openings for ears, eyes, nose, and mouth—but that's it. He could look straight up only, and his legs were held apart and immobile by an iron bar.

We set up a mike and a script directly over his face, Mrs. Blanc brought us all coffee and cookies, and Mel acted out his lines perfectly and beautifully. No one who would see the finished cartoon could possibly have guessed that Barney's words were emanating from a living mummy. For my part, I was moved by Mel's professionalism and commitment. To say he was trouper is the understatement of the century, but, maybe even more important, I am convinced that getting back to the show, getting back to being Barney, helped Mel recover sooner than he might have otherwise.

Right after its television premiere on September 30, 1960, the prospects for "The Flintstones" didn't look all that bright. Here was the first prime-time, half-hour, adult cartoon show, a cartoon populated with people instead of the customary talking animals—and the critics absolutely hated it.

The *New York Times* October 1 review called it an "inked disaster," complaining in particular that Fred and Barney were "unattractive, coarse, and gruff." (Hey, they're *cavemen*. You were expecting maybe Adolphe Menjou and Marcello Mastroianni?). *Variety,* five days later, predicted a lack of "staying power." Yet, by the end of its first season, the show garnered an Emmy nomination and received a Golden Globe Award as an Outstanding Achievement in International Television Cartoons. *TV-Radio Mirror* voted it the most original new series, and the National Cartoonists Society awarded it a Silver Plaque for "the best in animation."

Even more important, the audience loved it, and the reviewers, in subsequent seasons, fell into line behind the fans. Buoyed by the success of "The Flintstones," I started thinking about another half-hour prime-time cartoon show, loosely inspired by "You'll Never Get Rich," the hilarious army-life comedy series that ran from 1955 to 1959, starred Phil Silvers as the always-scheming Master Sergeant Ernie Bilko, and featured a supporting cast of his devoted motor-pool platoon at mythical Fort Baxter, Kansas. I quickly sketched a single drawing of a smart-aleck cat I dubbed Top Cat and handed it to Ed Benedek, who worked the sketch into a finished piece of artwork.

I walked into a meeting with ABC TV's Ollie Treyz, showed him the drawing, and said it was a cat who lives in an alley with a lot of other smart-aleck cats, all living by their wits and sheer guile, and all looking to Top Cat as their leader.

"The Flintstones" had taken eight weeks of forty-five- to ninety-minute dog-and-pony-show pitches to sell. Now Ollie Treyz looked at me, looked at the drawing, and said: "Okay. I'll take it."

Unfortunately, the rest of what I had to do was not as easy.

More than any cartoon we had ever done before—even more than "The Flintstones"—"Top Cat" would depend on characters, casting just the right voices, and that process proved to be even more of a time-consuming ordeal than usual. Perhaps it was because "Top Cat" was, in a way, closer to me than any cartoon I had done before. It came out of an urban milieu I knew very well. No, I didn't grow up in an alley, and, while my family was always short on money, we never had to cadge a meal. But, for me, New York was a place that demanded all your wit to survive, let alone get ahead. It helped if you were the kind of smart aleck who knew all the angles and whose smooth-talking charm would give you the force of personality that made you top cat. Damon Runyon knew all about this. Phil Silvers knew it, too. And so did I.

After auditioning a lot of actors, I ended up, logically enough, with an ex-cast member of "You'll Never Get Rich" in a key role. Maurice Gosfield, who had played Private Duane Doberman, became Top Cat's good-natured little sidekick Benny the Ball (if TC resembled Yogi Bear, Benny was the equivalent of Boo Boo). In addition, after much auditioning, I found Marvin Kaplin to play Choo Choo, Leo de Lyon as Spook and The Brain, John Stephenson as Fancy-Fancy, and Allen Jenkins—a veteran Warner Bros. character actor known for his gallery of supremely numbskulled small-time hoods—for the role of Officer Dibble.

But the character of Top Cat himself proved elusive. After months of casting, I settled on Michael O'Shea, who was known for his film roles as the kind of suave, easy-going leading man with a touch of Brooklyn in his voice that seemed just right for Top Cat. O'Shea, married to the glamorous Virginia Mayo, was probably best remembered as Jack London in the 1943 film of the same name, and he also starred between 1954 and 1956 in a successful TV series called "It's a Great Life," about a pair of recently discharged GIs trying to adjust to civilian life. My high hopes for O'Shea were confirmed in rehearsals, where he seemed to take to TC very naturally.

Then came the first night of recording (as with all our cartoons, recording always took place at night, at the end of a very busy, very tiring day). In walks O'Shea, duded up like a dandy from another age: old-fashioned three-button suit, big silk tie, archaic homburg hat, and gray suede gloves. Well, ordinarily, I don't much care how a man dresses, but something in the way he looked telegraphed trouble.

And trouble I got.

This man, who had been just fine in rehearsal, simply could not handle the rapid pace of cartoon television dialogue. His lines came out flat, or flubbed, or, at the very best, just plain wrong.

All I could think was how I'd just squandered months in casting only to come up with exactly the wrong man. And that's when I went home, thoroughly drained and dispirited, but just as completely unable to sleep, thinking, as I stared at the shadows shifting across the bedroom ceiling, *What have I done? And what am I going to do now?*

The answer came in the form of a great little actor with horn-rimmed glasses, pop eyes, a cockeyed smile, and a trademark bow tie. He *looked* not at all as I imagined Top Cat, but he sounded perfect: a nasal blend of streetwise expressiveness with just a touch of the carnival barker's whine. His name was Arnold Stang and he had been on radio since the age of ten and was a successful television comedian (a regular on "Henry Morgan's Great Talent Hunt," a very early comedy variety series, and on "The Milton Berle Show") and a great character actor, whose single most memorable role was as a derelict named Sparrow in *The Man with the Golden Arm.*

With the casting hurdle successfully cleared at last, we plunged headlong and happily. Recording sessions would not usually break up until 11:30 or even midnight, and we'd go across the street to the Naples Restaurant on the corner of Gower and Sunset, where I'd buy the cast dinner. Seven or eight of us would sit there, talking about the show and talking about our lives. I remember Maurice Gosfield—Bilko's stubby Private Doberman and now our Benny the Ball—consuming a huge plateful of clams on the half shell.

It was not a pretty sight.

He'd pick up clam after clam, suck in the solid contents and slurp in the buttery juice—or at least a portion of it. Much of the stuff never reached his mouth, running in rivulets down his wrist, over his wristwatch, into his sleeve, and onto his shirt. And through this all, he's talking, and always sounding in character, sort of an urban version of Andy Devine.

"I used to go with Anita Ekberg," he told us, amid exuberantly animalistic sci-fi slurping effects, fingers coated in butter, pausing to discard one spent shell and retrieve a fresh one. "But, you know, something was wrong with her."

Then a long interval of sliding and slurping until one of us finally said, "What, *what* was wrong with Anita Ekberg?"

"She had no class."

Then, dumbfounded and open-mouthed, you'd watch this little guy get up from the table, go out, get into his car, which was parked on Sunset, and pull out of his space. This he did in much the same way as he ate, throwing the car into reverse, stomping the gas, banging into the car behind him, making a little more room there, shifting into drive, stomping, banging into the car in front of him, making a little space there, repeating the process in reverse and in forward, then pulling back for one final impact before speeding off for a home without Anita Ekberg.

It was all a lot of fun, and I thought the show was going just great. Then, at about show number seven, Screen Gems's John Mitchell and Jerry Hyams came out to look at the material.

They did not like what they saw.

John pulled no punches. "What the hell is going on here? Where are the laughs?"

I was stunned.

But his next comment was insightful and a lot more helpful. "This isn't a cartoon. You're missing the cartoon laughs."

He was right. In one respect, we had made "Top Cat" look more like the traditional theatrical cartoons than, say, "Huckleberry Hound" or even "The Flintstones." Limited animation, of course, was still the order of the day—but, in "Top Cat," it was richer, fuller, more complex, and the backgrounds, too, were more detailed and elaborate. Yet, in another, more important way, I had taken a fatal detour from cartoon tradition. The great mix of urban alley cat characters had generated a lot of nifty dialogue, and I got carried away with it at the expense of the purely visual humor that must be a part of any successful cartoon. We might as well have been doing live action. There were no cartoon sight gags. I had committed the very crime for which I had earlier junked the "Flintstones" scripts by that ex-"Honeymooners" writer.

I had seven shows in the can, and, believe me, I had no desire to do any part of them over again. But I was honest enough with myself to know that John Mitchell was right, and if I let these shows go as is, "Top Cat" would evaporate in a single season or less. So I went over each cartoon and put in the kind of material that should have been there in the first place.

For example, there was one scene in which TC lays out a con game for the gang. As I had originally written it, it was just straight dialogue: talk, talk, talk. Now I went back in and gave Top Cat a golf club. With "The Flintstones," we had discovered the laugh potential of props that grew out of the show's major premise: a stone-age boulder for a bowling ball, a Stoneway piano, a mini-mastodon as portable vacuum cleaner, and so on. The prop premise of "Top Cat" was that, suave urban sophisticate that he was, TC would possess all the finer things in life—but translated into terms of the alley. His best-known prop was the telephone, indispensable to every wheeler-dealer, but in this case it was the official police call box mounted on a telephone pole and conveniently appropriated by TC whenever the need arose. Thus the golf club I gave Top Cat was a piece of pipe with an elbow joint screwed onto the end. Now, like many another self-respecting top exec, TC briefed his lieutenants while practicing his putting. Benny the Ball, as caddie, held a stick with a rag flag attached to mark the hole, and each time TC hit one his entire entourage would work like mad, laying pipe, screwing in angles and elbow joints to guide each and every ball to a hole-in-one. *This* was a cartoon gag—and all the while it went on, the necessary dialogue proceeded.

Even with the traditional cartoon gags installed, "Top Cat," for me, always seemed strangely close to life in the real world. One of the early "Top Cat" episodes was called "The Maharajah of Pookajee," and in it Top Cat and his gang disguise themselves as the maharajah and his retinue in order to gain access to a real maharajah, fabulously wealthy and ensconced in an elegant hotel, famed for casually dispensing rubies and diamonds. This was based entirely on an incident that had taken place at Hollywood's celebrated Ciro's restaurant. A local prankster circulated a rumor about an obscure Middle Eastern potentate known for tipping waiters not with coins, but with priceless gems. He then costumed himself and retinue appropriately, telephoned Ciro's, secured a prime table, and received the royal treatment generally.

After dining, on the way out of the restaurant, the potentate claps, his retainer produces a pouch, the maharajah reaches in, withdraws a handful of gemstones, and presses several into the palm of the open-mouthed maitre d'. In the process, a few jewels fall to the floor. A member of his retinue springs forward to retrieve them, whereupon the maharajah wordlessly raises a finger and shakes it dismissively, as if to say, "Don't bother with such trifling trash." With that, the potentate and his retainers leave Ciro's, and, in Three Stooges fashion, a dozen waiters, headwaiters, and Ciro's customers pounce on the fallen jewels.

Of course, the gems proved to be glass, the newspapers later revealed the prankster's con, and I sketched it out as the basis of a very funny TC episode—just one of many that, in terms of script, made this show probably the most sophisticated cartoon series Hanna-Barbera ever produced. Most of the very impressive scripts were written by Barry Blitzer and by the team of Harvey Bullock and Ray Allen, in addition to others.

I SAID THAT, for me, "Top Cat" frequently rubbed up against real life. Maybe it's just that "real life" in Hollywood was quite often awfully close to being a cartoon. My first wife, Dorothy, preferred the solidity of home and children to the gossamer glitz of the Hollywood most of the world (I believe) envies. Sheila, however, took to the social scene and proved a brilliant hostess at the many parties we gave in our Encino home.

I say what I am about to say at the risk of stopping the reader cold: These parties were not the sex orgies you might have heard were rampant in the Hollywood of the sixties. But some of these get-togethers were distinctly and inexplicably weird.

In 1964, we threw a formal outdoor party, attended by various friends, neighbors, and celebrities, among them Pamela Mason and her teenage daughter Portland—Porty. It was one of those balmy nights that can, from time to time, convince you that Southern California really *is* a paradise. Our pool was lighted and glowed a sort of nuclear blue-green. And, drink in hand, I look over toward the pool, where I see Porty, in a beautiful black dress, wearing black shoes, earrings sparkling at her ears, standing on the diving board, staring into the water.

Suddenly, with a cry of "Merry Christmas!" she jumps into the pool—dress, shoes, earrings, and all.

Pamela Mason sings out: "My earrings!"

But everybody else, what do they do? They jump in after her. Make no mistake, it's not to rescue her—she was fine—but to join her. One by one and severally, like lemmings, my beautifully attired guests not so much jumped as stepped off the side of the pool and into the water. Soon, various objects began to surface, mostly eyeglasses and wallets, which hands reached up and set out along the rim of the pool. Then came the shoes—Guccis don't take well to water.

At length, I roused myself from a stunned stupor and went into the house, digging through drawers in search of dry clothing—socks, t-shirts, bath robes, towels, napkins—which I began to distribute like some disaster relief worker.

That was our version of a Hollywood party, 1964, and, as I think back on it now, I wonder if I ever got any of those socks, t-shirts, bath robes, towels, and napkins back?

Pamela Mason, by the way, and her daughter Portland are two of the brightest people I know, whose conversation is always brilliant. Pamela was—and is—a great hostess, although her aged and obese dachshund frequently threatened to upstage her. You'd be at a party that absolutely glittered with stars and celebrities of all kinds, and, suddenly, all eyes would be cast downward, following this dachshund sailing calmly through the distinguished throng on his skateboard. It wasn't that her dachshund was athletic. It was that he had grown too fat to walk, and Pamela bought a skateboard, cut holes in it for the dog's legs, and she had the canine equivalent of a geriatric walker. Years later, I used the idea as a vehicle for Ferdinand, the dog in *Tom and Jerry: The Movie*.

BETWEEN "THE FLINTSTONES" and "Top Cat," we created "Hokey Wolf"—spun off into his own show from a featured role on "The Huckleberry Hound Show"—and "Snagglepuss," which, like "Yakky Doodle," had originated on the "Yogi Bear Show." All of these were premiered in 1960. Following "Top Cat," which debuted in 1961, came "Lippy the Lion," "Touché Turtle," and "Wally Gator," all first run in 1962. That same year, we also got to work on the next logical evolutionary leap forward from "The Flintstones." Called "The Jetsons," it took the prehistoric premise and translated it wholesale into the twenty-first century, which, in 1962, seemed like the distant future.

A typical middle-class family—George Jetson, a white-collar functionary with the firm of Spacely Space Sprockets; Jane Jetson, his wife; their teenage daughter, Judy; their school-age son, Elroy; and their dog, Astro—lives in a "skypad" apartment in Orbit City, a futuristic burg of high-rise towers (inspired by what was being planned for the New York World's Fair of 1964). Like everyone else, George commutes to work in a small bubble-canopied spaceship, passing signs that read: SPEED LIMIT: 5,500 MPH. The skypad can be raised or lowered to take advantage of the best weather, meals are dispensed from a computerized Food-a-Rac-a-Cycle, a shave and a shower are thoroughly mechanized procedures, and the family even has a maid, Rosie, who, like all domestics in the twenty-first century, is an automaton—albeit (in her case) a more-than-slightly used and quirky one leased from the U-Rent-a-Robot Maid Service. Judy, typical teenager, swoons over the dreamy boys at Orbit High School, and Elroy, taught by robot teachers at the Little Dipper School, enjoys pursuing his favorite hobby, building and operating an intergalactic radio set.

Like any number of sitcom fathers, George Jetson is locked in perpetual combat with his snarling boss, Cosmo C. Spacely (voiced by Mel Blanc). George's job description is simple enough. As a "digital index operator," he drives—or rockets—into work each morning, lands on a conveyor-belt "people mover" (ubiquitous in the Jetsons' world much as they are now ubiquitous in major airports), and folds his vehicle into something resembling a briefcase, which he deposits into his personal "parking space," no bigger than a post office box; George then sits at his desk, pushes a button, and puts his feet up.

Not a pretty job, but somebody's got to do it.

In reality, however, George is frequently required to do more than push a button, especially when he is caught between the demands of his family and those of Cosmo C. Spacely, who is engaged in an unending struggle with his business rival, Mr. Cogswell, chairman of Cogswell Cogs.

In familiar television tradition, "The Jetsons" was a spin-off from a highly successful formula, a variation on a theme. If "The Flintstones" featured the likes of Stony Curtis and Ann Margrock, the Jetson family could go see Dean Martian perform in a Las Venus hotel such as the Sonic Sahara, the Riviera Satellite, or the Flamoongo.

As if this formula approach weren't enough to assure success, we—for the first time in our history—ran audience tests at a high-priced state-of-the-art testing facility on Sunset Boulevard. They ran a trial episode of "The Jetsons" for six focus group audiences, recording their responses second by second on long rolls of graph paper that produced something closely resembling an electrocardiograph. After the test screenings, Bill and I were brought into a room, where the six rolls were unreeled side-by-side across the floor. We were walked along the rolls, the consultant pointing with his pencil to the seismic high spots.

"Here's a laugh. Here's a really big laugh. Here's a tremendous laugh. Here's a non-stop laugh."

He looked at us. "According to what I see here, you've got a giant-sized hit on your hands."

We were elated, as was ABC, who had bought the show.

What we hadn't anticipated is that ABC would slot "The Jetsons" against two well-established family shows on NBC and CBS: "Walt Disney's Wonderful World of Color" and "Dennis the Menace." It is a testament to the fundamental strength of "The Jetsons" that it wasn't simply creamed by these shows. What did happen is that the Nielsen share split neatly into three virtually equal parts—something like a sixteen or seventeen share for each show. But doing relatively well like that was not good enough, and, as a prime-time show, "The Jetsons" lasted no longer than a single season, twenty-four episodes. Run the next season in a Saturday morning slot, the show did very well, proving highly durable, and we created another forty-one episodes in 1985, ten more in 1987, and two feature-length specials that same year.

The failure of "The Jetsons" to achieve its full potential wasn't our only disappointment during this period. Ever since 1957 and "Ruff and Reddy," we had enjoyed a terrific relationship with Screen Gems, for whom our shows were making very nice money—twenty-eight million dollars in four and a half years. In 1962, we were getting ready for a fifth big year with them, and Bill was not surprised when Jerry Hyams, president of Screen Gems, called. What did surprise—shock and dismay—Bill was the tenor of the call he received.

"We want to talk about a deal. You want to make a buck. We want to make a buck. Why don't you come into New York and let's talk about it?"

Bill was stunned, and so was I. We had a right to expect better treatment. In fact, we had a right to expect *royal* treatment, and, indeed, we later learned that Jerry Hyams had been instructed to invite us to New York, foot all the bills, and sign us up pronto. Apparently, however, the accountant's voice within him whispered, *Make them pay, make them pay*, and he called Bill, reducing some twenty-eight million dollars to a matter of "making a buck" while saving the price of a hotel bill.

We were being courted during this period by Ted Ashley, who ran Ashley Famous Agency. When Ashley requested a meeting, he fetched us to it in a limousine, and, in contrast to the crackerbox headquarters of Screen Gems, Ashley's offices were elegantly decorated with antiques. More important, Ashley was a sharp and skillful agent, and we left Screen Gems—though we always kept up cordial relations with John Mitchell. When Ted Ashley became president of Warner Bros., federal regulations dictated that he divest himself of his agency, and one of his salesmen, Sy Fisher, was assigned to us. Sy served as Hanna-Barbera's agent for some seventeen years.

Despite the scheduling sabotage of "The Jetsons," Hanna-Barbera was booming. In 1964 alone, we introduced "Magilla Gorilla," the title character of which was voiced by Allan Melvin, another Phil Silvers alumnus, who would later go on to featured roles in the long-running "Gomer Pyle, U.S.M.C." and the groundbreaking "All in the Family"; "Peter Potamus and His Magic Flying Balloon," "Ricochet Rabbit," "Breezly and Sneezly," "Punkin Puss," and "Yippee, Yappee, and Yahooey," all of which were widely syndicated.

For ABC that year, we created our first adventure-hero cartoon series, "The Adventures of Jonny Quest," about an eleven-year-old boy (Jonny) who travels the world on various urgent and special missions with his father, Dr. Benton Quest, and their bodyguard, Roger "Race" Bannon. It was a major departure for us, but both Bill and I had been hooked on adventure stories and superheroes since we were kids. As I've said, Bill and I really don't have much in common, but we both spent our nickels and dimes on movie serials and had read Frank Merriwell and Tom Swift novels as kids. I particularly admired Milt Caniff's long-running newspaper comic strip "Terry and the Pirates," and that was the main inspiration for "Jonny Quest"—not only for some of the characters (our Race Bannon resembled the good-looking blond hero of Caniff's strip), but also in the sharp, angular look of the artwork, the emphasis on scientific gadgets and high-tech hardware, and the far-flung, exotic locales for the action.

Because the series was something new for us, we decided that we needed something more than a concept and storyboards to sell it, and we produced a short film. For this, I hired Doug Wildey, a comic-book artist, to create the character models. He also contributed to the stories. The casting was also top notch. Jonny was voiced by Tim Matheson, who had already appeared in a CBS sitcom called "Window on Main Street" and who would go on to a highly successful television and film career, with featured roles in "The Virginian," "Bonanza," and as the star of an ABC sitcom called "Just in Time," as well as appearances in movies like *Drop Dead Fred*, *Magnum Force*, and *National Lampoon's Animal House*. He would also later voice a number of other characters for us.

The result of the "Jonny Quest" promo film was even better than we had hoped for. It blew the clients out of the screening room, and they bought the series right away. The only elements I added to what was already present in that short were a dog, Bandit, and an exotic turbaned, Nehru-suited Indian boy loosely fashioned after Sabu, the young actor who had been popular in *Elephant Boy* and other Eastern adventure films of the late 1930s and early 1940s. The dog was needed because every boy should have a dog—besides, Bandit would make a very cuddly and eminently marketable stuffed toy. The boy—Hadji—would give young Jonny somebody his own age to talk to, and he was a master of Hindu-style magic. There was but one sour note in all this, when somebody pointed out that "Jonny" was the brand name of the Jonny Mop, a toilet-cleaning implement. True enough, but the kids never made the connection, and we stuck with the name. The series ran for a year, from 1964 to 1965, in ABC's prime-time line-up and was picked up for Saturday morning by CBS in 1967, running until 1970, when ABC took it for two years. In 1979, NBC bought the show for Saturday morning and ran it for a year. In the course of all of this, the show attracted a lot of fans, and even today I am frequently asked when we plan to make more episodes.

The economics of creating cartoons in high volume for television meant that I was always on the lookout for formulas and shortcuts, yet I also wanted us to keep exploring entirely new directions. "Jonny Quest" opened up a brand-new genre to Hanna-Barbera. Shortly after it premiered, I got an idea for opening up a whole new medium for us.

Lee Rich, who eventually became head of Lorimar Pictures and now has his own successful production company, was working for the Leo Burnett agency in the late 1960s and had sold their client, Kellogg's, on the idea of sponsoring an entire "Kellogg's Hour." Now all he had to do was find something to fill that hour. Lee flew in from Chicago and told me that he had come out to speak to every producer in town, lay the deal on them, and see what they came up with.

I went to lunch that afternoon with my agent, Sy Fisher, and raised the question: What can we do that will be really different? Lee Rich is going to get thirty or forty proposals, almost all of them for this cartoon show or that. What can we do that will make our proposal stand out from the crowd?

We talked about it, and then it hit me. Why don't we take the same characters that we would ordinarily animate and do them live instead? We could design the characters, get costumes made, and put real people inside the costumes.

From this discussion, we developed an hour format featuring a combination of cartoons and live action—the live action being people in character costume and acting as the hosts of the show. Watching "The Tonight Show" one evening, I saw Johnny and Ed demonstrate a new type of personal amphibious vehicle that had just been put on the market. It was called an Amphicat—a little thing with six soft balloon tires with about two pounds of air pressure in each—and my jaw dropped when Johnny Carson lay down on the floor of the stage while Ed McMahon got into the Amphicat and drove *over* Johnny's prone body.

Soon after seeing this, I contacted the Amphicat people and worked out a publicity deal whereby they let us use the vehicles as transportation for these characters, whom I decided to call the Banana Bunch. The basic idea was to shoot the Banana Bunch on location all over the place, in playgrounds, amusement parks, at the beach, always doing wild things. Then we would cut to a song, and there would be one or two new songs composed for each show.

That was the plan. We showed the artwork to Leo Burnett and his people, and we showed it to NBC. Now the next make-or-break step was selling the project to Kellogg's itself, which meant, of course, a midwinter flight to Leo Burnett in Ice Station Chicago.

SO OUT I WENT, with a bundle of drawings in hand, landed in a raging snowstorm, and fought my way to the Ambassador East Hotel. There, in the Pump Room, I started talking to Sy about the presentation. Each time I had shown the drawings before—to the agency people and to the network people—it was a regular labor of Hercules to make them understand that what I was showing them was *not* a fully animated show, but a combination of live-action characters in costume. I did not want to blunt my final pitch by having to explain that very basic aspect of the concept again. There was always a lot riding on these presentations, but this one was really big. It was a chance to sell twenty-six one-hour shows to a major sponsor on a major network. What could I do to make this presentation work, to close this sale once and for all and with a minimum of explanation?

I said to Sy, "Why don't we use a costume—at the pitch?"

"Joe, there are two things wrong with that idea. First, the pitch is tomorrow. Second, we don't have a costume."

But we did have a costume. At the studio, we had a Yogi Bear costume, which we used for various promotions. I told Sy that we could get Jerry Eisenberg to fly out tonight with it. Kellogg's had sponsored Yogi Bear, and Kellogg's loved Yogi Bear. I could use Yogi, a familiar character, to sell the "Banana Bunch" costume idea, an unfamiliar concept.

It was two in the morning before Jerry arrived at the Ambassador East. We went up to the room and started talking about the pitch, which was now a scant six sleepless hours away.

"Now, what we'll do is this. I'll introduce you. I'll say, 'We have here in the flesh—I should say, in the fur—an old friend of yours.' Then you'll come in, wave, and we'll do a little soft shoe together. I'll say something like, 'Don't call us, we'll call you,' but instead of walking out the door, you go over to the first lap you see, sit in it, and put your arm around the guy's shoulder."

So, about 7:30 in the frigid A.M., we took Jerry and the suit in a cab to the Prudential Building, took the elevator up to Leo Burnett, and I secreted Jerry in a men's room across the hall from the conference room. He climbed into all of the suit—except for the head—and sat down on the john to await his cue.

At eight, all the troops filed into the conference room and deployed themselves on three sides of a massive table: Leo Burnett and his staff along one side, the NBC brass along the other, and the Kellogg's crew, including the company chairman, along the third end. In the meantime, I saw out in the hall, waiting for *his* turn at the plate, my competition, none other than Grant Tinker, who had just left NBC for a high-level position with Universal. (I later learned that the project he was promoting had a price tag 50 percent lower than our show. I'm glad I didn't know that going *into* the pitch.)

I began my presentation with the artwork, which everyone, except for the Kellogg's people, had seen about forty-two times by now. Out of the corner of my eye, I caught the Kellogg's chairman nodding—not in assent and approval, but in a vain effort to fight off sleep. (It was never *my* idea to hold these meetings at eight in the morning!)

"Now I want to make it clear that this is not an *animated* show. It is something brand new, and to illustrate this, I've brought with me in the flesh—I should say, in the fur—an old friend of yours."

I opened the door, and in walks Yogi Bear. The minute he comes into the room, everybody sits up, and we break into our soft shoe.

At this point, Mort Werner, of NBC, takes a piece of paper, scribbles a note, and slides it to the president of the network: JOE BARBERA JUST SOLD THE SHOW.

"Don't call us," I say to Yogi, "we'll call you," and I push him toward the door. Instead, as rehearsed, he sits in the first lap he sees and throws his arm and paw around the shoulder . . . of the somnolent Kellogg's chairman, who, beaming, is now anything but sleepy.

Without a bear suit, Grant Tinker didn't have a chance.

As usual, though, we were not quite home free. A short time later, I got one of those phone calls that make you feel like the captain of the *Lusitania* watching the approach of the torpedo. It seems that Kellogg's was having second thoughts about "The Banana Bunch," and Roy Lang, the Leo Burnett account executive handling Kellogg's, asked me to fly out to Phoenix, where the cereal giant was having a corporate meeting, to squelch doubts and shore up confidence.

I dropped everything at the studio, caught a ride to the airport, and, in effect, pitched the whole thing over again, sans Yogi. It worked, and I started breathing once again.

That is, until I got another phone call.

We were well into production when our merchandise man phoned me from Scotland, where he had been vacationing. He had run across a children's book, written by a Scottish author quite unknown outside his own country. It was, unfortunately for us, called *The Banana Bunch*. There was nothing to do but trace down the writer and work out a deal to use the name. It's something that's done all the time.

But not *this* time. The author was a dour Scotsman, who, for reasons known only to himself, had decided he would share the name "Banana Bunch" for neither love nor money.

What do you do in a situation like this?

You begin by going into a panic. Then you come up with another name. We decided on "The Banana Splits," which was certainly as good a name for the series as "The Banana Bunch." The only snag in this was a little matter of Kellogg's having already printed up cereal boxes featuring "The Banana Bunch"—one-and-a-quarter million boxes, to be exact.

What did *they* do in a situation like this? They trashed 1.25 million boxes and reprinted every single one of them. The show ran successfully on NBC for two years, from 1968 to 1970.

Chapter Eight

ON THE MAP

WHENEVER I WATCH the drawn and colored images of one of our cartoons dance and race across a movie or TV screen, I am always well aware of just how hard we all had worked to get those images up there. Yet they are, after all, nothing but lights and shadows, whereas, it seemed to me, there was something solid, something unarguably real and absolutely undeniable about building your own building. You looked at it, you walked through it, you sat in your office in it, and you said: *Now we're here to stay.*

Buying six acres of Hollywood and putting up a studio on them literally put Hanna-Barbera on the map, but it was our growing inventory of hit shows that put us on the equally important financial map. By 1964, even before we moved into our new quarters, we were getting feelers from various interests who wanted to buy the company.

It was a heady experience, and I remember Bill slapping his thigh and saying, "All anybody has to do is put one million dollars in my pocket right here and they got it!"

Screen Gems came up with an offer that was a very good offer—for Screen Gems—and others approached us as well, but, for me, the visions of dollar signs danced in my head the day in 1965 that Lou Wasserman, chief of Universal Studios, our new neighbors, asked for a meeting. Wasserman was regarded as one of the giants of our industry and the toughest, shrewdest deal maker in town. His office at Universal was furnished with exquisite antiques, as were all the executive offices there. He prided himself on an immaculate desk, as if to suggest that only the most important matters came before him and that none of these ever sat and waited, but were acted upon immediately.

We spoke for a time in his office, and then he took me out to his Bentley so that he could give me a personal tour of the Universal lot. A master showman, he concluded the tour by driving up to the crest of a hill across from our studio. He got out of the car, and I followed him to the edge of a cliff. Lou Wasserman put one a hand on my shoulder and spoke in a voice as suave as it was seductive.

"Down there is you," pointing toward our brand-new six acres. "And over here is us," making a sweeping gesture that took in all four hundred acres of Universal. "I want you to be a part of us, and I'll tell you something: Money is no object."

Here was the toughest deal maker in Hollywood telling me that money was no object. Even at that moment, with his arm on my shoulder and our studios spread out beneath our feet, I couldn't help thinking about that famous painting of Christ being tempted by a devil who offers him the world. I drove the short distance back to our studio in a state of euphoria, talked to Bill, and got our financial people to send Wasserman our numbers.

It so happened that we had a great deal of detailed financial information all laid out and ready to go, because at this same time we had entered into negotiations with the brokerage firm of Loeb, Rhoads, who wanted to take us public and put us on the New York Stock Exchange. The figures I sent to Wasserman had already been seen by a Loeb, Rhoads financial analyst, who told us that our net profit picture was better than that of most major companies in the United States. In fact, shortly before my meeting with Wasserman, I had gone to New York at the invitation of Loeb, Rhoads to talk about the creative side of Hanna-Barbera. It was a kick to be taken by limousine to their offices at 42 Wall Street, less than a block from the site of my six years' enslavement at Irving Trust, and it was even more fun when we sat down to lunch in a richly paneled executive dining room, attended by white-gloved men in blue livery.

I was not entirely surprised when the questions I was asked had less to do with the creative directions in which we were taking our company than with my personal knowledge of this or that movie star, starlet, or television personality.

Shortly after my meeting with Lou Wasserman, he asked me to come back to see him. I entered his inner sanctum, where he was engrossed in scribblings on a yellow legal pad. He set the pad down on his unsullied desk, looked down at it meaningfully, and sighed a deep and heavy sigh, shaking his head. He looked up at me. "It's a shame to have to say this," he said, "but, after looking at these figures, I just don't see how we can make a deal."

I've never been much of a poker player, and I'm sure Lou had read the mixture of greed and bliss that had spread across my face when, from on high, he assured me that money was no object. But this time, armed with what Loeb, Rhoads had said about our numbers, I played it as close to the vest as any card shark of the Old West. That was because I knew that what I had was a front-row center seat at a performance by one of the industry's legendary deal makers positioning himself to make the best possible deal—for himself.

"Look, Lou, you think about it, and we'll think about." And that was all I said before I left.

While this deal remained hanging in mid air, we worked with Loeb, Rhoads to prepare something called a "red herring," in essence, an elaborate (and, at seventy-five thousand dollars, expensive) pre-offering prospectus describing our company in financial terms. Our great expectations were dashed, however, when the stock market took a sudden downturn, and we had to pull back.

IN THE MEANTIME, we were running our company, and in 1965 introduced "Precious Pupp," "The Hillbilly Bears," "Secret Squirrel," "Squiddly Diddly," and "Winsome Witch," all for NBC's ambitious children's programming schedule. "Sinbad, Jr." was distributed by American International Television (AIT), and Wolper Productions distributed our animated "Laurel and Hardy" series.

As we forged ahead while were reconsidering our financial alternatives, Loeb, Rhoads introduced us to the people from Taft Broadcasting, a Cincinnati-based company that owned and operated several television stations. They made an immediate offer, and in 1966 Bill and I sold Hanna-Barbera Productions for twelve million dollars.

Of course, you have a lot of trepidation and second thoughts about selling something you've sweated and worried to build up from absolute zero. But twelve million dollars was a nice round figure back in 1966, and, besides, Bill and I were part of the deal, staying on as vice-president and president, respectively. Better yet, we not only had the financial backing of a highly successful company, it was a company that knew enough to leave us alone. Bill and I just kept working.

ONE OF OUR MANY COMMITMENTS to NBC during this time was to produce an animated special. In 1963, while he was working on "Going My Way," an ABC sitcom based on the 1944 Bing Crosby movie of the same name, Gene Kelly had talked to us about collaborating on another animation-live action combination. The night after we spoke, I called him.

"Gene, why don't we do 'Jack and the Beanstalk'? You dance,

mesmerize the giant with your dancing, while the boy steals the magic harp and the giant's gold."

He sparked at the idea, and we secured a production budget of four hundred thousand dollars from NBC. Now that may sound like a princely sum. Each half-hour "Flintstones" episode cost fity-two thousand dollars to make, so you might think we could do an hour for twice that much, and, therefore, NBC was giving us four times what we actually needed. Unfortunately, it didn't work that way. Mixing live action with animation is far more complicated, demanding, and labor-intensive than doing straight animation. To begin with, limited animation techniques are out, because you've got to match the live action frame for frame, providing a drawing for each frame. And making the animated movement to mesh convincingly with the live action is in itself an excruciating exercise. Getting Jerry Mouse to dance with Gene Kelly for seven or eight minutes in *Anchors Aweigh* had cost a quarter of a million dollars in 1945. Twenty inflation-driven years later, we were being asked to do a whole hour of this sort of thing for less than twice that amount. Moreover, not only would the action consume much more time, the amount of artwork required was far greater. We were supplying several characters and the backgrounds—an entire animated world.

As usual, we swallowed our misgivings and accepted the miserly budget. By 1964, the project got under way. Kelly directed the live action himself, turned the footage over to us, and then went about his business.

We had gone into the project knowing that the job would be a tough one, but, in fact, it proved horrendously difficult. Nobody can deny that Kelly knew how to dance and that he was an exciting choreographer. But he did not appreciate the difference between what he could and could not do when he had to share the stage with cartoon characters. Some sections of the footage he produced were unworkable for our purposes. We spent a great deal of time culling out the material we could not use, then rotoscoping, frame by frame, what we could use and working in the animation.

More than a year went by before Gene Kelly, affable and smiling as always, came back to see the rough cut we had prepared. Bill and I ushered him into the screening room and ran the picture. At its conclusion, Kelly got up from his seat and motioned for us to follow him into the projection booth.

"Can you step in here? I want to talk to you two guys."

He closed the door and proceeded to lash into us. I cannot recall his words precisely, but there was talk of our having "really screwed" him with a "terrible job." He said that the picture was unacceptable to him and that he would inform NBC accordingly—tell them that they did not have to accept the picture.

We were stunned. Given the budget we had to work within, we did a far more creditable job on that picture than anyone had a right or even a reason to expect.

True to his word, Kelly told NBC that he wasn't accepting the picture and that they need not, either. We received an official-looking telegram from NBC: *WE RESERVE THE RIGHT TO REJECT THE PROJECT.*

Or words to that effect.

The telegram was sent, however, before anyone from NBC had actually seen "Jack and the Beanstalk." After some anxious days, we showed it to a delegation from the network, whose scowls were rapidly transformed into smiles. They accepted the show, ran it in 1966, and, in one of those delicious ironies that often occur in fantasy but practically never happen in real life, the show was nominated for an Emmy.

You can imagine that Bill and I would relish the moment we looked Gene Kelly in the eye on award night.

Two days before the Emmy show, our PR man, John Michaeli, called. "Listen, I've got to tell you, Joe. If you win the award, you can't have it."

"What?"

"Gene won't share it. As producer, he doesn't have to."

We weren't barred from the awards show, of course, and could have gone anyway, but neither Bill nor I had the stomach for it, and we each sat at home, watching the proceedings on TV. That's when another of those little ironies occurred. "Jack and the Beanstalk" won. Gene Kelly, beaming, accepted the statuette. And I have to admit that he didn't take *quite* all the credit for himself. I don't remember exactly what he said—except for a single phrase: "a lot of little hands." A lot of little hands, he said, went into the making of this show.

Something like this can make you bitter and resentful, if you choose to let it. I can't say that it didn't hurt, but through the years I've learned what all Hollywood survivors must *learn* to remain survivors. You *learn* that you aren't working with people, you're working with egos—and they're working with yours. Once you realize that, you start taking all the slings and arrows less personally. You understand that they come with the territory. After all, you're not dealing with store clerks and bank tellers and toll takers, who do their job, and pack up and go home at the end of each day. You're dealing with an assortment of artists and con men and combinations of them—very powerful people, whose power nevertheless hangs by the thinnest of threads. At a dinner party we hosted, Ernie Borgnine put it in the frankest terms I've ever heard. "Secretly, you feel that each part you get—each job—will be your last."

AND THAT BRINGS ME TO working with the legendary Fred Silverman. The first show I sold to him was "Space Ghost," in 1966, which was the start of seven intensely creative, highly profitable, and incredibly agonizing years of our working together.

In the tradition of Irving Thalberg, Fred started out as the classic boy wonder. In his very early twenties he was already a minor program executive at WGN-TV in Chicago and WPIX in New York, two independent stations. He took a master's degree in television and performing arts at Ohio State, producing a graduate thesis that analyzed ten years of programming at ABC. Most dissertations get the writer nothing but a diploma. This one got Fred a career. It brought him to the attention of the networks, and, in 1963, when he was twenty-five, CBS hired him as director of daytime programs. One of his chief responsibilities was children's programming, and that meant our paths would inevitably cross.

By the mid 1960s, Silverman was excited by the commercial potential of superheroes. His genius as a programmer was that he was a veritable trend barometer, or, more accurately, he was the equivalent of a super-sensitive weather satellite, able to make long term forecasts with uncanny accuracy. In 1966, he felt that the time was ripe for hard-action, high-tech superheroes, who would at once recall the heyday of comic-book superheroes like Superman and Batman while tapping into the space race and the explosion in technology that were shaping the decade.

What was even more brilliant about Silverman is that he didn't merely predict these trends, let alone follow them; *he made them happen.* He decided to totally remake the CBS Saturday morning schedule, which, like that of the other networks, was characterized by what he called "soft" shows. "It was either live action or it was lots of little animals running around," Silverman later observed. His idea was to transform Saturday A.M. into a "superhero morning," and he turned to us for the required product.

I started sketching ideas, but very soon ran into a problem. Our staff artists had been working exclusively on funny cartoons—precisely what Fred would have called "soft" shows. I needed to find an artist thoroughly tuned in to the superhero genre, and I hired Alex Toth, a great comic book artist, to produce some designs for an as-yet nameless superhero. He produced about forty variations on a character, and, when Fred was in L.A., he came to the studio to look at them. I spread the drawings—all painted in vivid colors on cels—across the floor. With a cigarette between his lips and a Tanqueray martini in hand, Fred tiptoed among them, agonizing over just the right combination of costume and color.

With Fred on the verge of buying the show—whatever it would be—we had yet to come up with a name. He had chosen a central superhero clad in white, with a black hooded mask, and a flowing yellow cape. Talking to Fred on the phone, the name hit me: Space Ghost. He bit on it.

The next step was to supply some scripts. I realized that some of our staff writers would likely have the same problems as our artists, and I hand picked two of our writers, former film editors Joe Ruby and Ken Spears. I explained some concepts, and they went to work. Fred loved the material, and he bought the show.

"Space Ghost" premiered with another series we created, "Dino Boy," which revolved around a youngster named Tod, who, escaping a plane crash, parachutes into a Stone Age world that time forgot. A friendly caveman named Ugh rescues him from hostile Neanderthals, and the two become allies in battles against an assortment of unsavory adversaries, including the Worm People, the Ant Warriors, the Rock Pygmies, and a host of other entities who, fortunately for us, are extinct in the modern world.

"Frankenstein, Jr." and "The Impossibles," two more series Fred bought for the 1966 season, took the superhero genre in a more comic direction. Frankenstein, Jr., a fifty-foot-tall purple-caped robot, bore only the slightest resemblance to Boris Karloff and fought evil-doers with the help of his creator, a boy scientist named Buzz Conroy, who activated the robot by means of his radar ring. Sharing the time slot with "Frankenstein, Jr.," "The Impossibles" were a teenage rock group (this was the year in which the tremendously popular bubble-gum rock band the Monkees, confected explicitly for television, premiered on NBC prime time) who were also—secretly—superheroes ("the world's greatest fighters for justice").

Of all these, "Space Ghost" was the runaway success, garnering a phenomenal 55 Nielsen share. The next year, Fred bought "The Herculoids," which combined what a later generation would call "family values" with the superhero-fantasy genre. The action takes place on the planet Quasar, where a collection of bizarre creatures—Zok, a flying dragon, who didn't breathe fire but who did shoot laser beams from his eyes and tail; Tundro the Tremendous, a ten-legged rhinoceros with a hollow horn that doubled as a super cannon; Igoo, an Incredible Hulk-like gorilla; and Gloop and Gleep, a pair of blobs who could change shape and size at will—defend the planet's royal family (King Zandor, his wife Tara, and their son Dorno) against would-be invaders, including Raider Apes, Destroyer Ants, Electrode Men, and the Faceless People (a species familiar to anyone who has worked with network executives).

"The Herculoids" nabbed an unbelievable 60 Nielsen audience share, which—I think, unfortunately—prompted Fred Silverman to stop ordering new "Space Ghosts" and throw the bulk of his budget behind "The Herculoids." It was good for that show, but it was an either/or decision that nipped the gross of "Space Ghost."

This series of successes makes working with Fred Silverman sound much more easy than it was. Satisfying it was. Easy it wasn't.

In our business, everything starts with a deal, and deals are born in meetings, so it soon becomes icily clear to you that your life and livelihood depend on the outcome of this or that meeting. Unfortunately for the faint of heart, a meeting with Fred was never a comforting or conventional business experience. On one occasion, I was in a CBS conference room waiting with an assortment of network execs and my agent Sy Fisher. Fred operated by his own clock and was frequently late for meetings.

What did you do about it? You waited.

Finally, the door opens, Fred walks in, fixes my agent with a brutal stare and fires off: "Sy, I'll never forgive you for that letter you wrote. It was unforgivable, and, mark my words, I'll never forgive you. Never." Flushed and panting, he trails off with: "And, with that, let's start the meeting."

I had about thirty pieces of artwork to show, which I flipped through at eighty-five miles per hour. "Here's a duck, here's a dog, this one's a monkey, here we have a gorilla, this is a cat. . ." Because all that was left to do was pack, hop a plane, get back to L.A., and wrap myself around a Rob Roy. That meeting was a forlorn hope and a very dead duck.

Then there was Fred Silverman after he got married. When I first started working with him, Fred was a free soul, who expected you to set aside all thought of hearth, home, and family in order to accommodate him anyplace, anytime. If that meant waiting in the office until midnight for a meeting that had been scheduled at the dinner hour, so be it. You waited.

Fred had a terrific assistant named Cathy Kihn, with whom he seemed to be engaged in perpetual argument. Seeing this situation, I could draw only one conclusion: The two were meant for each other. After they were indeed married, Fred's attitude toward time changed. Not his attitude toward *your* time, but toward his. He doted on his firstborn, Melissa, and, one day, when Sy and I were in Silverman's conference room at CBS doing a pitch, Cathy opened the door.

"I have to run an errand. Can you mind the baby?"

"Of course," he answered.

With that, little Melissa was deposited among us and toddled over to the piano, the keyboard of which she could just barely reach.

Plunk, plink, clink, twang, plunk, plink, plink, plank, ploonk, plonk, plink, plunk.

And I'm trying to make with the storyboards. "Over here is this bear, then he skids across the street— and you're really going to like this, Fred—he flips over backwards like this, and I'm going to kill that kid, and these mice start running all over hell . . ."

Finally, Sy took Melissa up in his arms, while Fred, clearly alarmed, concentrated all his attention on her and nothing on me. In an effort to keep her occupied, Sy pulled a cellophane-wrapped cigar from his pocket and gave it to her to play with.

"And the bear and the dog start talking to the turtle . . ."

"Sy!" Fred shot out. "What are you doing? What's the matter with you? Are you crazy? Don't give her that!"

End of pitch.

Sometimes you weren't even lucky enough to catch Fred in a room. In 1966, the film *Born Free* was a popular sensation, and I had an idea for doing a series based on it. It would use realistic drawings of lions—not cartoon-looking lions—and we would dub ordinary voices over them to make a sitcom about a family, a perfectly normal family, who just happened to be a family of lions. I went ahead and put together a short piece of film using the voice of Tom Bosley, and, when it was finished, I called Sy Fisher. He said that we should get it to Fred Silverman right away and that we could nail him at the Beverly Hills Hotel. We drove down to the hotel, where, sure enough, we found Fred poolside, supine on a chaise longue, taking in the sun, smoking a cigarette, and sipping a Tanqueray martini.

We sidled up to him. "Hiya, Fred. How're you doing?" I greeted him.

"Hmmph."

"Fred, I've got a really terrific idea for a show. It's based on *Born Fr . . .*"

"Naaaahhhhhh."

Like a quiz show buzzer.

End of pitch.

ONE OF THE MOST SUCCESSFUL, original, and enduring shows we developed with Fred Silverman was "Scooby-Doo, Where Are You?" It started out as an idea for an animated supernatural/whodunit series Fred wanted to call "House of Mystery," and I remember working like mad to get some artwork whipped up to show him, then running to get it to him before he left L.A. for New York. As usual, there was no time for a formal meeting, so I caught a ride with him to the airport, and he looked at the artwork on the way.

But that was not enough. These were the days before airport security guards, x-rays, and metal detectors. Nor did airports have those telescoping enclosed "jetway" ramps that take you right up to the airplane door. Instead, you could escort your party out the terminal door, up a set of ladder stairs, and right into the plane. And that is just what I did with Fred. Only he stopped in the middle of the aisle and began propping the artwork on empty seats, lighting a cigarette (that was most definitely not allowed, at least not on the ground, even back in 1968), puffing, and deliberating over the drawings—"Hmmm. Hmmm? Hmmm."—entirely oblivious to the other muttering passengers who jostled and squeezed past him.

And I'm saying to myself, *I'd better get the hell off this plane before they close the door.*

The original artwork, which Fred took with him back to New York, sparked such a debate at CBS that it went all the way to the Chairman William S. Paley's right-hand man, Frank Stanton, who recoiled from it in horror, rejecting it on the grounds that it was just too frightening for children. According to Fred, Stanton looked at him and said, "We can't put that on the air."

This presented a rather major problem, since Silverman had already made the show the centerpiece of Saturday morning, giving it the 10:30 slot and planning the rest of the schedule around it.

Fred called us, said he was hopping a plane right away, and set up a meeting for six that evening.

At this point in the evolution of the show, the title of which Fred had changed to "Mysteries Five" then "I'm S-s-s-s-s-scared," we had a cast of four teenage detectives who cruised around in a van called the Mystery Machine, solving not ordinary crimes and misdemeanors, but supernatural mysteries. Shaggy (a scruffy latter-day beatnik voiced by Kasey Kasem, who went on to become a phenomenally successful radio DJ), Velma (a Plain Jane whiz kid), Daphne (a pretty and stylish redhead), and Freddy (the good-looking blond lead) were accompanied by an awkward and gangling Great Dane dog. Like Jonny Quest's miniature bulldog, Bandit, the detectives' dog was conceived as a requisite adjunct with possible merchandising potential. However, as Ken Spears and Joe Ruby started blocking out scripts, it was becoming increasingly apparent that the Great Dane was taking over the show.

This was clinched when Don Messick gave voice to the character. In a stroke of inspiration, Don invented a unique canine dialect by transforming entire lines of dialogue into a cross between intelligible human language and a dog bark. That was impressive enough in and of itself, but the absolute genius was in the way Don did what he did in a way that kids could imitate. He just added a kind of growling "r" sound to key words. For example, the phrase "Hello, how are you?" became "R-r-rello, how are r-r-roo?" It was precisely the kind of gimmick that burrows its way into the collective consciousness of an audience, thoroughly delights the kids, and drives their parents slowly insane.

As Fred Silverman tells it, he was winging his way back to L.A., Stanton's rejection still stinging his ears, when he tried to relax by listening to some music on the earphones. That's when he heard Frank Sinatra singing his big hit of the year, "Strangers in the Night." I imagine that, today, only the most dedicated of Sinatra's fans can render all the lyrics of the song, but almost everyone who wasn't comatose in the late 1960s can sing on demand the nonsense syllables Frank inserted into the second verse: "scooby-dooby-doo."

We had dutifully assembled in my office at six P.M., only to learn that Fred's flight had been delayed. It was midnight before he came in, I handed him his Tanqueray martini, and he announced triumphantly, "I got the title: 'Scooby-Doo, Where Are You?'"

"Terrific!" I yelled. Actually, at that hour, he could have said anything, and I would have responded in much the same way.

Along with the title, Fred had come to the realization that making the dog—now called Scooby-Doo—the star would in and of itself soften the scarier aspects of the show and satisfy CBS management.

He was right. The series premiered in fall 1969 and ran for seven years on CBS.

FRED SILVERMAN WAS UNNERVING to work with, in part, because you were always aware that you never quite had his undivided attention. It has been said that Mel Blanc's repertoire of voices numbered nearly three thousand—but I don't believe that figure included the incredible range of weird talking automobile sounds he could do. When I first heard these, I just knew we could build some kind of show around them. What I came up with was a series about a talking VW beetle, called "Speed Buggy," and I set up a meeting with Fred Silverman to pitch the show with a piece of soundtrack featuring Mel's car effects.

I was convinced that all I needed to do to sell the project was to play the tape for him. It was that good. But each time I started the tape recorder, Silverman was interrupted by a phone call, a secretary, a messenger, an earnest young man with an urgent question, another phone call, then a call he remembered he absolutely had to make.

Your life hangs in the balance at these meetings, and the guy who's got all the power is off in a million places at once, as indifferent to you, it seemed, as a force of nature. But here's the thing. Three weeks after this totally frustrating meeting, Silverman calls me and says, "You know that Mel Blanc tape you played? It was a very good idea." And he bought "Speed Buggy" for CBS in 1973. A fraction of Fred Silverman's attention was worth more that 100 percent of most other people's.

IN 1970, Silverman was promoted from vice-president of program planning and development to head of the entire program department at CBS. Shortly after his promotion, I ran into him in a hallway at Black Rock, the network's glowering monolith of a headquarters building in Manhattan. He ran up to me, threw his arm around my shoulder, and said, "Remember, you put me here. I'll never forget it. Mark my words, I'll never forget that you put me here."

While I would still deal directly with Fred on numerous occasions, he hand-picked Duke Ducovny, a former Superman comics editor, to be his successor as director of daytime programming.

I did not get off to the greatest of starts with Duke. We used to have a lot of our client meetings at the Beverly Hills Hotel. We'd take an entire suite and settle into it the day before the client's arrival in order to prepare for the meeting.

Here we all were, nervous about shifting gears from Silverman, a mercurial but known quantity, to Ducovny, an unknown, when, in the middle of our pre-meeting discussion, the only fly that ever called Beverly Hills home started buzzing around the room. He was as jumpy as we were, stubbornly refusing to light anywhere for long. Finally, it became apparent that the shade on the elegant table lamp held an attraction he found irresistible. The conference came to a halt as the eyes of a half-dozen very creative and highly paid professionals focused on the fly in anticipation of what it would do next.

I went into the bathroom, retrieved a heavy Turkish towel, and folded and refolded it into a kind of billy club. As everyone in the room watched, I sneaked up on the fly with the stealth of a cheetah. I raised my club, and with the unerring aim born of a killer instinct, I struck. The undoubtedly very costly glass lampshade shattered into four hundred pieces. The now jagged rim was spinning, and the fly was buzzing more fiercely than ever.

I felt like a goddamn fool, and, the next day, when I walked into the meeting we had supposedly been preparing for, my thoughts, which should have been entirely devoted to selling shows to the new man at CBS, were still preoccupied with the question of what we were supposed to do about the lampshade: Tell somebody? Offer to pay? Or just shut up?

I opened the door, only to be greeted by a noxious wall of cigar, cigarette, and pipe smoke. Seeing Sy Fisher with a pipe in his mouth, I tore into him: "Jesus Christ, this is terrible. What kind of person would smoke a pipe? Pipes are an abomination. I can't stand pipes . . ."

Then, just getting started on a serious roll with my tirade, I looked away from Sy for an instant and beheld Duke Ducovny earnestly puffing away on a pipe.

" . . . except *that* one." I pointed. "*That*, Duke, is one hell of a pipe, a great pipe, and that tobacco is straight from heaven. Sy, what's the matter with you? If you are going to smoke a pipe, why don't you take a lesson in class from Duke here? Get yourself a pipe just like his, ask him what kind of tobacco he's smoking, and buy yourself a load of it."

LATER, IN 1972, I pitched a show directly to Fred called "Amazing Chan and the Chan Clan," revolving around an animated incarnation of the venerable detective but also featuring his "clan" of a dozen children. Fred bought the project and set us to working with Duke Ducovny, who had the responsibility of reading and approving the scripts.

The problem was that we got very little input from Duke. Now, in most cases, I would have been delighted with the absence of network interference, but by the sixth script that came in to me, I didn't need any client to tell me that the thing was a stinker. The scripts had bad problems, and I knew we were in trouble.

I said to Bill, "Duke may not be looking at this stuff, but when Fred reads it, the shit's really gonna hit the Chan."

Sure enough, Fred called Sy Fisher to tell him that the material was unacceptable. Sy responded by telling him that everything had been approved by Duke Ducovny.

"Don't you start picking on Duke!" Fred burst out. "I'll tell you what. You guys are never going to work for me again, and I'm calling every studio in town and telling them that. Mark my words, you'll never work for *anybody* again!"

This from the man who had told me that Hanna-Barbera put him on the top at CBS.

WELL, SPEND EVEN A LITTLE TIME in this industry, and you get used to the ups and downs, the blanket accusations and mortal curses that, in the end, mean nothing at all—except for what they do to your blood pressure and nervous system.

We did, in fact, continue to sell Fred and Duke shows after this, including "Jeannie" and "Speed Buggy" in 1973, and "Valley of the Dinosaurs" and "Partridge Family: 2200 A.D." in 1974. Later, after Fred left CBS to become president of ABC (whose stock rose two points the day his hiring was announced), I sold him a series called "Superfriends," which featured Superman, Batman, Robin, Wonder Woman, and Aquaman—all together.

With a lineup like that, it was hard to see how we could miss. But when the show was delivered, it was just awful, and Nick Nichols, producing it for ABC, called for a phenomenal nine hundred feet of fixes. Staggered, Bill Hanna turned down this request, and the ABC rep working with us complained to Fred Silverman.

This was on Tuesday. Silverman, we were told, would be at our studio, in person, on Thursday. Bill asked me to look at the footage.

There was no doubt about it. The stuff was bad, lackluster, plodding, and featuring the worst Superman drawing I had ever seen. This was not the drawing of the "real" Superman, but what was supposed to be a giant duplicate of the real thing concocted by evil underground creatures. What it looked like, however, was a rendering of the Man of Steel as the proverbial ninety-pound weakling. Deflated and wimped out.

What could I do in the forty-eight hours I had before Fred was due to show up?

I began by making all the changes that were big and obvious yet relatively easy to do, like reshooting a fire scene through a red Burgess cel so that the whole sequence was in vivid red. I reedited as much of the show as I could, taking interminable scenes of the superheroes streaking through the sky and frenetically intercutting these with shots of people looking up at them. Reverting to the hoariest tricks of limited animation, I underscored explosions and impacts by reshooting them while shaking the camera. And then I ladled on the sound effects. Each and every impact was accompanied by a huge effect, one bigger than the next.

If you know the business, you can add the touches that make all the difference, that double the impact of each gesture, gag, explosion, or scene. And, what's more, you can do it for pennies. The trouble is, the bigger you get, the less personal control you have over everything you produce. I was able, for example, to intervene in "Superfriends" at the eleventh hour. But sometimes a good show just gets away. In 1972, we sold into syndication an animated series called "Wait Till Your Father Gets Home," which was inspired by the very popular "All in the Family" and my own life, in which that very phrase was a familiar refrain until my father simply stopped coming home at all.

The show was based on a very good idea: Harry Boyle was a conservative businessman father at odds with his hippie son and his sexually liberated daughter. On his side were his younger son, dutiful and obedient to a fault, and his neighbor, Ralph, who was constantly training to defend himself and the neighborhood against an impending Communist invasion. Harry's wife, Irma, struggled to remain neutral in all of this.

Harry was voiced terrifically by Tom Bosley, and the show frequently featured other celebrity voices, including Don Knotts, Phyllis Diller, Don Adams, Rich Little, Jonathan Winters, and Monty Hall. We produced and sold forty-eight episodes, which were run between 1972 and 1974, so I can't say the show was a failure, but it *should* have been a runaway hit. Why wasn't it? The production values just weren't there. We subcontracted production to a small company working out of Detroit to save a buck and, in doing so, sank the show.

That one, as I say, got away and, in consequence, failed to realize its potential. With "Superfriends," however, I got to the footage, specified the changes on Tuesday, we shot them that night, recut the picture on Wednesday, and we showed it on Thursday to Fred Silverman and a crew of ABC executives, poised for the kill. None of these people had any idea of the frantic work that had gone into doctoring the picture.

We started running the show, and as soon as I saw Silverman jump and cringe with every crash and hit, I knew we were home free.

The lights went up, and Fred turned to his lieutenants. "Hey, you've got to remember that this is the guy producing the picture."

For us it was just business as usual.

Chapter Nine

RISKS AND REWARDS

T'S 1976, AND SCOOBY-DOO, where are you?

The answer is ABC. And it all started the year before, when Sy Fisher and I met with Duke Ducovny at Black Rock on Fifty-second Street in Manhattan. There were several people in on the meeting, and at some point, Sy leaned over to me and said, "Ask him about 'Scooby-Doo.' "

It was true, CBS hadn't yet picked up its option on the show, but since it had been running on high octane for six years now, I took it for granted that Duke would, sooner or later, simply renew. It is, of course, just those things you take for granted that have a way of turning around and biting you in the ass.

"By the way, Duke," I said, "are you picking up 'Scooby-Doo'?"

Duke Ducovny eased back in his chair, took a few contemplative pulls on his pipe, and seemed to lose himself in thought. Finally, he returned to our planet and said, "Well, we may . . . we may . . . we may pick up six or something."

Thanks to Silverman, CBS had become *the* powerhouse in children's programming. So what Duke was saying left me dumb. But that's what you have an agent for.

"Duke," Sy said, "we do have other interest." That was news to me, and it was followed by a dead pause.

Whatever else you might say about Duke Ducovny, he was a nice fella and customarily a genial man. But now the pipe came slowly out of his mouth, his eyes narrowed, and his voice went low and cold.

"Are you *threatening* us?"

Sy and I started backpedaling like demented unicyclists. "Ohhhh, Jeeesus, Duke, no!"

"Not at all!"

"Don't even think about it!"

And we got the hell out of there, with poor Scooby-Doo hanging by his collar.

What I saw in my imagination at that moment was straight out of a cartoon, a corny cartoon, and something I'm sure I must have drawn for Paul Terry a hundred times. It was a money bag, with a big dollar sign on it, sprouting wings and flying away.

"Sy, what are we going to do?"

"We're going to get into the elevator."

And we ride the elevator down, get off at the lobby, walk through the lobby, go out the revolving doors, cross the street, walk into another building, get into an elevator, and take it up.

"We're going to see Mike Eisner."

Most people know Michael Eisner as the genius who became chairman and CEO of the Walt Disney Company in 1984 and, within a half dozen years, jacked up earnings from something just shy of a hundred million dollars a year to something more than *eight hundred* million. But before he joined Disney, Eisner was briefly president of Paramount and, before that, senior vice president of prime-time production and development for ABC. In 1975, he was vice president of daytime and children's programming, serving under Fred Silverman, who had just left CBS to become president of ABC. Fred had been Eisner's boss back at CBS in the 1960s, when Eisner was working in the programming department. By 1976, Sy and I had been working regularly with Mike Eisner for about three years.

Sy nudged me. "Ask him. Ask him about 'Scooby-Doo.' "

"Mike, are you interested in 'Scooby-Doo'?"

He looked at me, wide-eyed. "Why? Is it available?"

"It is."

Without saying another word, Eisner punched up a number on the phone, mumbled a few words, hung up, and turned back to us. "We'll buy two years—that's twenty-six shows—and three specials."

It was just that fast. And so "Scooby-Doo" lumbered over to ABC, sharing his first time slot with a new show we had developed called "Dynomutt."

This is the way the business worked. You always had to be hoping or wishing. Sometimes it worked. More often it didn't. But you couldn't stop trying. For instance, on another occasion, I was leaning over Mike's desk, trying to intimidate him into catching my pitch.

"Mike, you're going to love this show," I said, practically breathing in his face.

He was sitting there just as cool as can be.

I said: "This gorilla . . ." But I hardly got the word out.

"I hate gorillas," Eisner quietly snapped.

I turned to Sy.

"Sy, why did you say that? This *bear*—terrific bear—not like Yogi, but a whole new concept . . ." And I recast the show on the spot.

When Mike and Sy subsequently fell to arguing about costs and price, I, sitting on an office chair with wheels, kicked my feet out, grabbed the edge of the desk, and shot-swiveled myself around to Eisner's side.

Putting my arm around his shoulder, I announced, "I'm with him."

On another occasion, after a hard day of selling to Mike Eisner, Sy and I went to dinner, had a few drinks, and, about eleven at night, were standing in front of the Park Lane Hotel talking. A man and woman were walking toward us. Suddenly, as she passed us, the lady turned to Sy.

"Don't you know me?" she asked.

"No," said Sy.

With that, she took his lower lip between her thumb and index finger and pulled it down.

"Recognize me now?"

"Nuuuh."

"I'm your dental hygienist," she said, letting his lip snap back into place.

As she walked away, Sy turned to me.

"Thank God she wasn't my proctologist."

From roughly 1972 until he left ABC in 1976 to become president of Paramount, Michael Eisner, Sy, and I used to get together in Malibu on every available weekend to kick around ideas. I like to think it was genius time, because something—usually two or three things—generally emerged from each of these sessions.

Years later, about 1984, when Mike first went over to Disney, I phoned him and went out to his office. Mike called in Roy Disney, and we chatted. "You know, Roy, this guy and I, we used to get together in Malibu on weekends and come up with two and three ideas at a time. Joe, if you ever have an idea we can use, we'll break all the rules to work with you."

The fact is, we continued along our separate creative ways, and that was the last contact I had with Mike Eisner until 1993, when I went out to Disney World in Orlando, Florida, for a premiere of the Tom and Jerry feature film. When I got back to the studio, a giant bouquet of flowers was waiting in my office, with a card that read:

From Mickey to Scooby-Doo, Sorry I missed you. Mike Eisner.

There is no law that says a man who personally earned a hundred million dollars in his first half-dozen years on the job has to be a decent human being, but Mike Eisner is that and more. Over the years, we learned to respect one another tremendously, and, like Fred Silverman, he is one of a very small handful of executives who, demanding a 100 percent effort from you, still give you back something more each time you work with them.

Eisner is also a prime example of the high-reward, high-risk nature of our business. Hailed as the conquering hero who octupled Disney's earnings between 1984 and 1991, Mike, as I write this now, presides over the disaster that is Euro-Disney, the mammoth theme park outside Paris, which has been hemorrhaging money since it opened.

How Mike will weather this storm remains to be seen, but, unfortunately, one of the very few constants in our business is the unalterable fact that the guy who takes the accolades also takes the heat. The same thing happened to Fred Silverman, who, after putting CBS on top, did the same for ABC, then moved to NBC as president and CEO in 1978. Struggling in third place behind the other two networks, NBC was betting on the legendary Silverman touch.

DURING FRED'S TENURE AT NBC, we sold the network a slew of shows, including "The Galaxy Goof-Ups," "The Galloping Ghost," "The Buford Files," "Godzilla," "Jana of the Jungle," "The New Shmoo," "The Super Globetrotters," "Casper and the Angels," "The Thing," "Astro and the Space Mutts," and "Teen Force," and I saw a good deal of Fred.

One day in 1979, I went into the Polo Lounge at cocktail time and saw Fred Silverman sitting all by himself in booth number one. After a year at NBC, he had not reversed the network's downward spiral, and almost daily he was suffering the slings and arrows of the press and others condemning him for having failed to furnish his customary miracle.

"Hi," I said.

Fred perked up. "Hi, hi. Come on and sit down," he said. "Boy, have we got a show going now. *You* should be doing it. It's called 'Supertrain.' "

This was a drama/comedy anthology set in a gigantic two-hundred-mile-per-hour luxury train that was appointed like a great ocean-going passenger liner. It had a swimming pool, an elegant restaurant and bar, a disco, gym, steam room, and even a completely equipped medical center. At ABC, Silverman had developed the phenomenally successful "Love Boat," and he hoped "Supertrain" would be a "Love Boat" on rails. The network was banking heavily on it.

"I just went on the set—fantastic set—two fully furnished, ultra-luxurious railroad cars. You know how you kick the tires when you're buying a car? Well, I went over and kicked one of the train wheels. And, do you know what? It was iron!"

He paused. "That's when I knew we were in trouble."

Fred went on to explain: If they had bought and paid for real iron train wheels, how much money had been poured into the rest of the production?

The answer to that one turned out to be *a lot.* "Supertrain" lasted about six months, and, though long forgotten by the viewing public, it is remembered by NBC to this very day as quite possibly the most expensive failure in the history of any network.

And so it went for Fred Silverman at NBC. Yet it was also in 1979 that Fred came to us with the seed of what would prove to be the most successful cartoon series the network ever ran. Fred had been attending a network meeting in Aspen, Colorado, and had taken his young daughter Melissa with him. During a break in the meeting, he took her to a toy shop, where she was captivated by some little blue stuffed figures. Fred was quite taken with them himself. He brought some of the figures back to us. He had never seen them before, and neither had we. They were called Smurfs.

"Get the rights to these Smurfs, and you have an on-the-air commitment."

To be perfectly honest, I was hardly blown away by the characters: little blue guys, all looking alike, each wearing a kind of white diaper and sporting sort of floppy cones for headgear. But if Fred was ready to make a commitment, well, who needs more enthusiasm than that?

We investigated and found out that the Smurfs had actually been around for about twenty-five years and were the work of a Belgian illustrator named Peyo Culliford. His children's books were not well known in the States, but the toys licensed from them had just begun to show up here. We secured the rights and put the series into development.

At one point early in the development, an NBC executive named Mickey Dwyer vigorously championed the notion of making the Smurfs all different colors in order to distinguish them from one another. Fortunately, I was able to argue this down. Not that there was any particular genius behind my position. To begin with, I just didn't want to complicate production by introducing a lot of different colors, and, even more important, I was sure Peyo would object and that that would throw a monkey wrench into the whole licensing deal. However, as I look back on it, maybe I should claim to have been moved by brilliant poetic insight. A big part of the Smurfs' charm—and staying power—is that, while they all look basically the same and, indeed, are almost nondescript, they each have unique personalities that kids quickly recognize and identify with. Making them all different colors would have given them nothing more than superficial identities—"This is the red one, he's the green one, she's the pink one"—which, really, would have been no identity at all. Making them all look pretty much alike forced us to develop characters with genuinely distinctive personalities.

I pulled a real coup when I managed to get the show upped from the standard half-hour format to a full hour. I congratulated myself on this, and we forged ahead until, near the end of production on the first batch of shows, I learned that NBC's new daytime programming director, Irv Wilson, had raised a protest with Fred, telling him that the hour format was a big mistake. In response, I wrote a long letter to Fred, who finally asked me to come to a meeting in New York to argue my case in person.

Well, what, exactly, *was* my case?

I searched my soul and searched it some more, and all I could think of was that my reason for wanting to make the show an hour instead of a half-hour was that it meant twice as much business for Hanna-Barbera Productions. But I knew I couldn't present it quite that way. There was nothing left to do but get on the plane and hope that something better would occur to me.

What it came down to was me at one end of a long conference table in NBC's Rockefeller Center offices, Fred at the other end, and Irv Wilson and other execs along the sides.

"Why don't you go ahead, Joe, and tell us why we need an hour," Fred began.

"Well," I said, "look. This is a new show, right? And what is in this new show? Little blue characters." Nothing Irv could deny so far—but then, of course, I hadn't said anything yet. My mind kept spinning. "Okay. So you're a kid, right? And you happen to be flipping around the channels and you catch part of the first half-hour of the show. Now, if you've only got a half-hour show, by the time you get to it—this show with the little blue characters—you've only got a few minutes left. You watch it for a few minutes, it's over, and you forget about it. But, if you've got another half-hour to go, you stay with it, because you've got thirty more minutes to figure out what's going on. You get wrapped up in it, you hang in, and you stay with the show."

Don't think for a minute that a person can babble something like this and fail to realize that it is absolute, unadulterated double-talk.

The thing of it is, though, it worked. Irv was not happy about it, but Fred elected to keep "The Smurfs" a one-hour show, we made more money than we would have made with half-hours, and NBC—well, it saved NBC's badly faltering Saturday morning. Those little blue guys were like the cavalry riding in to the rescue, the show was a blockbuster hit for seven years, and it was eventually expanded to an incredible hour-and-a-half.

The kicker is that, whatever I said or failed to say at that NBC meeting, I think I was right about making the show an hour—and not just because it meant more cash in our pockets. In its way, "The Smurfs" was as new a direction for Hanna-Barbera as our venture into the genre of superheroes had been. The show was an excursion into fantasy. Effective fantasy requires you to create and populate an entire world, and that takes time. The great fantasy writers wrote long novels. Just think of J.R.R. Tolkien's *Lord of the Rings* and so on. Letting "The Smurfs" have an hour to do their thing gave the show enough time to create a convincing realm of fantasy.

The characters were vitally important, too. Papa Smurf has actually become a hero—as real as any living hero—to millions of children. Perhaps the only Smurf more popular than he is Smurfette. She was an afterthought, who was not part of the original concept, and key to her success was a woman named Lucille Bliss, who gave her a voice.

Lucille had been coming to the studio regularly for maybe fifteen years, auditioning for voices. Unfortunately, we were just never able to use her. Then we came up with the character of Smurfette, Lucille showed up for an audition, and she was absolutely perfect for the part. You could not have dreamed up the voice any better.

If Smurfette was a new character for us, she was also something new for the Smurfs themselves, who had never encountered a female Smurf before. When she appears among them, one of her very first lines is: "Do you like what you see?" It was a line Lucille delivered with a husky coyness and allure that worked beautifully, and it was from the moment of her introduction that the show really took off.

UNFORTUNATELY, all of this was too late for Fred Silverman. As of June 30, 1981, he was out of a job at NBC after three years of ceaseless battle, during which you'd read an attack on Fred in the trades and the popular press almost every other day.

Sometime before the end came, Sy and I were sitting in a Chinese restaurant in New York, which was a restaurant we used to go to with Fred.

Sy said, "Let's call him. See if he's still in."

This was nine o'clock at night, but we called, and, by God, he *was* in.

"Come on up, come on up!" Fred said, clearly eager for the company.

Sy and I walked over to Rockefeller Center and the RCA Building, which was silent, dim, and completely deserted. The only elevator running was the service elevator, its walls hung with quilted padding. We got off at Fred's floor, went into his office, and saw him at his desk, brooding, his fingers wrapped around a Tanqueray martini. Before him, on his desk, a copy of *Weekly Variety* was spread out.

"What do you know?" he said, looking up at us. "They've finally said something nice about me."

"No kidding?" I said.

"Yeah. Here. Go ahead, read it."

"You mean out loud?"

"Yeah. Go ahead."

I don't remember the article, but it did go on across two or three pages, and, while it certainly wasn't positively laudatory, neither was it damning. For Fred, at the time, this was praise enough. I continued to read it, aloud, acting it out with as much enthusiasm as I could summon up.

After I had finished, Fred said to Sy and me, "Stick around a few more minutes. I want to play a piece of tape."

The tape he ran showed a kid—he looked like a well-groomed college freshman—and Fred explained that this was his new vice president of programs making his maiden speech to the NBC affiliates.

I watched and listened, and I thought to myself, God almighty, this kid is brilliant. He was Brandon Tartikoff, who not only proved himself a great executive, but became a personal ally and friend. Year after year, he supported me every time I went up to NBC to argue for keeping "The Smurfs" going for another season. With his help, the show remained a hit year after year.

Tartikoff, who became president (and subsequently chairman) of NBC after Silverman's ouster, succeeded where his mentor had failed, taking the network from the number three to the number one position with such shows as "Cheers," "The Cosby Show," "Hill Street Blues," "The Golden Girls," "Miami Vice," and "L.A. Law." He then went on to head up Paramount. That Tartikoff pulled off the NBC miracle that had eluded Silverman is, if anything, a tribute to Fred, part of whose genius was a knack for recognizing and promoting genius in others.

FRED SILVERMAN was not the only victim of his demise at NBC. Inspired, in part, by the hilarious and highly successful "Rowan and Martin's Laugh-In," which was a big hit for NBC between 1968 and 1973, I developed an animated series I called "The Joke Book." It was unlike anything that had ever been done with a cartoon before. The feeling I was looking for was the animated equivalent of stand-up comedy, and the show was a series of unrelated gags or gag segments, ranging in length from ten seconds to a minute and a half or so, one right after the other, fast-paced, and each in a different style of art. They were a blend of visual puns, absurd or surreal situations, and slapstick as well as more traditionally verbal jokes.

When I pitched it to him, Silverman got very excited, and he subsequently called to tell me that "The Joke Book" was the "talk of the RCA Building." He was so eager to get it on the air that, almost immediately after my having pitched it in November, he asked for an April delivery and slotted the show in his prime-time schedule, doubtless hoping that it would recapture some of the magic of "Laugh In" and serve as the CPR his network desperately needed.

We delivered seven half-hours—the pilot plus six more shows—in April 1979, but by that time Silverman was already so thoroughly under siege that he could pay virtually no attention to launching the series. An ambitious, thorough, and carefully planned PR and ad campaign is critical to the success of something as innovative and different as the "Joke Book." Unfortunately, that just didn't happen. There was no PR, no advertising, no preparation for the show, which was simply dumped unceremoniously into its slot, where it was misunderstood and generally ignored. Those first seven half-hours were our last.

Harry Love, who worked closely with me on "The Joke Book," commiserated on its demise, saying that the concept was ahead of its time. True enough. But a good publicity and ad campaign educates and informs the public, allowing them to catch up with the concept. When a giant like Fred Silverman stumbles, a lot of people and projects fall.

Of course, Fred Silverman ultimately—and in remarkably short order—gave the lie to all those who, full of praise during the CBS and ABC years, dumped on him after the NBC fiasco. In 1982, he set up an independent production company and launched such hits as the "Perry Mason" specials, "Matlock," "In the Heat of the Night," and others.

IN THE LATE 1960S, Hanna-Barbera deviated from our customary routine of creating animated series to produce a number of specials, most notably the piece we did with Gene Kelly, "Jack and the Beanstalk," and an adaptation of "Alice in Wonderland." But it was in the 1970s that the networks really became interested in programming specials in an effort to inject some variety into the regular schedule of series, and we produced our fair share of specials during this period. Usually, we adopted children's stories, which had proven their value as enduring classics. This was, in part, because Bill and I liked the stories, but, since specials called for elaborate production, they were far more expensive to produce, foot for foot, than an ongoing series, and that meant we and our clients had to get the maximum mileage out of them.

We animated such perennials as "Oliver Twist and the Artful Dodger" in 1972, "The Count of Monte Cristo" and "Twenty Thousand Leagues Under the Sea" in 1973, "Last of the Mohicans" and "Davy Crockett on the Mississippi" in 1975, "Five Weeks in a Balloon" in 1977, "Black Beauty" in 1978, and "Gulliver's Travels" in 1979. Seasonal occasions also helped to ensure a substantial audience for specials, and typical of these were "The Thanksgiving That Almost Wasn't" and "A Christmas Story," both first aired in 1971. Sometimes, we created animated specials based on popular live-action series, including "Gidget Makes the Wrong Connection" in 1972 and "Lost in Space" the next year.

We also starred various of our own regular series characters in specials from time to time, especially Yogi Bear and the Flintstones. While we did a number of these in the 1970s, the most ambitious projects got under way in the 1980s, when Kevin O'Sullivan, of the distribution giant World Vision, called to ask if we could do ten two-hour TV specials featuring our characters. My favorite of these was done around 1987 or 1988 and started with an idea Harry Love gave me. Yogi Bear is the driver of a tour bus carrying a load of our best-known characters—Boo-Boo, Quick Draw McGraw, Huckleberry Hound, Snagglepuss, Scooby-Doo, and so on—to see the "Spruce Goose," the mammoth wooden-bodied seaplane Howard Hughes designed and built during World War II and which is now housed at Long Beach, California, where it is a major tourist attraction. You need to know two things about the Spruce Goose: First, it is the biggest airplane ever built, which is saying a lot, as anyone knows who has ever flown on a 747 or watched on TV as the air force landed its Lockheed Galaxy cargo planes during Operation Desert Storm. Second, the Spruce Goose flew only once, and that for only a short distance and a few feet above the water, piloted by Howard Hughes himself. After that, the plane was parked and allowed to disintegrate over the years until an entrepreneur bought it, refurbished it, and opened it to the public—as a strictly earthfast attraction.

Yogi takes his cartoon tour group up into the Spruce Goose, where the attendant warns him that it's late and they have only a few minutes to look around before closing time. Yogi is also cautioned not to touch anything in the plane, but, of course, he heads straight for the controls, tries out a few levers, presses a few buttons, and, suddenly, all eight prop motors kick over and rev. In a panic, Yogi and the other characters start frantically turning other knobs and pulling other levers, which not only fails to stop the motors, but starts the plane rolling forward. The immense hangar doors slide open, and the plane, picking up speed, takes off—takes off on a series of adventures, including the rescue of a whale trapped by Arctic ice, the rescue of a flock of stranded penguins, who walk across the plane's enormous wings from a drifting ice floe to the safety of shore, and many more such episodes. But more important is the fact that Yogi Bear, a mere cartoon character, becomes the second pilot in history to fly the legendary Spruce Goose. The cost—besides production, of course—was a $10,000 licensing fee paid to the owner of the airplane for the right to use its name and likeness.

I'm happy to say that this special and the other nine World Vision ordered were very successful and were the animated stars of the NATPE convention, where production companies exhibit their wares to syndicators and independent television stations.

Of all the television specials in which I was involved, a handful stand out as personal high points for me. "The Last of the Curlews" appeared in the fall of 1972 as an ABC After School Special. It was a moving story, based on a book by Fred Bodsworth, with a strong environmental message told in a way that kids could appreciate. The narrative focused on a single Eskimo curlew, a migratory bird who is all but the last of a species that once numbered some 35 million, before hunters annihilated the birds, often clubbing them to death en masse as they slept on the ground. The particular curlew in our story is followed as he makes an epic 9,000-mile seasonal flight from wintry Alaska to the Orinoco swamplands of South America, where he searches for a mate. At the end of his journey, the curlew does, in fact, find his mate, who, however, is soon killed by a farmer, and the bird, now truly the last of his kind, is left to return to the North alone. The picture ends with the narrator intoning, "And so they were two, now there is one, soon there will be none."

A bare plot summary hardly does justice to the cartoon, which, beautifully scored by Hoyt Curtin, is really more lyrical and evocative than narrative, full of images of flight, and of nature in its loveliness and its violence. The special was a labor of love and received an Emmy as Outstanding Achievement in Children's Programming.

Two years later, I directed an adaptation of one of my favorite plays, Edmund Rostand's *Cyrano de Bergerac*. At the time we were getting the special into production, a company was touring the play, with Richard

Chamberlain in the title role. My idea was to use the cast voices in the one-hour adaptation, which we would call, simply, "Cyrano," but, much as I admired Chamberlain, the only Cyrano I could imagine was José Ferrer, who had created the role on Broadway and who subsequently starred in a great film version. I called Ferrer—he was in London at the time—and, to my delighted surprise, he agreed to voice an animated Cyrano.

It was my project, and I was slated to direct it, but, I thought to myself, How can I presume to direct José Ferrer, especially in the role he *owns*?

On the first day of recording, I asked him: "José—uh—Mr. Ferrer, would you like to direct it?"

"Oh, no, no, no. You do it."

It was an utterly gracious, totally professional response. Of course, as I might have guessed, with that company and that star, very little in the way of "direction" was needed from me. Mainly, I just told them when to start and when to stop. They did the rest.

I was thrilled with the finished hour, which was shown on ABC in 1974 and garnered an Emmy nomination, and my dream was to make "Cyrano" the first in a series of highly produced yearly specials based on such classics as Sir Walter Scott's *Ivanhoe* and Mark Twain's *The Prince and the Pauper*. ABC and Hanna-Barbera could have amassed a most impressive and solidly perennial library, but, disappointingly, the network never ordered any more.

Another disappointment was the *Rock Odyssey*, which, I'm sure, none of my readers have heard of, since it has yet to see the light of day. My idea was to do the rock equivalent of Disney's classically oriented *Fantasia*, using the best rock music from the 1950s, 1960s, the 1970s, and the opening of the 1980s—the picture was conceived at the beginning of the 1980s. I asked the advice of my good friend Dick Clark to consult on the selection of the songs, we lined up the music and some terrific stars, and Sy Fisher, flying back to New York from a visit with us, lost no time in pitching the show to a fellow passenger, who happened to be an ABC executive. The network bought the idea.

This, obviously, was the beginning of a success story, and we got the go-ahead to start production. That's when things began to fall apart. The story line was the subject of continual and totally fruitless argument, and our director took the concept further and further away from my concept of the *Fantasia* model, which was simply one segment, one animated mood piece, following another, each set to different music. Instead, it changed to a single narrative thread based on the odyssey of a mysterious woman, who springs from the earth and embarks on a search for her lost love. She travels through the fifties, sixties, seventies, and early eighties.

It actually sounds better than it worked out, despite great music and some quite wonderful segments. The show was under-budgeted at two million dollars for a two-hour movie, and it included grisly, graphic animation relating to the Vietnam War, which some in the network doubtless found objectionable. *Rock Odyssey* was completed and delivered to ABC, which, to this day, more than ten years later, has yet to show it.

Among our television specials, none is closer to me than "The Gathering," which was first shown in 1977 on ABC and has been rebroadcast regularly ever since. It is not a cartoon, but a full-scale, live-action, made-for-television movie, and I want to say more about it, but, first, I have a confession to make: The truth is, I would like to have done many more live-action features, whether for television or for the big screen.

As it is, our studio did produce more than a dozen live-action movies, mostly for television. One of the strangest—but, to me, most thoroughly enjoyable—was a picture we did starring Ace Frehley, Gene Simmons, Paul Stanley, and Peter Criss, better known collectively as the rock group KISS. This was the wildly costumed Heavy Metal group popular with younger rock audiences during the late seventies. They were real showmen, comically Satanic in their darkly grotesque make-up, and they somehow managed to balance themselves precariously on the tallest platform boots in the history of footwear.

The plot of *KISS Meets the Phantom of the Park*, which was aired on

ABC in 1978, pits the group, which is the star attraction at an amusement park, against a mad scientist who lives under the park. This fellow hates KISS and their music and therefore makes robot clones, turning them loose on the unsuspecting park visitors. We shot the action on location at Magic Mountain, a vast amusement park about thirty miles from our Hollywood studio. KISS brought in all of its special-effects lighting and sound paraphernalia—a cool million dollars' worth of equipment—and we invited thirty thousand "extras" to come to the park for free. Logistically, it was the most complex production Hanna-Barbera had ever undertaken.

A short time after the picture aired, I was having lunch at the Sunset Marquis in Westwood, and I was sitting at the table, pitching an idea to Phyllis George. I was telling her about shooting the picture, and how great it was working with KISS, who, of course, were the bane of parents everywhere and who had assiduously cultivated a reputation as bad boys at best and Satanic freaks at worst. Granted, they never permitted you to see them out of their make-up, but they were, in fact, professionals and highly considerate professionals at that.

I was carrying on in this vein when two gentlemen sitting at the table next to ours got up to leave. One of them stopped at the table and introduced himself as Gene Simmons. "Excuse me, I heard you talking, and I just wanted to thank you for what you said."

As the pair walked out, I said to Phyllis George, "Jeez, suppose I had been negative about the whole thing. I'd have ended up with a bowl of soup on my head—or a lump."

MY LIMITED EXPERIENCE with live action encouraged me to do more, and I contacted a good friend of mine, Samuel Z. Arkoff, who was co-founder and chairman of American International Pictures (AIP). This was a highly successful studio, which, for the thirty years of its existence, had never lost a dime—a lot more than most studios can say. I pitched him a number of ideas, he sparked at all of them, and he proposed a nine-picture deal in which his studio and ours would split financing and profits fifty-fifty. I came back to our studio, bubbling with enthusiasm. Here was a chance to get into the live-action field with a pro who had a proven track record.

Now, AIP had reputation for producing low-budget films, which many would label "exploitive" (*Reform School Girl*, *Terror from the Year 5000*, *The Premature Burial*, *How to Stuff a Wild Bikini*, to name just a few), and that was quite enough to turn off a lot of folks at Hanna-Barbera, but the real problem was that most of my colleagues, Bill Hanna included, just did not want our studio to be in the live-action business.

We're a cartoon *studio*, they all said, and they couldn't understand why in the world I wanted to go into live action.

What's wrong with cartoons? they asked.

The answer was—and is—*nothing*. There's *nothing* wrong with cartoons. I love doing cartoons. But why should that mean I can't do live action, too—or, for that matter, write a play and get it produced on Broadway?

Nobody, including Taft, our parent company, came out and told me that I *couldn't* do live action. They were polite and assured me that the deal was in the works. But with each frustrating exchange between lawyers, exchanges that produced absolutely nothing, the handwriting on the wall became increasingly legible. This deal was not going to happen.

Nevertheless, during this period of calculated foot-dragging, I did manage to get clearance for one theatrical release in association with AIP. It was called *C.H.O.M.P.S.* The film was developed from a story I wrote about a boy (played by Wesley Eure) who invents a computerized robot watchdog called C.H.O.M.P.S.—Canine HOMe Protection System—which he tries to sell to Norton Security Systems, a company owned by the father of his girlfriend (Valerie Bertinelli). A rival inventor (Jim Backus) tries to sabotage him, but the young inventor ultimately triumphs.

My original idea was to make the dog a robotic Doberman pinscher with super-canine powers. It could, for example, crash through a concrete wall or outrun a getaway car and was totally impervious to bullets. Thus the concept drew on a number of themes that were particularly hot in the late 1970s, including an obsession with home security and an interest in superheroes and in robots and robotic toys.

I had a three-dimensional model of the robot Doberman built, showed it, and everybody was sold on the idea. We started production, which began with a series of conferences. After half a century, I've finally learned that the minute you have a conference consisting of more than two people, you're in big trouble. And in our business what you always have is a *tableful* of people, each of whom has ideas. In this instance, Louis Arkoff, Sam's son, came in and declared that he didn't see how anybody would go for a picture with a Doberman in it. What we needed, he said, was a Benji type of lovable cute dog.

My mistake was that I compromised and agreed to this. This meant that most of the supercanine appeal of the original concept would have to be scrapped. If I had thought harder about it, I would have realized that turning our Doberman into a Benji clone named Rascal didn't just compromise the image of a superdog, it defeated the very idea of a *guard* dog. Who would invent a robot guard dog that you wanted to cuddle with instead of run away from? Nevertheless, we made the picture, which did okay and is still available on videocasettes, but it never made the splash it should have, and I could not build a case among my colleagues to do any more.

IN CONTRAST TO THIS VENTURE with AIP, "The Gathering," which was made for television, drew universal critical acclaim, earning an Emmy as Best Drama Special of 1977, and receiving recognition from the Christophers, an ecumenical mass media organization, as a contribution to the portrayal of "the highest values of the human spirit." The American Council for Better Broadcasts gave our sponsor, Eastman Kodak, a special award as well.

The project began when James Poe, a highly respected writer entirely new to television at the time, came to talk to me about an idea for a Christmas special. He walked into my office, looked around with a distinct air of suspicion, and when we began to talk, he was aloof, as if he felt that he would be speaking to somebody obviously too stupid to appreciate his idea. He was far too gentle and decent a man to put on such an air deliberately, but I got the message nonetheless.

In fact, as it turned out, he couldn't have come to anyone *more* appreciative of and receptive to his idea. "The Gathering" is a story about a father who deserted his family and, four years later, learning that he is terminally ill with cancer, contacts his estranged wife, who helps him gather the family, including their spouses and children, for a final Christmas together. It is a tense, painful, and emotionally charged reunion, but in the course of this "gathering," the family members come to terms with the father, with one another, with themselves, and with the past.

What made—and makes—the show so good is that the themes and emotions are universal, yet, of course, for me they struck a chord particularly bittersweet. My father left us. I could identify very directly with that. But the father of our story seeks reunion and reconciliation, whereas my old man simply made himself, at least as far as any of his family was concerned, disappear.

I did not speak to James Poe about that. Rather, I told him how I had celebrated Christmas with my own children, year after year, rushing to put up the tree and decorations the night before, so that it would all appear as if by special Christmas magic, telling him how I used to climb a ladder outside the house and shake sleigh bells under my children's windows, and telling him how the Christmas ornaments were wrapped in newspaper, the same newspaper, year after year, so that you read and reread the faded news of ten, fifteen, twenty, thirty years before. I told him about the Lionel train I'd bought, secondhand, when I was maybe sixteen, and how I'd set that up, year after year, running it on a small loop of track under the tree, and how, each year, the darn thing ran just like new.

That's when Jim Poe warmed, saying to me that Christmas was very much like that for him and his family, and that's when we both knew we were going to have a deal. The script, when it came in, was as perfect as any script I have ever read. There weren't half a dozen lines to change.

Sy Fisher and I went to New York, where we pitched the special to Ed Vane, a delightful executive in charge of special projects at ABC. Ed and I shared the sacred bond of a high regard for the Rob Roy.

At the meeting, Sy nudged me. "Tell him about James Poe."

I told Ed that James Poe was our writer, and a look came over his face as he suddenly snapped to attention. "James Poe? You got him?"

"Yeah," I said, failing fully to comprehend the importance of this until, within about two seconds, I found that I had sold the show to ABC.

Everyone who worked on "The Gathering" came to believe in the material passionately. My executive producer, Deke Heyward, assembled an extraordinary cast, which included Edward Asner, Maureen Stapleton, Lawrence Pressman, Stephanie Zimbalist, Bruce Davison, Veronica Hamel, Gregory Harrison, John Randolph, and Gail Strickland. Heyward also brought on board a fine producer, Harry Sherman. Randal Kleiser, a very young man at the time, made a spectacular directorial debut with the picture, much of it shot on location in an idyllic upstate New York town, which obliged us by keeping its Christmas decorations up for the two or three months of shooting there.

As if the experience of making "The Gathering" weren't reward enough, to walk up on stage at the Emmy Awards ceremony and accept an award in the most prestigious category, beating out such giants as Paramount, Universal, and Fox, was the crowning thrill.

It would be wonderful if all creative experiences were like this one, but what I've been doing all these years is as much a business—a very hard and unforgiving business—as it is a creative endeavor. In the crush and crunch of cash, it is easy to forget the creative, magic, joyous side altogether. Doing "The Gathering" helped balance my perspective. It was good for me, it was good for everyone who worked on it, and I like to believe that it has been good for all who have watched it.

Chapter Ten

TAKE AND GIVE

WHEN I WAS A YOUNG MAN shivering in winter-bound, Depression-gripped Brooklyn, I dreamed, as many others dreamed, of picking up and moving to the very source of heat and sunlight and skies of boundless blue: California, golden California. And, as I've already said, when I at last trekked out to Los Angeles, I arrived in the worst part of what was a gray, rundown city that was gripped by the Depression no less brutally than Brooklyn or anywhere else. I almost turned around and went back home to the East, but I stayed, worked like hell, found a terrific business partner, had some incredible good luck, and earned, bought, and paid for my place in the sun—several places, in fact.

But in California, things have a way of getting *too* hot. I was living in Bel Air when a terrible wildfire burned thirty or forty houses around mine. In those days, few homes had stone or slate roofs. Mine did, so we were saved from annihilation, but I remember vividly how the pillows on our veranda *exploded*, as did the convertible top of my car, the embers of which landed hundreds of feet away, some of them on the roof of Walter (Woody Woodpecker) Lantz's house, which burned to the ground.

I've often cursed my insomnia, angry that this or that business or creative problem keeps me awake some nights until two or three in the morning. I was lying awake on just such a night, my family sleeping soundly, when I heard a terrific roar, went to the window, and saw the trees and brush aflame around the house. A tanker truck had turned too sharply, jackknifed, and thirty thousand gallons of gasoline ignited.

I woke the household, got everybody out, and then, as my house began to burn, went back in to get a few personal items, photographs, and the like. Incredibly, seated at my piano was a stranger—a stranger seated at my piano and playing my piano as the smoke thickened in the room.

"What in hell are you doing here?"

"Uh, oh. I was just trying this out."

"Get out! Get out of here!"

He was a perfect Southern California looter: aggressive enough to arrive even before the house had really started to burn, yet laid back enough to enjoy even what he couldn't possibly take with him. Fortunately, quick action by a fire department helicopter, which dumped flame retardant on my roof, saved the house.

Then there was fire number three, a few years after that. This time I was at the studio when I got a call that my house was on fire. I rushed home and arrived to find the place surrounded by police and rubberneckers. We had hired some redecorators to strip the old paint off the walls. Fumes from the stripping agent accumulated, and when one of the men switched on the air conditioner, the spark ignited a fireball, which set one of the workers on fire. He saved himself by jumping into another fixture of Southern California life, the swimming pool.

Fire number four began some time after a dinner party we hosted. It was about eleven o'clock, our guests had left, I had changed into my pajamas, and I was shutting down for the night, turning out the lights, when I saw the shrubbery aglow and the surrounding trees just starting to flame. Our floodlights, it seems, had ignited an accumulation of dead leaves. By this stage in my California sojourn, I had learned to be prepared. After calling the fire department, I got out the pump we had purchased for just such an emergency. It was a gas-powered motorized thing that drew water from the swimming pool and sprayed it out at high volume through a hose. After quickly setting the machine up, I pulled on the starter cord—the kind you use with a lawn mower or an old-fashioned outboard motor—and nothing happened. I pulled again. Nothing.

The fire was spreading. I was sweating, pulling again, sweating, working furiously, never giving up, but thinking: *Yes, yes, this is when the heart attack comes.* Just as my panic attained critical mass, the motor at last kicked over, and a stream of water gushed. By the time the firemen arrived, I had the situation under control. A strapping young firefighter, arrayed in helmet, boots, and heavy black slicker, came over to me, arrayed in soaking wet pajamas, and patted me on the head.

"Good work, kid"—pat, pat—"good work."

I felt like a wet cocker spaniel, but was universally hailed as a hero. Only later did it occur to me—and I reveal this for the first time here—that I could have put an end to the whole thing much sooner simply by turning on our lawn sprinkler system.

THEN THERE ARE THE EARTHQUAKES. The first one I remember woke me up at 6:10 in the morning (I looked at the clock) with the house shaking, and, out the window, I saw a fifteen-foot wave—in our *pool*. It was unbelievable, but I didn't let it stop me from keeping a hard-to-get 8 A.M. appointment with my dentist. Of course, as I was sitting in the chair, my dentist delicately probing and drilling and scraping, all he could talk about were the dreaded and unpredictable aftershocks, and how the one place you didn't want to be during an aftershock was in a high-rise—much like the one we were in at that very moment.

The next earthquake I experienced hit when Sheila and I were spending the weekend in our Palm Springs house. This one shook the house like a terrier ragging its prey. We didn't find any damage, and although this was my fourth substantial earthquake, it left me more than usually terrified.

Sheila was far more fatalistic. "If the house didn't come down this time, I'll never be afraid of earthquakes again!" she swore, whereupon a fierce aftershock rolled in, terrifying the both of us.

Then came the wee hours of Monday morning, January 17, 1994. Earthquakes do not observe polite and reasonable schedules.

In the pre-dawn hours, there were, authorities later said, actually *two* earthquakes, which struck within four seconds of each other, one that pushed up and another that thrust sideways. All I know is that I woke to total blackness—not just our house, but the whole city, which, since we are perched on a hill in Sherman Oaks, is usually seen spread out below us like a carpet of lights.

Now it was like being blind. But there was also the violence, not just of motion and thrust, but of a room gone insane as curios, keepsakes, lamps, mirrors, books didn't fall but *flew* from their places as if propelled by demons. What woke Sheila up was not the quake itself, but a bedside lamp hitting her in the head, followed by a framed picture that sprang at her from the wall.

When it was over, I couldn't see, and when I tried to get up and walk, I found that everything was smashed and jagged under my bare feet. I groped for shoes and a pair of jogging pants and, thank God, I finally found a flashlight. I struggled over knifelike shards of debris and went to my wife's door. I had heard nothing from that room.

I began banging on the door. I could not open it. The house had twisted—corkscrewed—and nothing that used to move moved anymore. It was as if the door had been flash-welded shut.

Then, at last, Sheila banged in response, and the two of us started shouting instructions at one another. Finally, I told her just to stay where she was. What you have to imagine is that she was in a room that was pitch black—no light whatsoever—and she was feeling her way, cutting her feet on smashed crockery and glass, all invisible to her.

"I'm going to try to get you from outside," I shouted through the unyielding door. With that, I found my way through the dark to a window, fought with some drapes, and was able to pry open a small sliding patio door that went out to a little balcony in the back. Once outside, I had to straddle the balcony's iron railing and walk along a Spanish tile roof for about fifty yards to Sheila's windows.

With the house, neighborhood, and city blacked out, I could see nothing, but I was very much aware of the roof tiles breaking beneath my feet as I inched across the roof. I also found myself stumbling over bricks that had shaken loose from the chimney. (There is a good reason to build nothing of brick in earthquake country. Later, after sunup, when I was able to survey the devastation of our hillside neighborhood, I saw house after house that *seemed* almost perfectly normal—except for the presence of an exploded brick chimney on the front lawn.)

As I groped from window to window, I was unable to slide any of them open, and, disoriented, I really had no idea of where Sheila was. The last narrow window I came to had a screen over it, and I found Sheila. She was able to push the window open, but the screen over it was bolted in place. I got my fingers into a corner of the screen and was trying to rip it open while Sheila kicked at it.

It was frantic time: Two terrified people clawing and kicking at a piece of metal, feeling all alone, cut off from help and from light itself. But the thing is, we were not alone. Tens of thousands of people found themselves—in less than a roaring, rumbling minute—thrust into similar or far worse predicaments.

When the screen finally yielded, I got Sheila to put her leg over the windowsill while I hung on to her—as well as to the precious flashlight—and pulled her up onto the roof with me. Then we had to make our way back to the place where we could ease down onto the balcony and reenter the house. If we fell off, we had a concrete patio underneath us and a half-filled swimming pool, much of the water having instantly drained through a fissure that shot through the bottom of the pool. Once inside the house, we groped our way through the wreckage and descended the stairs. We learned later that we were very fortunate we hadn't had a fire or explosion, since gas and water pipes had ruptured all over the neighborhood and throughout the city.

With the dawn, what you saw was war-torn Bosnia, not on TV now, but all around you and with you, live and in-person. Looking at it all, you knew in your head that there was no way to repair the damage, but in your heart, you said, *maybe*. We had twenty-five years invested in the Sherman Oaks house—furnishings, bronzes, the wonderful English china and glassware Sheila had long and lovingly collected.

It was, really, an unassuming house, a home rather than the Hollywood extravaganza you might expect from the "Sultan of Saturday Morning" (as *60 Minutes* once called me). Nevertheless, many guests over the years have been generous enough to tell us it was a showplace, and Sheila and I were very proud of it and wonderfully comfortable in it. But the architect and structural engineer agreed: It had to be torn down.

So we'll tear it down.

And we'll start again. Just like many others.

FIRE, EARTHQUAKE, FLOOD, RIOT. One of the wags at the studio dubbed these the four seasons of Southern California. As I write this chapter, I'm still reeling from the Mother of All Earthquakes. But I'm alive, Sheila is alive, and my children are unhurt. The loss of things, precious things, brings plenty of heartache, I can tell you, but

I've been a lot luckier than many others in coming through our region's smorgasbord of disasters, natural and otherwise. Over the years, I've even fought back, in a very modest way, by creating a special program for the city of Los Angeles. It started with a city councilman, Hal Bernson, and his assistant, Margaree Klein, who wanted to use one of our characters in an earthquake preparedness program. We decided on Yogi as a spokesman—or spokesbear—and developed an instructional comic book and video material to be used as part of a mobile program carried in a huge, decorated van called Yogi's Quakey Shakey Van. Inside the van were desks arranged as in a classroom, and the kids would sit at these desks and watch a three- or four-minute animated piece showing what to do in case of an earthquake. Then the van operator would throw a switch, activating a hydraulic system that would send the van pitching and rocking like an earthquake. The vehicle was capable of simulating various degrees of intensity on the Richter scale, and kids would line up for blocks to get their turn in the van.

NOW, I COULD DO JUST AS WELL without having to suffer any of the thousand natural shocks that flesh is heir to, but these things do teach you something about who and what you are. My point is that making cartoons is as real a business as stamping steel into automobiles, or cobbling shoes together, or selling groceries. The money you make from the creation of fantasy is just as real as the money you make from doing any of these other things. Your children grow up like other children. They—and you—suffer the same pressures and stresses as most other high-stakes, time-eating careers generate. And life—regardless of who you think you are or what you believe you've achieved—touches, caresses, and smacks you around, just as it does everyone else.

I was getting off a plane in New York one day in 1974 and found a message waiting for me at the gate. My Uncle Jim had been trying to reach me. He wanted me to hurry out to the house in Brooklyn because my mother, who lived alone at the time, had collapsed, and he had found her on the floor. She was a small woman, but, unconscious, had become what they call a dead weight, and he couldn't get her onto the bed. I helped him lift her, and we called an ambulance, which took her to Brooklyn's Swedish Hospital, where my Uncle Michael was on staff. My mother died three days later.

My uncles and I went through her house. I wasn't interested in taking anything for myself until I saw the old mahogany cabinet and its precious contents, the twenty-one volumes of *The Book of Knowledge*. That piece of furniture and those books were, perhaps, the start of my creative life, and they certainly held many dear memories of my mother.

I opened the cabinet, pulled out a book, and flipped through the pages.

A twenty-dollar bill fell out.

I flipped through some more pages. Tens, twenties, and fifties seesawed to the floor like so many autumn leaves. I flipped through more of the books, and there was money in every single one of them.

Over the years, I had sent my mother as much as I could. In later years, it was a check a week, which my uncle would cash for her. Not trusting banks, she didn't have an account herself, and nobody knew what this very frugal woman did with the money I sent her.

Now we knew.

There were thousands of dollars in these books, the books she had bought for me at $1.49 a volume when I was eight years old. She had given me these books, shared their treasures with me, and now she was even giving back to me what I had shared with her.

MY MOTHER RAISED ME as a Catholic, but I cannot say I have ever been a very religious person, at least not in any traditional sense. Yet, when I think about it, I realize that my business has a lot to do with faith and belief. Faith and belief are essential to making cartoons, key to giving substance to fantasy and imagination, to creating entertainment for children. Not that I mean to trivialize religious faith by saying this. After all, even Christ advised his followers to make themselves "as children," and spoke of a little child leading the faithful.

Certainly, it was a childlike thrill of wonder I felt when I met Pope John Paul II during Easter week of 1989. I'm sure there are millions of people who dream of meeting the pope. I wasn't one of them. I mean, the thought never entered my imagination. Yet, when it happened, it was electric.

Bill and I were negotiating with RAI, an Italian television company, which was interested in doing a cartoon series with us. What we came up with was something called "Don Coyote and Sancho Panda," which pleased RAI so much that they invited us to Rome to discuss doing an hour special based on our characters. It was decided that we would produce it in Bologna, at the ultra-modern studio facilities of the University of Bologna, which, I understand, is the oldest university in the world. The university is staffed largely by Jesuits, who proved to be very gracious hosts and, in the course of working with us, asked if we would like to meet the pope.

I may not be quite the good Catholic my mother had hoped I would be, but I was damn excited, and, besides, what else do you say when somebody asks if you want to meet the pope? "No, I think I'll just take a pass on that one"?

What you do is jump up and down, and what you say is *yes!*

We were staying at the Excelsior Hotel on the Via Veneto in Rome, and on the day appointed for our papal "audience," a young Jesuit strode through the lobby, his hand extended toward Bill and me. He was the kind of good-looking, sharp, well-groomed type I had encountered in any number of high-powered ad agencies—except, of course, for his brown vestments and scarlet sash.

He drove us to St. Peter's, and we were ushered into the awe-inspiring basilica. Pope John Paul II addressed an Easter week crowd of 22,000, greeting and blessing them in twenty-two languages. He finished his address, walked up the aisles, blessing the faithful, who extended hopeful hands toward him. Then he returned to the podium and sat back down.

"Well," I said to Bill, figuring that there was no way we were going to meet the pope, "let's go."

At that point, one of the Jesuits motioned for me to wait, and the pope stepped down from the podium, descended some stairs, and headed down the aisle, straight for me. *Whoa*, I thought to myself.

He extended his hand, and we shook hands. I had brought a rosary with me for him to bless, and then we chatted about what he pronounced as "Holy-wood, California."

It was, as I said, electricity time. I looked into these vivid blue eyes, almost icy in their blueness, but set in a face of intense gentleness. And all around us were people reaching out, wanting to touch him. I don't care who you are or what your religious beliefs are, you would have felt it, had you been there: the adoring, reverential vibrations emanating from 22,000 people. The air hummed with them.

When I got back to L.A., I sent my brother Ted a copy of a photo showing me shaking hands with Pope John Paul II. "Hope some of this rubs off on you," I wrote on the picture.

He phoned me. "Can you believe it?" he said, thoroughly awed. "When you were six years old in Brooklyn, could you have imagined that you'd be in Rome holding the pope's hand? About 750 million Catholics would *kill* to have been in your place."

SO WHILE I HAVE NEVER BEEN a regular churchgoer, I'm anything but immune to the power, the wonder, and the majesty of the religious experience. I believe that people who know me understand this, and, back in 1969, my closest friends and colleagues were not entirely surprised when, that year, I first pitched the idea of doing a series of cartoons based on Bible stories.

They weren't *surprised*. But they didn't much like it.

I tried to point out that the Bible was an incredible source of action-adventure stories. Brother kills brother, a guy gets thrown into a lions' den, an entire cavalry force is drowned in the Red Sea. What more can you ask for? Certainly, Cecil B. DeMille knew and fully exploited the commercial potential of the Bible. I mean, what I was pitching was hardly a new idea.

I was turned down flat.

In contrast to what schoolbooks and Horatio Alger tales teach us, in the cartoon business, when at first you don't succeed, you quit. It almost never pays to re-pitch a project that failed to go over the first time. If you're rejected, you don't come back with the same thing. You bring 'em something else.

But not this time. Not for me. I kept pitching the Bible project to anyone who would listen. I'd pitch the usual gorilla cartoon show or cat-and-mouse show or superhero show, then I'd end with a pitch for the Bible—at which point, I'd be shown the door. Bud Grant, in charge of new development at NBC, reacted faster than most other executives. For him, my launching into the Bible pitch was his signal to end the meeting.

Despite the rejection, and in violation of all the rules, I came back year after year. On one occasion, we had a meeting with the Mattel toy company people. We were pitching the usual cartoon fodder, when the man who was president of the company at the time turned to me and said, "You know what I'd really like to do? I'd really like to do the Bible."

I almost flew ten feet up in the air. Telling him not to move, I raced into my office and gathered up all the research and artwork I had been presenting year after year. I showed it to him, and he loved it.

Before anything got going, however, he and Mattel went their separate ways. But soon after this, Mattel hired Joe Taritero to start up a TV unit for the company. He, too, was interested in doing something with the Bible series. Then, after four or five months, Mattel pulled out of the television business altogether, without ever having really gotten into it in the first place.

As it turned out, I pitched the Bible for a total of seventeen years. It became a kind of industry joke. *Let Joe Barbera in the door, and he won't leave until you've heard the good word for the Good Book.* I'm sure that, long about the end of the first decade, I was thoroughly resigned to the fact that the project was doomed, but I kept at it anyway.

Finally, perhaps out of sheer embarrassment, our parent company, Taft Broadcasting, invited me to fly out to their headquarters in

Cincinnati to pitch the series directly to upper management. Gathering up all the artwork—and there was a ton of it by now, beautiful, impressive stuff—I boarded the next flight out for Cincinnati.

I sat in a large conference room, waiting while the troops were mustered. I could hear them coming down the hall.

"What's this all about?"

"Joe Barbera's in from the Coast to make a pitch."

"Pitch for what?"

"The Bible."

"Uhhhh, no!"

And I knew they were thinking, *It's looney bin time*. But I had the pleasure of seeing their faces change as they looked over the terrific artwork I had put up on the walls.

I made the pitch, stressing, as always, that these were great stories and that the cartoons were perennial and would run forever. Two of the execs said that, if they had this artwork, they'd quit their jobs today and start selling. Most important of all, Charlie Mecham, head of Taft, took to the project immediately, got behind it, and started pushing.

Even after I started production, many of the folks back at our own studio remained skeptical. Bill Hanna himself said he wouldn't touch the project with a ten-foot pole. But, secure in the knowledge that we were all doing what Charlie Mecham wanted, production went forward.

Harvey Bullock turned in a fine script for the Noah's Ark episode, and I began by telling him so. "It's a darn good script," I said, "but there is no reason for a cartoon company to be doing it. This might as well be live action. Can't we add something to it?"

What I suggested was that we stop to think about the physical *reality* of what we were dealing with and follow that through to its logical conclusions. "Look," I said, "here's this ark, seven hundred feet long and made out of hand-hewn planks. It's seven hundred feet long and loaded with animals. It *had* to leak. All boats leak, and this one just had to. You know it, and I know it. What can we do with this fact? Let's get the animals to stop the leaks. The rhinoceros uses his horn to plug a hole. The monkeys stuff cracks with their hands and tails, and so on.

"Then, was it a smooth voyage? In the middle of a forty-day flood? No. The ark would be pitching and heaving. What will happen? The big animals, elephants, cows, bulls, will s-l-i-d-e slowly across the deck with each swell."

Harvey and I thought of dozens more touches like this, transforming a great story into a great *cartoon*, without, however, altering the biblical narrative or, indeed, one word of the Bible. In fact, I hired five members of the clergy, representing Judaism, Catholicism, and the major Protestant religions, to act as advisors in order to keep us honest.

The religious community welcomed the series with open arms. We previewed some of it at a convention of Lutherans in the Sports Arena in downtown Los Angeles. An audience of seventeen thousand roared and shrieked at the activity in Noah's ark. Later, I was invited to attend the National Religious Broadcasters Convention in Washington, D.C. I was practically stopped at the door by a convention organizer telling me that one of their scheduled speakers was ill and asking me if I were willing to fill in.

I stammered for a second or two, then found myself agreeing. I showed up at nine the next morning, facing a large audience, and sitting at the dais next to Steve Allen, who had been a neighbor of mine when I lived in Encino. Steve was studying the ton of research and notes heaped in front of him. I didn't have any notes. I didn't have anything.

I was introduced, ad libbed a few lines, then took a question from the audience.

"What's to prevent people from taping your material off the air instead of paying for cassettes?"

"That can't happen," I answered. There was an uncomprehending pause.

"What? What do you mean? Why not?"

"Because, up there is a lightning bolt with your name on it, and the minute you rip off one of my videos, you're going to get it right in the butt."

The audience exploded in laughter.

THE NEXT YEAR, I was invited back to the convention and awarded a special medal and the association's first Golden Eagle award for excellence in religious broadcasting. Other major religious organizations asked me to make appearances as well, and I was the guest of Pat Robertson at his Virginia Beach, Virginia, headquarters; of Mother Angelica, the Catholic broadcaster operating out of Birmingham, Alabama; and of Robert Schuller in his Crystal Cathedral.

Anyone who has seen one of Reverend Schuller's television programs has some idea of the immensity of the Crystal Cathedral, which, I believe, is the largest house of worship in the world. Standing with him in the pulpit, looking out at the cavernous structure, I felt about as significant as an insect.

"How is it that you kept going back with the Bible series for seventeen years? What made you do that?" It was the first time anyone had ever asked me this question, and, in front of thousands of people in the Crystal Cathedral and hundreds of thousands of television viewers to whom Schuller's services are broadcast, a light bulb clicked on over my head.

"Look, I am an ordinary person—a human being. You don't think it was me who kept coming back for seventeen years, do you? Obviously, it had to be a force bigger, stronger, more powerful than I ever could be."

Applause broke out.

I hadn't intended to say anything like this at all. I hadn't even thought about it. But here I was, preaching from a pulpit, telling the world that God had said, in effect, *J.B., get up, get that artwork, go out, and try to sell it again.* What's even stranger is that it was all true. I had never flogged a project like that before. I wouldn't have thought of doing such a foolish, unprofessional thing as bringing a rejected show back and back again. Yet, this time I did it. Not once, not twice, but for seventeen solid years. I had no other explanation for it. Later that day, I presented two of the half-hour episodes to about two hundred children at the Crystal Cathedral's Sunday school.

Now, I remember Sunday school in Brooklyn very well. It always brought to my mind the name of Jesus Christ. I said to myself, *Jesus Christ! Why do I have to spend a beautiful day in a classroom when everybody else is outside playing ball?* When I showed the films at this Bible class, however, the children asked to see them again, right then and there. They wanted to make Sunday school twice as long.

I don't want to give anybody the impression that *The Greatest Adventure: Stories from the Bible* was some kind of altruistic religious crusade. God knows, I've taken no vow of poverty. I always thought that, whatever good the Bible series might do, it was first and foremost very good business. At this point, the series stands at twelve episodes, has enjoyed about $20 million in home video sales, and will continue to make a lot of money because the material is, spiritually as well as commercially, eternal.

I AM PROUD OF *The Greatest Adventure*, just as Bill Hanna and I are proud of every cartoon we've done. I think that's a remarkable statement to be able to make—honestly—at this point in a half-century career. This is not to say that everything we've done has been a terrific financial success or great entertainment—but it has *all* been entertainment, and it has all been crafted with high regard for our young audience. We have never been tempted to go the way of some of the recent violent, emotionally exploitive, and generally irresponsible cartoon series, one of which may have even prompted children to acts of arson.

We never had a serious run-in with censorship or the network standards and practices people because, instinctively, we steered clear of problematic content—unless you consider a pie in the face violent.

And the networks do employ some people who, while letting pass acts of sexual, moral, and physical mayhem on prime-time live action, mount impassioned campaigns against one animated character hurling animated baked goods against another animated character. I recall one occasion on which we were compelled by network police to make Yogi throw a big layer cake he was carrying on the ground rather than on top of Ranger Smith.

I once attended a meeting in Beverly Hills with standards and practices people and was asked to state my position on what they called "responsible programming."

"I'm aware of the importance of vigilant standards and practices," I said, "but I hope we don't get to the point where we have to have the cat stop chasing the mouse to teach him glassblowing and basket weaving." It was my way of saying that I hoped we wouldn't kill cartoons by burdening them all with phony "educational content." I guess at least one of the standards and practices people present got the message. My comment prompted her to up and walk out of the conference.

Animated cartoons like the Bible series or "The Last of Curlews" are, by necessity, few and far between. To begin with, broadcasters may claim they want such material—but it took me seventeen years to sell *The Greatest Adventure,* and while "The Last of the Curlews" won an Emmy as Outstanding Achievement in Children's Programming, its "meaningful" and "educational" content also elicited some outraged letters from parents, one mother complaining that the story of a bird who loses his mate to the brutality of man had so upset her twelve-year-old daughter that she was unable to sleep at night.

There is a wonderful old movie directed by Preston Sturges called *Sullivan's Travels*. It's about a movie director, who, tired of making fluff, sets out with nothing more than a dime in his pocket to experience what he thinks of as "life in the real world." What he discovers is that what the "real world" of 1941 needs most is the release and relief provided by laughter. The best most cartoons can hope to do is entertain, provide welcome relief in a world of personal and public anxieties and amid a televised parade of disasters and acts of cruelty, bigotry, stupidity, and greed.

I happen to think that "best" is good enough. This does not mean you ignore the realities around you. I don't live in a cartoon, I live in a community, and, like most everyone else I know in the entertainment industry, I have tried to give something back to my community. I serve on the advisory board of the St. Joseph Medical Center, to which my wife and I have contributed some facilities, something we have also done for the extraordinary House Ear Institute. I work with the Greater Los Angeles Visitors and Convention Bureau and have been involved in the Cousteau Society; the Wildlife Way Station; Friends of Animals, Inc.; Child Health U.S.A.; and many other charitable and community-oriented organizations.

Our principal stock in trade has been entertaining children, and a few years ago it occurred to me that we could use that stock in trade directly to help children. I don't know anyone who enjoys going to the hospital. In fact, for most of us, a stay in the hospital is an anxiety-producing experience. No matter how bad an adult feels about this, however, think how much worse it must be for a child—sick, hurting, separated from his parents, brothers, sisters, friends, pets, and home.

To help remedy this, I got an idea to create what I called a Laugh Room in the pediatric ward of hospitals. It would be a special room, decorated with our characters and where our cartoons would be run on a continuous basis. I mentioned this notion in the course of a number of interviews, and, one day, I was called by an executive at the UCLA Harbor Medical Center. I met with him, and I agreed to donate a Laugh Room to the hospital. Iraj Paran, who had for many years served as an art director at Hanna-Barbera, designed the decor for the hall leading to the Laugh Room—Fred Flintstone pointing the way to the door—and for the room itself.

The press and city officials showed up at the opening of the UCLA Harbor Medical Center Laugh Room, and what they all saw was children—many desperately ill and all clinging to their mothers in terror—suddenly break into smiles and laughter when a costumed

Huck, Yogi, and Scooby-Doo came in to officially open the Laugh Room. Those smiles remained as they watched the funny, familiar, and reassuring cartoons in a setting and situation that were otherwise terrifying and sad.

The nurses in this pediatric ward—wonderful, caring, dedicated people—asked me to talk to one boy in particular who, terminally ill, was scared, withdrawn, and depressed. What made it all the worse was the fact that his mother had not come to visit him for six months.

I didn't tell him how very sorry I was, and I didn't tell him that everything would be all right. I knew he didn't care if I were sorry or not, and I knew he knew that everything was *not* going to be all right. What I did was to talk to him about Tom and Jerry, and I drew them for him, showing him in the process some of the old tricks I had learned as an animator—speed lines and such. And this little boy, who had nothing to smile or laugh about, smiled and laughed—in contrast to the nurses, who were in tears. One, who had been working at the hospital for thirty years, told me that this was the most incredible, moving experience of her professional life.

I wish I could say that the Laugh Room idea took off from there. The Shriners, who fund a network of children's hospitals nationwide, loved the idea, but, as so often and so stupidly happens, political and financial feuding broke out between the Taft Broadcasting executives and Shriner officials, and the idea stalled.

I still wanted to go across the country with it, and Great American Communications, which had purchased us from Taft, brought in a merchandising specialist to secure a major sponsor to enable us to install Laugh Rooms in hospitals nationwide. Yet nothing ever came of these grand plans, and once again the project stalled. UCLA Harbor Medical Center has its Laugh Room, and I still hope to get a larger national program under way.

NOT ALL MY COMMUNITY-ORIENTED activities have taken place in my own community. In June 1984, the Duke and Duchess of Westminster invited me to be their guest at the Grosvenor, a Tudor-style inn they own in Chester. The couple's favorite charity, the

National Society for the Prevention of Cruelty to Children, was conducting its "Centenary Appeal" in association with the Cinema and Television Benevolent Fund, and as part of this they staged a Scooby-Doo event, for which our studio loaned original artwork, which was put on exhibit, and character costumes. And me—I accompanied all this to England.

Up until the January 1994 earthquake, I had been living in the hills of Sherman Oaks—quite comfortably, if I say so myself—but I've never shed my Flatbush roots, and we enjoy living like folks, even though my wife, Sheila, is the daughter of a British army colonel. Not only is Chester the home of the Grosvenor Inn, but it is also the seat of what television's Robin Leach would certainly have called the couple's "fabulous country estate"—all ten thousand English acres of it—and, as I boarded the Britain-bound plane, I felt a bit like a little boy trussed up in a stiff Sunday suit and told to be on my best behavior while I visited some wealthy strangers. It was more than a little intimidating.

Well, the estate was everything I had expected—and then some. There was the customary household staff and—hardly customary—the British army—or, at least, five members of the Duke of Westminster's regiment, who volunteered to exchange their uniforms for the Scooby, Yogi, Huck, and other outfits we had brought, and mingle with the children. It was a hot day, and the suits are very uncomfortable, and I remember seeing them during a break with the suits unzipped to their waists. They were sitting, but sitting at attention, stiff and very military. Not very promising cartoon character material, you'd think, but one thing I've learned over the years is that, put *anybody* in a Yogi costume, and they are transformed—no matter how shy, proper, or uptight they may be in street clothes. And such proved to be the case with the members of the Duke's regiment.

As to the Duke and Duchess of Westminster, they were anything but what I had expected. Wealthy? Absolutely. I'd kill for the Duke's Lagonda—a particularly exotic and beautiful version of the Aston-Martin, capable of cruising along at 170. But this couple was hardly the stereotypical English gentry. They were dressed in sport clothes, very easy-going, utterly charming, and perfectly gracious, by which I mean that they made me feel completely at ease.

The Duke sent a note to the inn, inviting me to his house for lunch, and telling me that his two daughters, the Ladies Edwina and Tamara, were "very much looking forward to seeing me." From the titles and the way the note was phrased—"very much looking forward"—I expected to be greeted by a pair of young ladies verging on teenage. I was surprised when I was welcomed at the door by delightful little girls, ages four and six (the Duke and Duchess were themselves in their mid-thirties), and we all sat informally in the dining room, eating lunch, while I held the younger daughter on my lap and drew for her picture after picture of Tom and Jerry. Drawing them is as familiar an act to me as signing my name.

We also tussled with the family's huge dog. "Do you know what his name is?" asked the Duke.

"What?"

"Scooby-Doo."

"No kidding? That's great!"

"You can have him," the Duke drily suggested.

"No, thanks."

The easy mingling of opulence and graciousness, the happy charm of the young Ladies Edwina and Tamara made a stark contrast to what the program was, at bottom, all about. I have built a business, a partnership, and a career creating as well as sharing in a fantasy world for children, a world of superheroes and slapstick, to be sure, but, I hope, a world more of gentleness and love. I was horrified by the realization—documented in chilling photographs—that the abuse of children is an international epidemic, hardly confined to the poor or to a handful of demented individuals, but practiced, it seems avidly, in every country, neighborhood, and stratum of society.

IF MY LIVELIHOOD, cartoons, put me in a unique position to reach out to the community, and to children in particular, my secret passion, the stage, motivated another kind of involvement. I became acquainted with James A. Doolittle, a remarkable man who had been raised and educated in Los Angeles and whose own passion for the theater began when he, by pure chance, took a Shakespeare course during his senior year at the University of Southern California. He did not go directly into the theater after he left USC, but worked in the retail business. Later, he began producing for the Hollywood Bowl, then, in 1952, leased the deteriorating open-air Greek Theatre from the city of Los Angeles and founded the Southern California Theatre Association to run the facility.

Falling apart, poorly equipped, thoroughly uncomfortable, and long dormant, the Greek Theatre was an unlikely venue in which to establish a center for the performing arts, but Jimmy did it, staging a host of opera and ballet productions, followed by very exciting and distinguished theater.

The Greek Theatre became so successful that the city renovated and enlarged it. Next, in 1959, Jimmy was party to the purchase of the aged Biltmore Theatre in downtown Los Angeles, which, under his direction, saw a series of wonderful plays directed by the likes of Peter Brook, Tyrone Guthrie, John Geilgud, George Abbott, Dore Schary, Joshua Logan, Elia Kazan, Moss Hart, and Jerome Robbins. In the 1960s, Jimmy moved the Theatre Association's operations to the Huntington Hartford Theatre, which, over the years, has featured such artists as Henry Fonda, Helen Hayes, Zero Mostel, Nicol Williamson, Glenda Jackson, Lily Tomlin, Anthony Hopkins, Ann Miller, Julie Harris, Jack Lemmon, Eli Wallach, Anne Jackson, Marcel Marceau, Richard Harris, George C. Scott, Twyla Tharp, Richard Dreyfuss, Jane Alexander, James Earl Jones, and many more.

My relationship with Jimmy ripened into a close friendship, and he invited me to become president of the Huntington Hartford and Greek Theatre. I claim absolutely no credit for anything that took place during the glittering decade in which I served as president of these organizations—Jimmy, as always, did all the work—but Sheila and I did throw some damn good parties with guest lists that were something different from what you might expect to find in the suburbs. We hosted Maurice Chevalier, Charles Aznevour, Hedy Lamarr, Eli Wallach and Anne Jackson, Harry Belafonte, Gail Patrick, Ann Sothern, Tony Newley, Sir John Gielgud, Paul Anka, Englebert Humperdinck, Barbara Rush, Helen Hayes, José Greco, Herb Alpert, and many others.

A regular guest at our house—and not just at the theater parties—was Zsa Zsa Gabor, a neighbor who has been a good friend to Sheila and me for some twenty years. She has a reputation for being difficult—most recently with young traffic cops—and that reputation is not entirely undeserved.

I once gathered Marshall Karp and Chuck Jones, who were serving at the time as ABC daytime executives, together with Pamela Mason and Zsa Zsa Gabor for dinner at my house. Jimmy Doolittle was with us as well. I had an idea for a talk show in which Pamela and Zsa Zsa would sit on one side of a table, and a couple of hapless males, a different pair of celebrities each week, would sit on the other, and the four would go at each other on the subject of female versus male. I wanted to call it "The War between the Sexes." But what I soon found myself witness to was a war between Pamela Mason and Zsa Zsa Gabor. And I mean war.

I was just about to propose my idea for the show when, apparently, Zsa Zsa made some offhandedly disparaging remark about Pamela's former husband, James Mason. The two exchanged words, and more words, and then the words gave way to action, a full-fledged brawl. Jimmy circled around the pair, cooing, "Now, ladies. Now, ladies, we're all friends here," but it was Sheila's heroic intervention—she stepped between the two—that finally brought peace.

Zsa Zsa, after gathering the pieces of her blonde fall off our floor, made her exit—though, before she left, I made everyone promise that not a word of the incident would be breathed. The next day it was on TV.

Needless to say, my show idea died a-borning, but, true to form, neither Zsa Zsa nor Pamela held any grudges and were soon once again the best of friends.

Aside from this episode of fireworks, I never had anything other than delightful experiences with Zsa Zsa Gabor and have, in fact, found her to be a sort of natural politician whenever charm is called for.

During the two decades that Hanna-Barbera was owned by Taft Broadcasting, we had any number of meetings, and I was always looking for new ways to entertain this really great bunch of guys from Cincinnati. Well, on one occasion, I invited a group of executives up to the house for drinks and dinner. Now, I thought, what can I do to make this more interesting?

I got on the phone and called Zsa Zsa Gabor.

"Zsa Zsa, I'm having six or seven executives from Cincinnati to dinner. Why don't you come on over and host it? They'd love to meet you."

"Of course, dahhhling, I'll come."

She arrived at the house before anybody, looking glamorous as always: a movie star and queen of love and beauty. She sat at our bar, which is right off the entrance, and was chatting with Sheila. I was behind the bar. Then we heard a lot of yammering and laughing, which meant that the contingent of already amply lubricated Cincinnatians had arrived. Sheila opened the door, and there they were, all yelling and laughing until, all of a sudden, they froze—coming to a skidding halt, their mouths open.

There's Zsa Zsa Gabor!

This is somebody they don't usually run into on the streets of Cincinnati, Ohio.

Then I watched her work. One by one, she praised each of them as to looks and the brilliance of their conversation, and after another drink or two, they, in return, one by one, toasted Zsa Zsa. I could picture vividly each of them going home to their wives and saying, *You'll never guess who I had dinner with.*

Who?

Zsa Zsa Gabor.

What?

The amazing thing about Zsa Zsa was that her charm was

dispensed irrespective of sex. On another occasion, for example, I was entertaining Bud Rogers, the president of Taft, and his wife. They arrived before Zsa Zsa, and I told them that she would be joining us. Bud raised his eyebrows, but Mrs. Rogers did nothing more than sniff. Well, how else should a woman react to the news that Zsa Zsa Gabor, solo, was going to dine with her husband and herself?

The doorbell rang, and Zsa Zsa walked in. The first thing she did was to shake hands with Mrs. Rogers, look into her eyes, and say, "You are a beautiful woman."

That was it.

From then on, they were the closest of friends, and it was another terrific evening in Hollywood.

Chapter Eleven

A FULL CIRCLE

ILL HANNA AND I owe an awful lot to television, but we both got our start and built the first phase of our partnership in the movies, so it is no wonder that we were always thrilled when we had an opportunity to get back on the big screen. Our first feature-length theatrical release was *Hey There, It's Yogi Bear*, which premiered in 1964, and *The Man Called Flintstone* came to theaters in 1966. But the real feature-length breakthrough for Hanna-Barbera was *Charlotte's Web* in 1973.

It started this way. Edgar Bronfman, a delightful gentleman who was the president of Seagrams, the distilling and beverage giant, called at the studio to discuss a property he owned. It was the movie rights to *Charlotte's Web*, a book children as well as adults have treasured since E. B. White wrote it in 1952. The story, about a spider named Charlotte who befriends and, in a most unique manner, saves the life of a shy pig named Wilbur, combines charm, wit, and genuinely moving emotion. White himself described it as well as anyone ever has when he called it "a tale of friendship and salvation, a story of miracles—the miracle of birth, the miracle of friendship, the miracle of death."

Bronfman had made a deal with a Czech animation studio, which produced some very dark, depressing, and distinctly eastern European artwork. He was not pleased with it and came to us to see what we could offer instead. There was not a great deal of money in it for us, but the possibilities of the story were hard to resist, and we agreed to produce the picture.

The first step was to create the models for the characters, which included Charlotte the spider, Wilbur the pig, Templeton the rat, a very proper Goose, and the little farmgirl, Fern Arable, who befriends Wilbur. Part of the deal we had with Edgar Bronfman was to show the artwork to E. B. White to get his suggestions and approval. Accordingly, Edgar asked me to come to New York with the material.

I hopped a plane to New York and was instructed to meet Bronfman at the Pan Am Metroport, a heliport just north of the Fifty-ninth Street Bridge in Manhattan. If I hate flying in airplanes, I hate even the *thought* of flying in a helicopter. But, deceiving myself into thinking that Edgar had chosen the heliport as nothing more than a convenient meeting place, I took a limo to it. When I got there, no one was around. At length, Edgar drove up, said hello, went inside the little terminal building, and picked up the telephone. I overheard him saying things like "What's taking so long?" "When will you be here?" and "Where's the helicopter?"

Where's the helicopter?

I couldn't believe it. Then, all of a sudden, I heard this picka-pucka-picka-pucka, and I looked up and saw something that appeared to me like a large mosquito. It circled and then, with the engine sound getting louder and louder and the metal insect looking flimsier and flimsier, the bubble-canopied chopper set down on the pad.

Edgar called to me: "Let's go!"

Four of us—Edgar Bronfman, his assistant, the pilot, and I—were squeezed into this bubble, the picka-pucka-picka-pucka quickly picka-puckaed up speed and volume, the tail angled up, we lifted off backward, then forward, and we began heading up the East River, north toward Westchester. We never flew very high, and, looking out the bubble, I could see the faces of the happily earthbound gaze up to see what was making all the noise. I think we were somewhere over Harlem when I noticed that the plastic bubble door was held shut by a hook and eye—I mean a little hook and eye—which you would get from a five-and-ten, and, of course, it was shaking, rattling, and vibrating as the helicopter moved along.

As I had often asked myself during other flights to sell other cartoons: *What in the devil am I doing up here?*

We landed at the Westchester Airport, where a private business jet was waiting for us. It held about twelve passengers and was idling, as I was told, to keep the air conditioning going. We were greeted at the door by two men in sport coats; I would have been less unhappy if they had been wearing official pilot uniforms.

Edgar got in, and I got in. He started to do a crossword puzzle. I started to tremble. We taxied down the runway, turned around, revved up, rolled forward, and took off—it seemed to me—vertically. My cheeks, nose, and hair were pulled back by G-force like some test pilot. Then we leveled off and, after what seemed like an eternity, landed at Bar Harbor, Maine.

We piled out of the plane and into a waiting 6.1 Mercedes limo, then drove about forty-five minutes to E. B. White's charming little farm house, which was almost a duplicate of the sketch at the beginning of *Charlotte's Web*. We walked into what seemed like a Currier and Ives print come to life, and I could smell something baking. E. B. White shook hands with us as Mrs. White hobbled down the stairs on a cane. They were, at the time, seventy-nine and eighty-one, respectively.

Edgar was impressively gracious in thanking the couple for inviting us into their home, and, as he looked over the sketches and models I had brought, White was equally polite, almost overly formal. He did have one suggestion for improving the look of Charlotte herself, and, taking a pen and paper, shakily drew his notion of the arachnid. Naturally, I was very effusive in my comments on the drawing, swearing that it was the best spider I had ever seen in all my life.

Next, we sat down to lunch—an extraordinary feast, which included succulent Maine lobster just out of the water and was rounded out with a home-baked rhubarb pie. But the true miracle came before the food was served. Two, maybe three martinis were inhaled, and the Whites, who, hovering on either side of eighty, had been showing their age, were now transformed into a vivid, ageless couple. Formality, too, dissolved, and we were a group of people sitting in a Maine farmhouse on a pellucid summer afternoon, which blossomed into brilliant, sparkling conversation.

After lunch, Mr. White gave me a copy of *Charlotte's Web*, in which he had made extensive notes, marking in black ink those sections he felt we could alter as necessary, in green those passages subject to discussion, and in red the words he did not want us to change. Not only did I take his wishes as gospel in producing the picture, but I have treasured the book among my most valued and pleasurable possessions.

With that parting gift, we were driven back to the airport, flew back to Westchester, and, as we came in for a landing, were paced by a white Italian sports car running parallel to us. When the plane rolled to a stop, the car drove up, and Edgar Bronfman climbed into it.

"Gee," I said to him, "that lobster was great. Did you ever have Lobster Fra Diavolo?"

"No, what's that?"

"Well, you've got to have Maine lobsters."

"I'm coming out to California. How many do you need?"

"Oh, I suppose about a dozen."

About three weeks later, Edgar arrived in at the studio with eighteen Maine lobsters. I sent these to an Italian restaurant where I ate regularly and asked them prepare Lobster Fra Diavolo for a dozen of us, including Dan Rowan and his wife, Tony Quinn and his wife, Edgar Bronfman, and Zsa Zsa Gabor.

ONCE WE GOT INTO PRODUCTION, a marvelous writer named Earle Hamner did the script, and the picture was directed by Charles A. Nichols and Iwao Takamoto. As we were about to start recording the voices, I got a call from Debbie Reynolds, who said that she had heard we were doing *Charlotte's Web*.

"I'll do it for nothing," she said. "And if you want to pay me, you can give the money to charity." She was cast as Charlotte and brought along her good friend, the distinguished character actress Agnes Moorehead, who voiced the Goose.

I was convinced that there was only one actor to play Templeton the rat, and that was Tony Randall. I called him and shamelessly pleaded with him to do the part, no audition necessary. Finally, he agreed and flew in from New York. Tony Randall is a fine actor, but as soon as I heard him at rehearsal, I knew I had made a terrible mistake. He was all wrong for Templeton. He simply had too much class for the part, and he sang Templeton's song, "A Veritable Smorgasbord," like the accomplished opera buff he is, turning it into an aria. Out of respect for him, I tried him again, but, at last, thanked him, paid him, and recast in the role Paul Lynde, the acidic comedian who first came to fame in the movie *Bye, Bye, Birdie* and who was even more familiar to at least one whole generation of television viewers as a hilarious regular on the game show "Hollywood Squares." He was perfect.

Years later, I got my comeuppance from Tony Randall when he hosted a ceremony at which I was slated to present an award.

"And now," he said to the audience, "to present the next award is Joe Barbera—the only man who ever fired me." A chorus of mock boos rose up from the audience, and I hardly knew how to respond.

"No, Tony, you've got it all wrong. I just didn't have the heart to see you play a rat."

CHARLOTTE'S WEB was a great success with the public and critics alike, including even the iconoclastic *Village Voice* in New York, which called it a "terrific animated musical movie."

Later, in 1981, when I went over to pitch our next theatrical animated feature, *Heidi's Song*, to Michael Eisner, who was heading up Paramount, the distributor for *Charlotte's Web*, Eisner told me that he and the studio had loved *Charlotte's Web* and then called his accounting department on the phone. Some ledger books were brought into the office, Eisner looked at them, and then up at me.

"Yup. We made money on that picture."

We made a deal for *Heidi's Song*, and put the same kind of talent and devotion into it as had gone into *Charlotte's Web*. I wrote the story with Jameson Brewer and Robert Taylor, who also directed the picture, and we cast Lorne Greene, Sammy Davis, Jr., and Margery Grey (who played Heidi) as the starring voices. The music, by the classic team of Sammy Cahn and Burton Lane, was terrific. And, of course, we had Johanna Spyri's timeless story to work with.

Heartbreakingly, the picture was a box office disappointment. In retrospect, the title was probably all wrong. There were just too many *Heidis* around, with Disney's overshadowing them all. And distribution was uncharacteristically inept. The picture was dumped on the theaters and just sat there.

BACK IN THE MID-1960S, when Universal's Lou Wasserman came a-courting, he spoke about the studio's plans for an amusement park. By the 1980s, the Universal Studios theme park was a reality, and the television airwaves and cable currents were saturated with commercials showing delightedly terrified visitors getting snapped at by the four hundred billion teeth of the *Jaws* shark, being menaced by a King Kong-like ape, fleeing from a terrifying helicopter crash, suffering through the fire and flood of an earthquake (Hey, who has to pay to enjoy *that*?), bearing witness to Wild West shoot-outs, and the like. After weeks of seeing these images on the tube, I woke one morning at the customary hour of three with the thought: *They have nothing for little kids.*

Later that day, eyes bloodshot, I called Sid Sheinberg at Universal.

"Sid!"

"What do you want?" The question was not framed in a terribly friendly manner.

And I gave him my thoughts, concluding with, "*Our* characters should be in your park."

"I'll call you back," he said, and that is exactly what he did. There was, in fact, great enthusiasm for the idea at Universal, and the Taft people, who still owned us at the time, were excited as well. You'd never have known any of this once the business types got hold of the deal, but the idea survived negotiations, an agreement was hammered out, and in a publicity gesture born of an era in which the Berlin Wall was about to fall and the Cold War was in rapid thaw mode, our employees and Universal personnel joined hands to form a human chain across the overpass above the Hollywood Freeway, which separates our two studios. A helicopter circled overhead, filming the whole thing.

It was very sweet and lovely and seemed to foretell great things to come. Then out of left field came the news that, when it sold an amusement park it owned in Northern California, Taft had also sold the rights to our characters as well, which meant that no other amusement park within a certain distance from the Northern California facility could use them. And that, children, is why Hanna-Barbera has an attraction at Universal Studios in Orlando, Florida, but not right across the freeway at Universal Studios, Hollywood.

THE NEXT PRODUCT of our association with Universal was our next big animated feature, *The Jetsons*, to which I looked forward with great excitement. Doing a major feature in partnership with a big studio like Universal presents great opportunities, but it is also full of booby traps. It's like the big fish swimming in the same bowl with the little fish.

All things considered, it's better not to be the little fish.

Bit by bit, the Universal people tended to take over the project. They were promoting a singer named Tiffany, and they cast her as Judy Jetson in place of Janet Lee (whose stage name is Janet Waldo), the woman who had voiced the role in the television series and who, in fact, had already completed recording the movie. I know this broke Janet's heart, although she took it like the trouper and thorough professional she is. Nevertheless, having worked for so many years with Janet, I felt terrible about it, and I still do.

Later, another executive pressured us to make musical substitutions—and so it went. I won't chronicle the rest of the invasion, and it is not, in any case, an unusual story. The folks putting up the money have a very natural urge to take over everything. When I at last had had enough of it, I walked out on the production, and I can't really say much more about the movie, because I've never had the heart to go see it. I do know that, as of this writing, it's made about $23 million, not including proceeds from the lucrative home video market. So I can't lean over the parapet shouting *I told you so.* However, *The Jetsons* was not a happy experience.

BUT, OF COURSE, I went on from there. I was lying in bed, wide awake at three o'clock one morning, thinking about, of all things, Tom and Jerry. Here was something that had consumed seventeen years of my life, that had been a sensation, and that earned seven Oscars, beating out anything Disney or Warner's had to offer. Here was this great property, which had meant so much to me, and yet I had absolutely no idea what had become of it. Who owned the rights now? MGM had gone through so many sales, buy backs, and shufflings and reshufflings of material, I hardly knew where to begin. But, lying there, I thought, *something* should be done with Tom and Jerry, a great property lying fallow.

When I got to the studio, bleary-eyed as usual, I asked one of our business people to check on the Tom and Jerry rights, and I learned that Turner Broadcasting owned the rights. Turner had acquired MGM, subsequently sold back the studio, but retained the negatives of the MGM film library. I called Roger Mayer, Turner's vice president in L.A., set up a meeting, and drove out with my lawyer to a building on Venice Boulevard.

I had just that morning read in the trades that Turner was in the process of negotiating a mammoth five hundred million dollar deal, so on the way to the meeting I said to my lawyer, "Now, remember, they don't have any money."

"Yeah, sure."

Roger Mayer was a bright, astute industry veteran, who greeted us with a warm handshake and then announced, "Gentlemen, before we begin, let me tell you something: We don't have any money. Now, what can I do for you?"

So, after a knowing glance toward my lawyer, I began. "As you know, I was involved with the creation of Tom and Jerry, and it occurred to me, why don't we do some more Tom and Jerry? Maybe a TV special." Then I broached what I imagined was the far more remote possibility. "Maybe a theatrical feature."

Roger Mayer nodded slowly, sagely, and politely as I talked, but it was evident to me that I was lighting no fires. He concluded this most civil meeting with thanks and a remark that amounted to "don't call us, we'll call you."

Well, this is what you do. You keep pitching. Most of the pitches run wild. A few are caught. I was recently leafing through the pages of six very thick bound volumes I call *The Graveyard*. These are a collection of cover art for projects I pitched over the past thirty-three years and that have yet to see the light of day. I can't bear the thought of actually counting them. With my skill at numbers, the total would doubtless be inaccurate in any case. But I figure there are close to eight hundred projects buried in *The Graveyard*.

Creating fantasy is a very personal thing, but you can't take the process—an inevitable part of which is rejection—too personally. In order to keep a studio running, you keep generating ideas, like a tree broadcasting its seeds, even though only a very few will ever take root. Margaret Loesch, now the head of Fox children's programming but at one time a Hanna-Barbera staffer, recently told me a story she had been keeping to herself for some years. Back when she was working for us, it seems that Sy Fisher called her on the phone demanding one hundred new ideas on his desk by morning. Poor Margaret didn't sleep a wink that night, and, yes, it was an unreasonable and unrealistic demand—but not one that was unheard of. That's the way the business is. You are expected to be prodigal with ideas, as if they went for a dime a dozen. Nobody treats them like the precious natural resource they are.

But, just a few days after the meeting with Roger Mayer, he phoned. "We're interested in the motion picture."

"What?"

"Let's get together."

We met again and negotiated a deal for a seventy-five thousand dollar advance to develop a script, artwork, and a partial storyboard. When it was completed, I sent twenty pages of storyboard, in color, over to Roger, who, liking what he saw, packed it and us off to Turner's headquarters in Atlanta.

Ted Turner's offices are in a cavernously futuristic downtown Atlanta building called the Omni, and we were led into a large conference room, the corner of which was dominated by a stuffed lion. I don't mean a stuffed toy lion. I mean a taxidermified specimen of the King of Beasts himself, his tail stuck out the way a lion sticks his tail out when he is poised to charge. While I was staring at it, waiting for it to pounce, one of Turner's people, observing my apparent fascination with it, told me he had heard that whenever some outfit like the National Geographic showed up for a conference, about eight strong men had to lift the beast up and out to another room.

Ted Turner sailed into the meeting, and I mean *sailed*. He holds himself as if he were at the helm of his sailboat, in the process of winning the race. I did a little innocent ad libbing, my customary preamble to a pitch, until Ted, who had been eyeing me up and down, cut in with an abrupt question.

"How old are you?"

"Uh, um, seventy-eight." This was 1988.

And he eyed me some more, I assume in an attempt to determine what I ate or what I took to keep me out of a nursing home that long.

I launched into my pitch, and there really isn't much of a story here, because, inside of a quarter-hour, Ted Turner leaned back, looked at me, and said, "I like it. Let's make a deal."

I was so stunned that I must have looked catatonic. Roger Mayer, glancing over at me, said, "Why so gloomy? You just sold the show!"

As usual, at this point the battle was only half won. Turner had agreed to finance half the project, we had to finance the balance and, of course, get the picture produced.

I was in the process of pondering this when I went over to Fox to pitch another show. I stopped at that studio's commissary to have lunch, and, across the room, I saw Joe Roth, a colleague and friend who had just been made production head at Fox. I went over to him, and we did the customary Hollywood hugs as I offered my congratulations on his appointment. Then I went back to my table to finish lunch. After I got back to my office, I began to think. *I wonder what's going on at the Fox studio in animated features*? And I called Joe Roth.

"Do you have anything going in an animated feature?"

He said no. So I set up a meeting with Joe and Roger Birnbaum, his right-hand man. I did for them the pitch that had worked so well on Ted Turner, and they loved it. Great.

That's when Taft Broadcasting, who had been piloting us with great success across the treacherous seas of mass media since 1967, seemed finally to run aground. They had expanded and expanded, acquiring a group of television stations precisely at a time when television ad revenues had taken a nosedive. As I understood it, the cumulative financial pressures prompted the sale of Hanna-Barbera, as well as the television and radio stations, to Carl Lindner's company, Great American Communications. Bill Hanna and I were part of the deal, but the Great American people were concerned about the future. *What happens when you guys retire?*

With my approval, encouragement, and participation, Great American hired a headhunter and came up with David Kirschner to work with Bill and me in running the studio. The first thing David did was to come down to my office and say, "I don't want to do the Tom and Jerry feature." I hardly knew where to begin my response. *The show was sold!* The deal was made. Why abandon it?

"Look, Joe, if you're real passionate about it, we won't do anything about it," Kirschner said. Groping for a strategy, I asked him to let me think about it.

But he didn't wait. He went over to Fox and persuaded studio head Barry Diller that they shouldn't go ahead with the picture, and, in the meantime, I was told, he promoted a project of his own. This is not as underhanded as it sounds. What I mean is that it's strictly standard operating procedure in this business. When you're put in charge of a studio, you try to get as much of your own stuff in as possible. It's the law of the jungle.

Fortunately, the Turner organization still liked the project and was eager to go ahead with the deal. I recommended working with FilmRoman, an animation studio run by Phil Roman. I knew and respected Phil, whose studio does the production on "Garfield" and "The Simpsons," among other shows, and I had worked with him before. I set up a meeting, and the project moved ahead.

Given the choice of being credited as producer, co-producer, executive producer, dishwasher—essentially, whatever I wanted—I chose to be called creative consultant, and I had one of the best times in my life working with Phil and his people.

While the movie was in production, I met—in fact, I had a series of five meetings with—a young man who is very much in the news as I write this. Some time in 1992, Michael Jackson, an avid cartoon buff, contacted me to discuss the possibility of working on some project together. Who could say no? My thought was to make a deal for him to sing a song in the *Tom and Jerry* feature. During our first meeting in his apartment on Wilshire Boulevard, he asked me if I had really written all of those Tom and Jerrys. No, I said, I drew them.

"Do you want to see?" I asked.

He nodded, sprang out of the room, and returned with a pad and some markers. I took them and started making sketches of a cartoon—one of my favorites—called "Bowling Alley Cat," each depicting the action and the atmosphere. Michael looked over my shoulder, whispering in that high, thin, breathy voice of his, "Wow!" and "Wow!"

I stopped at the fifth sketch. "Would you like me to autograph them?"

"Oh, yes," he whispered.

"Now, how about me getting an autograph?" I asked. I pointed to a poster he had showing himself and a little girl. It was, he said, his niece Nicole.

"Could you autograph that?"

"Oh, yes," he whispered, and he began to write. And write. And he wrote some more.

"What is this, the Gettysburg Address?"

"You'll see. Please, read it. Read it aloud."

I read: "To my hero of yesterday, today, and tomorrow, with many thanks for all the many cartoon friends you gave me as a child. They were all I had.—Michael."

As it turned out, the executives Great American Communications had sent down to us had no interest in my doing a deal with Michael Jackson, and nothing further came of these meetings. Nevertheless, my meetings with him were delightful, and I found him to be laid back, courteous, and a gentleman—which is great deal more than you can say about any number of people in our industry.

Work on *Tom and Jerry: The Movie* proceeded rapidly. When our people bowed out of the co-production deal with Turner, that organization struck a deal with a German company to provide the other half of the financing. Part of the agreement was a world premiere in Berlin, in preparation for which Phil and I were flown first to London, where I gave seventeen major interviews in the space of a day and a half.

The next stop was Munich, where we stayed at the Four Seasons, which is a fine hotel in every respect, but, in one respect is a *great* hotel. They put spectacular down pillows on the beds. These were about two-and-a-half feet square, maybe two feet high, and when I lay down on one, my head just sort of floated into it. This was bliss after thirty-eight interviews in two days, followed by a night in a beer hall, where the steins were almost too big to lift and the only thing edible was potato soup. I reported to Jürgen Wohlrabe, our host for the premiere, on the glories of the down pillow, and before we left for Berlin, he had ordered a brand-new specimen of this miraculous pillow for me to take home.

In Berlin, we were checked into *the* Grand Hotel—the one that had inspired the 1932 movie with Greta Garbo and John Barrymore—and as we were eating an opulent breakfast, Jürgen came in to tell us that a one million dollar German video deal had just been concluded, which was a highly auspicious prelude to the premiere that night.

Phil Roman and I were picked up in a big Mercedes limousine and driven from the Grand Hotel, in what had been the Cold War's East Berlin, past the Brandenburg Gate to the theater in West Berlin. Long before we got there, I could see the skyline illuminated with a forest of powerful searchlight beacons, which brought to mind nothing more vividly than movie and newsreel images of World War II air raids.

"What the hell is all this?" I asked Jürgen.

"Why, it's the premiere!"

I couldn't believe it. *This* for a middle-aged cat and mouse who hadn't even been seen in theaters for thirty years?

The mob at the theater entrance was so thick that we couldn't open the limo door, and it took the efforts of a big, burly man who had been assigned to accompany us—now I knew why—to clear a path, parting a sea of pads and pens and autograph books. We're talking about Tom and Jerry. Not Clark Gable, Mel Gibson, Barbra Streisand, or Madonna. And we had to fight every inch of the way to get into the lobby. Once we started down the aisle, the entire theater stood up, applauding.

The response to the movie itself took me back to the days when Bill Hanna and I used to slip one of our new cartoons into a theater in Glendale or Pasadena and quietly sit in the audience to gauge response. What I remember is the very gratifying *roar* that would rise up when the Tom and Jerry title appeared on the screen. Multiply that by a factor of a thousand, and you have an idea of how well the feature was received by the Berliners. It ran, by the way, for months in Germany—and, for all I know, may still be running as I write this.

We had a post-premiere party at the Palais, which, like the theater itself, was jammed, and I signed autographs while everybody else got to eat. Suddenly, the lights went out, and we were plunged into total blackness. Then four men in chef's outfits came in bearing a huge cake—each layer a foot-and-a-half high—resting on a pair of poles and surmounted by sparklers that fizzed with the intensity of road-accident flares.

This was beautiful, and I felt like a little kid. Jürgen and I were asked to make the first cut together, and it was with no little gratitude that I accepted a piece of the cake—at last I had been given something to eat—but, in the ongoing crush of autograph signing and interview giving, even that disappeared before I could get it into my mouth.

We were ferried back to our various hotels in a double-decker bus, and I was sitting next to the film's French distributor. Reminding me that the French premiere was just three weeks away, he pleaded with me to come to Paris for the event. He didn't have to plead very much.

In Paris, we stayed at the Ritz, which, in every respect, lived up to its legendary reputation, and we also spent an evening at the Crazy Horse Saloon, renowned for its beautiful women and its free-flowing champagne. This and some twenty-seven interviews the next day—from nine to five, without a break for lunch—prompted me to tell Phil that I was going up to my room for a nap before dinner.

The Ritz is big on elaborate detail, and among the details are handles—golden swans for turning on and off the sink and bath water and elongated dueling pistol grips for opening and closing doors. My room had two doors, each with a dead bolt lock and a chain. I twisted a swan, washed my face, gripped a dueling pistol, closed both doors, threw the bolt, hooked the chain, peeled back the bed covers, and totaled out into a blissfully comatose slumber.

The next thing I was aware of was a voice—Phil Roman's voice. "Joe. Joe, are you all right? Joe?"

All I could answer was, "How the hell did you get in here?"

I mean, it was like Houdini. Two doors, a dead bolt, a chain, and there's Phil Roman hovering over the bed.

"We tried to call you, but the phone was off the hook," Phil said, "and we knocked and knocked at the door, but you didn't answer. We got worried."

"You mean you thought I was dead?"

"Well, if you must know . . ." Phil went on to explain that, after getting a busy signal from the phone (which had, in fact, somehow fallen off the hook) and failing to rouse me by pounding on the door, he flagged down a passing chambermaid and explained the situation. She used her pass key to open the dead bolt, and, when they found the door chained, Phil was on the verge of calling for somebody with a wire cutter. But the resourceful chambermaid was also a very tiny woman, with slender arms and hands. She slipped her hand through the opening the chain allowed and flipped the chain off its track.

The long and the short of it is that I lived to attend the Paris premiere, which took place the next Sunday morning at ten—the French wanted to make their premiere a family event—and the picture was met with the same adulation it had received in Berlin.

Back in L.A., I was having lunch one afternoon with Roger Mayer, who had not attended the Paris event.

"I'm sorry I missed Paris," he said. "You know what would be great? To go back to Paris for a week—no pressure—eat at the finest restaurants and go to the museums."

"What I want to do is go back to the Crazy Horse Saloon," I said—also agreeing with him about the museums, of course, but having only the most secondary intentions of visiting any of them.

THE ORIGINAL RUN OF "The Flintstones" was 166 episodes over six years, from 1960 to 1966 on ABC, with reruns on NBC from 1967 to 1970. In 1971, we premiered "The Pebbles and Bamm-Bamm Show" on CBS and then "The Flintstones Comedy Hour" (1972–73) and "The Flintstones Show" (1973–74), also on CBS. NBC acquired the Flintstones property in 1979 and redubbed thirteen of the original shows as "The New Fred and Barney Show," which was later expanded to an hour as "Fred and Barney Meet the Thing." NBC brought out a *ninety-minute* "Flintstones Comedy Show" in 1980.

In the later 1980s, when the outrageous demand for Cabbage Patch dolls was creating shortages that many parents, driven insane by their clamoring children, took harder than the gas-station lines that came with the great OPEC oil embargo of 1973, I sat down with Squire Rushnell, head of ABC daytime programming, to sell a Cabbage Patch Kid show.

It was, understandably enough, an easy sell—*and* it was for a highly lucrative hour-long show. The deal made, however, Rushnell admitted to me that he was having trouble securing the rights. He made a phone call to check on the situation. I sat there, listening as the conversation melted into pleading, and I could see that hour dissolve right before my eyes. It wasn't a simple cartoon bag of money sprouting wings and taking flight. At an hour, it was Fort Knox tied to a rocket and the fuse was lit.

I was sitting there, praying, and finally he hung up and looked at me. "It's no use. I can't do a thing with them."

"You mean *no show*?"

"Yeah."

Then my old friends came to the rescue, and, *boom*, I just blurted out: "Why not do 'The Flintstone Kids'?"

Why not indeed? We turned Fred, Barney, Wilma, and Betty into little kids and turned them loose on Bedrock. My hour was saved, the show premiered in 1987, and was a great success.

THERE WAS DESTINED to be yet another Flintstones incarnation. The next Hanna-Barbera-related project Universal got behind was *The Flintstones*, a live-action, very big-budget movie starring John Goodman as Fred and Rick Moranis as Barney. Now, the idea for this movie did not originate with us, but with Steven Spielberg's Amblin Productions. I was enthusiastic about it from the beginning, and, as it was taking shape, Universal called me, pleading with me to confirm Spielberg's direct and personal participation in the movie.

"Hell, yes," he said. "I want to do it."

I was given a berth as one of the film's executive producers, which, along with ten cents, will get you a job behind an elephant. I did look at script draft after script draft, and I understand from a recent *Variety* story that the film involved the services of no fewer than thirty-five writers. This, according to the article, eclipsed the previous record of the twenty or more writers who had worked on *Godfather III*. "Almost as many people participated in the writing of *The Flintstones*," *Variety* observed, "as signed the Declaration of Independence."

But the picture became a reality for me when I visited the incredible set that had been constructed at a place called Vasquez Rock. Spielberg's people had wrought a live and living duplicate of Bedrock as I had always imagined it, a dream come true, right down to a stone toilet with a stone lid on it.

I also found myself assigned a cameo part in the picture. I play a bigshot—that's what we call in the business typecasting—who drives up to an elegant prehistoric nightclub called Cavern on the Green at the wheel of his Mersandes automobile and in the company of a "bimbo" (That's what the script calls her.) It's a speaking part, naturally, consisting of the following:

"*Take care of the car*," spoken to the doorman while I toss him some stone money.

And: "*Only the best for you, babe*," spoken to the "bimbo" as we walk through the door of Cavern on the Green, which is all done up in elaborately detailed Rock Deco.

And, oh yes, I'm *costumed*—in a black *Flintstone* skin, formalized for evening wear with a dickie bosom and black tie.

Now, this Mersandes I was driving is a vehicle made out of wood and stone. It has no motor but is rolled down a slight incline. It has a steering wheel but no steering, nor brakes, nor anything, except for a button to start the car rolling. It weighs four tons. I was half terrified through rehearsal and then through take after take, rolling along in something more massive than my own car, but lacking any means of control. Not surprisingly, the vehicle repeatedly overshot or undershot the place where it was supposed to stop. We did ten or a dozen takes before we got it right.

Then there was the pleasure of standing around bare-armed in the cold desert air of nighttime at Vasquez Rock, and the equally amusing experience of walking barefoot across the gravel path to the door of Cavern on the Green. Struggling to remember my two lines, I thought that what the script *should* have said was "Ouch, ooch, eech, ouch, yow," and I could have ad libbed it from there.

At this point in my Hollywood Horatio Alger story, who would have believed that this lad of eight decades, who thirty-three years earlier had been holed up in New York's Sherry-Netherland Hotel hawking the world's first prime-time television cartoon series, would now be shivering in a three-dimensional incarnation of a cartoon dreamed up so long ago?

Standing there in my Flintstones skin, watching the actors and technicians and grips make a fifty million dollar movie (each original "Flintstones" half-hour had cost fifty-two thousand dollars to make), my eight-week Manhattan sojourn at the Sherry seemed light years away, hazily visible through the mists of a television career begun in middle age. But, standing on the streets of Bedrock, I could no longer tell whether that beginning was centuries in the past or eons in the future.

PROLOGUE TO THE NEXT VOLUME

AS I CONTINUE to develop new characters, other production companies are creating a host of new characters and shows that are innovative and refreshing. These shows are not always to my liking, and, in some cases, I believe they are even questionable as to their emotional impact on young viewers. Yet, I think animation is in the middle of a very exciting period, and new ideas are vital to maintaining that excitement as well as the interest of the viewing public. The success of "The Simpsons," for example, is largely due to the writing rather than to anything intimately related to the cartoon medium. A show like "Ren and Stimpy" I find even difficult to watch.

But I applaud these approaches, extreme though they may be, each in its way, because I feel they stimulate a growth in the industry that will open up chances for artists who might otherwise never find an audience. The importance of syndication (which is how "The Simpsons" got its start) and cable (which runs shows like "Ren and Stimpy") is that these outlets provide a creative, often innovative alternative to the networks.

As the first studio to make a business out of creating cartoons for television, Hanna-Barbera has been an innovator, and I'm proud to say that I have worked with a number of major figures in the animation and children's entertainment industry. Margaret Loesch had been an assistant daytime executive at NBC when she joined Hanna-Barbera as head of development. After a great stint with us, she went over to Marvel Comics and then to Fox, where she is now head of children's programming. Jean McCurdy, who worked at Hanna-Barbera as Margaret's assistant, is now head of Warner's children's programming. Judy Price directs children's programming at CBS and moved the network into the number one daytime position. When Squire Rushnell left ABC, Jenny Trias took over as head of ABC's children's department and has kept the network highly competitive in this area.

There is another wonderful woman I want to acknowledge as one of the greats in our business. She's not an animator or writer or director, but she's been indispensable to running my office for fourteen years now, as I write this. She is my secretary, Maggie Roberts. Don't ever make the mistake of criticizing me in front of her. She'll rend you limb from limb.

Mark Young, who now works for MGM, turning out the new Pink Panther series, not only worked for Hanna-Barbera, but is an alumnus of a unique training program I initiated in 1984. Nobody taught me how to write cartoons and how to animate them. Back when I got into the business, there was no one to teach you. You learned on the job, and you honed your craft after hours at home. I've done okay, and plenty of writers and animators have come into the profession the same way. But in 1984 it occurred to me that such a haphazard approach was inadequate to the demands of a most demanding business. By that time, there were a handful of academic programs offering the rudiments of animation, but nothing from the trenches, nothing offered by working animators and writers.

I called Harry Love into my office to discuss a notion I had of giving classes in animation. Harry is one of the great pioneers of animated cartoons. He started in the business in 1927, animating Krazy Kat when he was sixteen, and has served in the major studios, including Hanna-Barbera, where he was a producer and my assistant. Out of this meeting emerged a plan for a program of six-week classes in animation. Later, we added classes in writing as well. Harry directed the program, bringing in all the experts and, with me, evaluating the droves of applicants vying for the few spaces we could offer. Our evaluations were not based on experience or background—applicants might be bookkeepers, trash collectors, executives, what-have-you—but on how they handled a trial assignment. I would open each class personally with a welcome and random anecdotes.

The program ran for four years, until 1988, and was highly acclaimed and very successful, but Taft Broadcasting, suffering the financial problems that would soon prompt the company to sell us, decided the classes didn't pay. They couldn't say it cost them much. We didn't compensate the instructors beyond giving them an occasional dinner, but neither did we charge the students tuition or fees of any kind. Although we did hire a few of our own students, we were discouraged from this practice, largely because they "graduated" from the courses at a sort of intermediate stage of readiness and would have required an apprenticeship period of supervision before they could become fully productive animators or writers. There was nothing wrong with that, except, given the volume and pace at which we were creating cartoons, nobody could afford the time to give what the army calls OJT—on-the-job training. The result was that our competition hired away many of our best graduates, who, like the studios who hired them, were very grateful to us.

ONE OF THE MORE ATTRACTIVE things about writing your autobiography, as opposed to having someone write your obituary, is that you're not dead. However, that also makes the piece more difficult to end.

I have few regrets and none I can't live with. What I do have is a sense of great enthusiasm about the future. Our acquisition by Turner Broadcasting in 1991 generated incredible excitement at Hanna-Barbera because of the dynamism of Ted Turner himself and the exciting young executives who were brought into the company, Fred Seibert and Jed Simmons. With their leadership and Turner's commitment to our studio, I feel as if the baton has been well passed.

That doesn't mean I've stepped out of the race. As of this writing, having just finished sixty-five half-hours of the new "Tom and Jerry Kids" show and thirteen half-hours of the "Droopy, Master Detective" show, ordered by Turner and sold to Fox, I am continuing to develop many new projects. It gives me no little pleasure to point out that "Tom and Jerry Kids" had grown from an initial order of thirteen, then an additional thirteen, and, finally, another thirty-nine, for a total of sixty-five, which seems to be the number needed for syndication. When I was asked if I could produce the additional thirty-nine shows in a span of time originally allotted to produce thirteen, I gave the same answer I've been giving for more than half a century now: Yes.

Not everybody was happy about this, and I can't say that I blame them. Each half-hour show contains three stories, which means coming up with a total of 117 stories (3 times 39) in a very short time. The fact is, nobody had ever gotten out so many stories so quickly. I ended up two months ahead of schedule.

And now, with that behind me, I'm hard at work on developing "Jellystone's Most Wanted: Yogi the Fugitive Bear" and a dog show called "Smart Ace," with very fresh artwork by Marty Murphy, whose style I used in "Wait Till Your Father Gets Home," one of my favorite shows, which was regrettably ahead of its time in 1972. I'm also working on "The Pizza Crumms," a wild and wacky animated leap some several light years beyond, say, the Three Stooges.

This is a sampling of the ideas whirling around in my head. Will all of these projects find good homes? I hope so. That's what keeps me going: dreaming, inventing, then hoping and dreaming some more in order to keep dreaming and inventing and hoping. I've already mentioned my "graveyard," the bound volumes I keep, which contain artwork for more than eight hundred dreams and inventions that no one wanted to buy.

One of my favorite denizens of the graveyard is a show called "The Blackstones," which was created about 1966 or 1967 and featured a black Stone Age family who move nextdoor to Fred Flintstone with results so interesting and provocative that no network or syndicator would touch it.

Another is an idea for a live-action show called "Jump Start," set in world taken over by computers, which grow in power, take on lives of their own, fall into jealous electronic battles with one another, until one supercomputer becomes so powerful that it explodes. When the dust clears, we're back to scratch, left in a world without computers but, once again, controlled by human beings who, quite happily, produce nothing new, content instead to live off the salvage of the world they had let their machines destroy.

Then there are *The Lupezoids*, a live-action feature project based on two books by Will Henry about the *second* invasion of the Mongols, who descend from the North, not wearing chain-mail armor and mounted on steeds with flaring nostrils, but equipped with ultra-sophisticated weaponry and sitting astride super-fast hovercraft.

Like anyone who manages to survive in a creative business, I learned long ago to accept the fact that not everything I create will see the light of day. But the great thing about my "graveyard" is that no one knows for sure if the beings who inhabit it are really dead. Any number of them may come to life again.

And if I ever do feel discouraged, well, I can always go to the TV and watch a cartoon.

Or I can go to one of the many galleries that feature our artwork, and I can autograph cels. I've confessed elsewhere in this tome that high-level, big-deal publicity has a way of getting old for me, but what never fails to move and thrill me is when I make these personal appearances and look up from the table where I'm signing cels and see the faces of the many people who come up to talk to me, fathers, mothers, children, as well as grandmothers and grandfathers. Sometimes the children bring drawings they've done of Yogi Bear or Fred Flintstone or Scooby-Doo. Sometimes they bring drawings of Bugs Bunny. Oh, well.

Then the parents look at me like I'm somebody pretty important, they look at me, and they say, "We were raised on your characters, and now we're enjoying them all over again with our children."

The beautiful thing is that this happens over and over and over again. Who could ask for a more satisfying achievement than that?

WELL, MAYBE THERE'S ONE. Let me share just one more memory before I start the next installment of my life.

A while back, I invited about forty colleagues—the writers, storyboard people, and voice talent I have worked with for years and years—to my favorite Chinese restaurant, Fung Lum, a huge, rectangular Eastern palace of a place right across the Hollywood Freeway from our studio. What I wanted to do was simple: just thank them all.

What I got in return was far more than I had bargained for.

It happened very quietly.

Mel Blanc, who had at his command (they say) three thousand voices, was in fact a taciturn gentleman, a quiet man, who would come into a studio, do his job with spectacular skill, then leave.

We were all happily chowing down when, all of a sudden, Mel rose from his seat and asked for silence. The clack of chopsticks momentarily ceased.

"I want to say something," Mel began. "I've known Joe Barbera for thirty years, and I want to say that I have never heard in all that time one person say one bad thing about him."

You know, I have never been prouder, happier, or more pleased with myself than at that moment.